Real Life, Real Family

Real Life, Real Family

A Guide to Raising Empowered Children

RaaShaun "DJ Envy" & Gia Casey

Abrams Image, New York

Editor: Soyolmaa Lkhagvadorj
Designer: Diane Shaw
Managing Editors: Lisa Silverman and Kayla White
Production Manager: Kathleen Gaffney

Library of Congress Control Number: 2023946471

ISBN: 978-1-4197-7015-9
eISBN: 979-8-88707-120-6

Text copyright © 2025 Gia and RaaShaun Casey
Photographs courtesy of the Casey Archives

Jacket © 2025 Abrams

Published in 2024 by Abrams Image, an imprint of ABRAMS. All rights reserved. No portion of this book may be reproduced, stored in a retrieval system, or transmitted in any form or by any means, mechanical, electronic, photocopying, recording, or otherwise, without written permission from the publisher.

Printed and bound in the United States
10 9 8 7 6 5 4 3 2 1

This book is not intended to replace professional therapy or serve as a substitute for mental health treatment. The information provided within this book is for educational and informational purposes only. It is important to consult with a qualified mental health professional or therapist for personalized advice, diagnosis, or treatment for any specific mental health concerns. The authors and publisher of this book are not responsible for any actions taken based on the content provided. Readers should use their discretion and seek appropriate professional help as needed.

Abrams Image books are available at special discounts when purchased in quantity for premiums and promotions as well as fundraising or educational use. Special editions can also be created to specification. For details, contact specialsales@abramsbooks.com or the address below.

Abrams Image® is a registered trademark of Harry N. Abrams, Inc.

ABRAMS The Art of Books
195 Broadway, New York, NY 10007
abramsbooks.com

Real Life, Real Family is dedicated to our beautiful and cherished children, the Choo Crew: Peyton, Brooklyn, Jaxson, London, Logan, and Madison. Each of you is a testament to love's infinite wonders and life's most precious blessings.

We live for you, as you are our greatest gifts. You give life meaning, joy, and a sense of anticipation of what is to come. The excitement that we feel while watching you grow and succeed is unmatched. Know that, in everything that you experience, we will be right by your sides.

Contents

Introduction ... 1

PART 1: The Family Unit

CHAPTER 1: The Importance of Creating a Family Mission Statement ... 10

CHAPTER 2: Constructing an Unshakable Foundation ... 51

CHAPTER 3: Echoes of Wisdom ... 71

CHAPTER 4: Architects of Unconditional Love ... 89

CHAPTER 5: Strengthening the Foundation of Self-Esteem ... 110

CHAPTER 6: Creating Healthy Habits from the Ground Up ... 126

PART 2: Raising Children to Be Resilient to Stress

CHAPTER 7: Manifesting Patience ... 139

CHAPTER 8: Encouraging Greatness vs. Demanding Greatness ... 150

CHAPTER 9: The Alchemy of Actively Listening ... 159

CHAPTER 10: Building a Safe Environment ... 167

PART 3: Individuality

CHAPTER 11: Prioritizing and Savoring Quality Time with Your Family ... 180

CHAPTER 12: Cultivating the Seeds of Greatness in a Complex World ... 193

CHAPTER 13: Recognizing Individual Needs Through Heartful Parenting ... 202

CHAPTER 14: Challenges of Raising Children with ADHD, Autism, or Diverse Diagnoses ... 211

PART 4: Discipline and Self-Discipline

    CHAPTER 15: The Unbreakable Bond of a Parent and Child   219

PART 5: From Theory to the Practice of Living with Purpose

    CHAPTER 16: Unleashing the Power of Critical Thinking in Children   232

    CHAPTER 17: Navigating the Boundaries of Domestic and Public Spaces   242

    CHAPTER 18: Living Deliberately by Design   247

PART 6: A Parenting Guide to Course Correction

    CHAPTER 19: The Beginning of Disarming Potential Bad Behaviors   259

    CHAPTER 20: Resisting Negative Situations and Worldly Temptations   268

Conclusion: Real Love and Parenting   274

Family Resources   277

Our Gratitude   278

Acknowledgments   279

About the Authors   280

Introduction

While it's often said that "parenting doesn't come with a manual," *Real Life, Real Family* was written with precisely that idea in mind. In this age of abundant information, we can no longer justify not learning how to be incredible parents. This literary offering serves as a compass to help you navigate some of the complexities of parenting.

As Dr. Maya Angelou once said, "Do the best you can until you know better. Then when you know better, do better." It's unconstructive to blame others for our familial discord, the conduct of our children, or the quality of our relationships without first engaging in introspection and striving to be deliberate in adopting healthier parenting techniques as needed. In the current state of our society, filled with increasing division, hatred, and a range of escalating issues such as mental health concerns, substance abuse, and the many diverse challenges our children face, the responsibility of parenthood carries an urgent need to evolve and adapt. The reality is that methods that may have sufficed in the past no longer hold up under the weight of today's complex issues. Therefore, we must rise to the occasion and elevate our parenting strategies accordingly.

> "The reality is that methods that may have sufficed in the past no longer hold up under the weight of today's complex issues."

We've amassed a collection of widespread and seldom-discussed parental concerns, dilemmas, and inquiries from our real-life experiences and those of other families, presenting a remarkable mosaic of perspectives on parenthood. These short, insightful stories will equip you with a range of effective strategies, while also helping you identify practices that could be harmful or create dysfunction within your family. Whether you're looking to refine your parenting approach, need additional counsel, or anticipate nurturing children in today's environment, the narratives and methodologies explained in *Real Life, Real Family* can offer invaluable assistance.

With twenty-four years of marriage encompassing the nurturing of six beautiful children, ranging in age from three years to twenty-three (Peyton, two; Brooklyn, seven; Jaxson, nine; London, ten; Logan, twenty; and Madison, twenty-two), we are constantly flooded with questions from those seeking to fathom the origins and sustenance of our patience, focus, and time allocation essential for cultivating happy and successful children in a happy and successful marriage. In our first book, *Real Life, Real Love*, we spoke candidly of our partnership, how we've weathered the adversities and obstacles thrown our way, and how, despite those trials, we've built a family unit that's filled with what we refer to as magic.

In *Real Life, Real Family*, we delve further into that magic, revealing the secrets to how we raise children to be resilient to stress, or low-stress, while fostering a solid and thriving partnership in a healthy environment. Naturally, the ultimate aspiration for the majority of parents is to raise happy, healthy, and well-adjusted children who exemplify love, respectfulness, and kindness because that's who they truly are. Nevertheless, should children fail to witness these very qualities in their homes and their prioritization remains neglected, the likelihood of these qualities taking root dwindles—and we want to help change that or prevent it from happening.

We must acknowledge that we've encountered numerous well-mannered, respectful children whose parents have done a commendable job in their upbringing. However, while it's important to say that the experiences of children and young adults can significantly vary depending on their circumstances, there are many misguided children and wayward youth. The harsh disrespect we see parents endure from some of these children is devastating. We've found that some parents are conditioned to accept disrespect, others remain unaware of its presence, and some might choose to disregard disrespectful and negative behaviors, clinging to the hope that their children will eventually outgrow them. But is it a risk worth taking? Allowing problematic behaviors to manifest can adversely affect a child's life as a whole. Unaddressed, these behaviors can lead to long-term issues, such as difficulty forming healthy relationships, poor decision-making, mental health issues, and placing them at an elevated risk of substance abuse. Communities need our help. This society can't do what we can as parents, and when it comes to raising our children, we can do better. We know we can.

Alternatively, by improving our own behavior, this positivity spills over, and we're enriching our children's lives. Setting a positive example, teaching values, and providing resources give them the most favorable prospects for success. We can also open up new opportunities for them that we might not have been able to access ourselves.

Our objective is to ease concerns by answering questions you may have to assist in laying the foundational groundwork needed to have well-behaved and good-hearted children, through strategies to amplify your effectiveness as parents. Distinct from other parenting books, which often tell parents what they should and shouldn't do from a clinical perspective, *Real Life, Real Family* brims with real experiences from two parents (with RaaShaun, a host of the successful syndicated radio show *The Breakfast Club* and the *Casey Crew* podcast on all podcast platforms) with authentic connections that keeps us in tune with society so much so that we've practically seen, experienced, and heard it all! In addition, we share stories from diverse fellow parents giving their experiences, viewpoints, and encounters about successful and ineffective parenting methodologies covering various topics.

Often overlooked are the interactions between parent and child and between siblings, and the mother-and-father partnership, which are pivotal for a thriving family. We don't hold back when we delve into these relationships and explore ways to navigate and strengthen them. Recognizing our culturally diverse society, which includes an array of family structures—from single-parent and blended families to diverse and LGBTQ+ households—we aim to offer adaptable, healthy perspectives. These insights can be custom-tailored to suit and support your unique family dynamic. Recognizing the unique complexities of parenting, we understand that there's no "one-size-fits-all" solution. This is particularly true when facing the distinct challenges associated with raising children diagnosed with ADHD, autism, or other diverse health conditions. Each situation requires a personalized and respectful approach. We encourage you to embrace what resonates with you and your family and share the rest with others on a similar journey. Regardless of your relational circumstances or the number of children you have, this book will provide the tools to build a resilient family unit rich in purpose, intention, respect, and love.

When we look at society, whether in the context of a dual-parent or single-parent household, we bear the responsibility for rearing, educating, loving, safeguarding, and disciplining our children. Take a minute and observe your surroundings. You'll find that your children require unwavering reliability, compassion, attentiveness, and deliberateness in the lessons and examples you impart through consistent communication and conduct. In other words, they need the best part of you!

> **"We encourage you to embrace what resonates with you and your family and share the rest with others on a similar journey."**

As we watch the many troubling news headlines surrounding children today, they're a call to action to safeguard their physical and emotional well-being, instill within them a deep sense of self-confidence, build unbreakable bonds of trust, and devote ourselves to their growth and development through active listening and unwavering support. While the challenges we face may seem overwhelming, our shared mission is to create a brighter future for our children, which is an immense responsibility of profound significance. We're sharing narratives illuminating important moments, and some are just fun little lessons, but each of them possesses aspects of parenting that you can adapt because they're designed to help navigate your remarkable journey. It still takes a village to raise a child. A strong, competent, reliable, confident, and loving one. Given some may need access to resources and guidance, *Real Life, Real Family* is our contribution.

Faith holds an indispensable role within our family, and we'll tell you why. However, for those who do not subscribe to religious convictions, this doesn't signify an inability or failure to be wonderful parents. Our intent in sharing our approach to raising children within today's culture and the significance of a loving family unit is to supply parents with diverse circumstances and distinctive viewpoints that may inspire more effective parenting. So take what resonates with you as every reader of this tome shares a common aspiration for their family—*success and happiness*. Should even a single invaluable parenting technique or suggestion enhance your lives, adapt it as you deem necessary.

Children are susceptible to numerous vulnerabilities, both within the domestic sphere and beyond. For some, the dangers may lie with the parent(s) or the household environment, whereas for others, the problems stem from society at large. For this reason, our children must be at the forefront of our minds, with our actions and behaviors aligning accordingly. We know your home environment profoundly influences your child's mental and physical development, which is why we spent so much time building the foundation of ours. And while some children presently lack authentic self-assurance and many struggle with mental health challenges, it's not too late to initiate efforts aimed at assisting, correcting, better managing, or even preventing these issues. The journey commences within the sanctuary of your home—*with you*.

> **"It still takes a village to raise a child. A strong, competent, reliable, confident, and loving one."**

Unfortunately, with harmful or abusive parents, children may be predisposed to emulate such behaviors, display defiance, or adopt a demeanor diametrically opposed to their experiences. We've encountered children with both tendencies—some raised by alcohol-dependent parents. The crux of our argument is that no solitary predictor can determine the extent to which a child's environment will shape them, and, even when combined, these factors may yield disparate outcomes. Even then, we can't guess how they will turn out. Though a child's environment can significantly impact them, other factors like genetics, temperament, and resiliency play a role in their development. Nevertheless, this doesn't absolve us of our responsibility to provide our greatest efforts.

As a preemptive measure, *Real Life, Real Family* serves as a guide in recognizing risk factors. We can never be too knowledgeable or too prepared—right? Traumatic life experiences, unhealthy relationships, discrimination, mental health concerns, and financial instability often correlate with a heightened probability of unfavorable outcomes. The good thing is that we're not simply pointing out unsolvable problems or delivering negative news. Instead, our objective is to provide relatable and practical solutions that can help address the challenges at hand. Additionally, we're lifting the veil on social media with good reason. Its ramifications can undermine self-esteem, exacerbate insecurities, and enable cyberbullying unbeknownst to parents, wherein the impact on one reverberates throughout the entire family. Because of our interconnectedness as human beings, our actions, decisions, and behaviors can have far-reaching consequences beyond our immediate spheres of influence, so we also explore protective factors. Among the characteristics that can mitigate the influence of risk factors are enrolling your children in a quality education system, fostering moral principles, encouraging positive peer associations, nurturing community ties, honing coping mechanisms, developing problem-solving abilities, achieving financial stability, and providing parental support, to name a few. We will explain why evaluating whether your environment threatens a child's development or prepares them for success is necessary. While we may lack the ability to control these risk factors, we can help children understand and make meaning of them, transforming them into instructive and cautionary lessons. But first, they must trust *you*. So we explore the importance of actively listening, attuning ourselves to our children's needs, and engaging in honest conversations to better equip and safeguard them throughout their lives.

For the record, there is no singular, definitive, or perfect approach to parenting. As individuals, we wield a tremendous capacity to shape our children's growth and development through love and guidance. Though love is an essential ingredient, it is only through additional supportive measures that we can truly inspire and nurture greatness within our children. With six beautiful children, like most, we've been through our ups and downs and have had failures. And while these experiences are an inherent aspect of parenthood, we've adapted when necessary, seamlessly integrating changes by refining our parenting approach—just as you can. Change is an inherent part of our lives for ourselves and our children. Embracing the need to adapt and evolve allows us to navigate these inevitable changes with resilience and growth.

It's a common belief that financial abundance begets happiness, time, and the means to raise healthy, well-adjusted children. In reality, a combination of love, time, patience, honest communication, trust, and an abundance of affection can help achieve this goal. Of course, being financially secure or having a higher socioeconomic status can provide greater access to resources, making it easier to do things; however, it doesn't mean you can't raise a healthy and happy family with what you have. After we graduated from college, married, and were expecting our daughter Madison, we were living in a renovated basement apartment (in Gia's mother's home). Although we had the support of our parents that others may not have, that's where we began creating our strong foundation for raising our family. As our family expanded, this groundwork contributed to our continued success and enabled us to eliminate any barriers that arose between us and our children.

What are we trying to say with all of this? That what we have is awesome! Our home is so magical that anyone who walks through our doors can immediately see and feel it, and we want *you* to have that too! We want everyone to have the incredible experiences with their children that we have cherished and for the younger generations to reciprocate these experiences with their parents. People think what we do to achieve this is difficult, and some may perceive our endeavors as challenging. But the truth is that consistency and intentional living makes the process far more manageable. *We choose, and we execute.* You can learn to do the same.

Being a good parent isn't about the pursuit of perfection. At its core, it revolves around the expression of love—a sentiment that doesn't preclude challenges, hurdles, and discord but, rather, preserves progress and joy. As parents, it's incumbent upon us to exemplify positivity because we bear the responsibility of shaping our children's lives, and they rely on our persistent guidance. Regrettably, some children are born to parents who don't assume that responsibility. Some parents can't. However, our efforts are to continue elevating our standards and encourage you to break bad habits and the cycle of negativity to yield unprecedented benefits for your family. We want you to look internally at your family structure and identify where the problems are so you can work to effect meaningful change. Doing so can change the trajectory of not only your life, but also your children's. If we can change families for the future, we can create something extraordinary in society and achieve generational prosperity.

RaaShaun and I aspire to address questions you may have while disclosing parenting strategies to help raise children who are productive, respectful, loving, compassionate, and good-hearted members of both your family and the broader society. And our questions can help you nurture a successful family with healthier habits. Our goal in writing this book is to incite change. If we can convey a thought that we believe in and reside by and it lands, that's where the shift begins. Take the initiative to shape your children's healthy development. If you want to level up, you have to be motivated to think more deeply and make changes in your life and in the lives of your children.

Welcome to a solution-focused journey. With our Real Life Reflections closing each section, you'll find questions to help you determine the best path forward and discover solutions fitting your family's unique dynamics and lifestyle. So, get your highlighter, grab those sticky notes, and get ready! This book is set to become a cherished favorite. A "parental roadmap," offering an insightful perspective on each stage of parenting. With each chapter uniquely addressing varying ages, challenges, and preventive strategies, you're sure to encounter a different resonating message every time you delve in. Get ready. It's time to truly embrace the unexpected journey of parenthood! You will better understand *what to expect when you're parenting!*

"After all, we are nurturing the next generation of leaders."

If we want to create a resilient family legacy, we must be willing to adapt ways that encourage us to become better parents, children, and human beings. *After all, we are nurturing the next generation of leaders.*

PART ONE

The Family Unit

1. The Importance of Creating a Family Mission Statement

We are a unit.
We respect each other.
We always have each other's backs.
We always uplift each other and point out the good in one another.
We represent each other at all times.
Our overarching purpose is rooted in family, fun, and faith.
We are each other's soft place to land.

A mission statement is a concise statement that outlines the purpose of an organization and their reason for existence. Then the organization creates a strategy that aligns with their values and works to achieve it. Why shouldn't families do the same? A family mission statement can help your family unite around common values and aspirations. It can provide guidance and focus in decision-making, enhance communication, and ensure that family members remain committed to achieving their collective objectives. Furthermore, a well-crafted mission statement can improve or even dissolve sibling rivalries, fostering strong and nurturing relationships.

(Gia)

We've discussed our mission statement in *Real Life, Real Love*. However, here, we dive deeper into the importance of creating a family mission statement through conscious cultivation of your children's growth tailored to each member of your family. We have revised our mission statement to include our children's perspectives and needs. By creating a family mission statement, you can ensure that each family member is empowered to live a life congruent with your values and goals. We've discovered that when children have a role and a sense of a higher purpose within the home, their values invariably extend out into the world.

The Value of a Mission Statement

Why is a mission statement valuable for your family? When goals are articulated, a transformative effect ensues, and it can take on a life of its own. By explicitly expressing aspirations—whether pertaining to career, sports, family life, vacations, faith, innovations, or other pursuits—you enhance the likelihood of their realization. Consider the impact of an academic syllabus outlining objectives for a semester; you might find yourself regularly monitoring progress to ensure you remain on course. Similarly, when your values and identity are captured in words, their power intensifies. As these words crystallize into thoughts and, ultimately, actions, they come to life. You are deliberate in giving your children evidence that a rewarding life is possible. You are practicing *conscious parenting*.

When asked to describe the characteristics of your family, the very essence of your shared values often emerges. Perhaps you identify as hardworking, closely connected, nurturing, jovial, and mutually supportive—elements that constitute the core of your family identity. A mission statement articulates these meaningful facets, integrating them seamlessly into your daily life and bringing you even closer.

> **"Our family is steadfast in uplifting each member, and we never hesitate to illuminate the goodness in one another."**

RaaShaun and I discussed the impact of our mission statement as our family expanded yet again, and we revisited and refined it to achieve even greater effectiveness by allowing our children to weigh in. Our family functions as a cohesive unit, honoring one another and unfailingly providing support in times of need—regardless of the circumstances. Our family is steadfast in uplifting each member, and we never hesitate to illuminate the goodness in one another. No matter where we find ourselves or in whose company, we invariably serve as ambassadors for our family. As we say, our overarching purpose is to be rooted in fun, family, and faith. With an unshakable conviction in the divine principle that "with God, all things are possible," we embrace these values as the guiding force in our lives. You put your trust in something. This is where we place ours.

Our mission statement works because our overarching objective is to hold one another accountable, fostering closeness and fortitude within the family. If your family lacks established core values, take a moment to reflect upon your collective identity. Assess who you are as a family and envision who you aspire to become. Contemplate the changes that could enhance your home environment and family cohesiveness. How can you deepen connections with your children? What are their intrinsic needs? Does your family operate as a cohesive entity or as disparate individuals? Is there a shared foundation of respect and trust? Are you fully engaged in the practice of active listening, genuinely empathizing with one another's emotional experiences? We encourage you to sit with these questions before writing your statement and determine which values have the most significance and necessity within your family unit.

> **REAL LIFE REFLECTIONS**
>
> A Real Life Reflection is examining your experiences and actions and thinking critically about what you have learned in each *Real Life, Real Family* section. Our Real Life Reflections aim to help you gain insight into your thoughts, experiences, and needs and use that insight to make positive changes in your life and your children's lives. This can be valuable for personal growth, improving relationships, decision-making, and problem-solving skills. We've created these questions to help you determine what aspects of *Real Life, Real Family* you want to adopt and, based on your family history and structure, health goals, economic status, and culture, the solutions that will meet your needs.

1. In what ways can a family mission statement help maintain a sense of unity and purpose amid the challenges and changes that life may bring?

   _____
   _____
   _____

2. How do your family's shared values and characteristics currently shape your daily interactions and decision-making?

   _____
   _____
   _____

3. In what ways does having clear goals and aspirations contribute to the personal growth and development of each family member?

   _____
   _____
   _____

4. How might reflecting on your family's current environment and relationships help identify areas for improvement or change?

   _____
   _____
   _____

5. How does creating your family's mission statement help sustain a loving and supportive home environment?

   _____
   _____
   _____

> 6. In what ways can accountability within the family nurture closeness and resilience among your members?
>
> _____
>
> _____
>
> _____

Creating a Mission Statement

Our families deserve the same deliberations we give to purchasing a home or vehicle, selecting vacation destinations, and other endeavors. Take the first step and initiate the process by convening a family meeting to explore the values and aspirations most significant to each member. Listen attentively, and inquire further. Then weave these collective ideals into the tapestry of your mission statement. Your youngest child may tell you that they don't feel respected, so part of your mission statement may be to respect everyone's thoughts and ideas. Your eldest may want to help others as a family, so incorporate being rooted in family-centered philanthropy, community service, or faith-based activities. Once you've identified the actions or behaviors to adopt, discuss how to achieve these objectives as a family and infuse the experience with fun and creativity!

When you know what you want, act with intention to cultivate consistency in embodying your mission statement to its fullest extent. Establish goals and strive to achieve them so they become inherent for everyone. Embrace the family you aspire to be, remaining vigilant that there are many temptations in life that can cause you to veer off course.

> **REAL LIFE REFLECTIONS**
>
> 1. Encourage respect, value, and participation from your youngest child to your eldest.

2. Create an enjoyable and creative process for family objectives.

3. Utilize intentional actions to maintain focus and progress.

4. Each year, evaluate the family mission statement and progress toward goals for beneficial insights.

Establishing Lasting Goals for Your Family

In creating a family mission statement, the goal is to inspire our loved ones to live their most meaningful lives. Our intent is not to exert control but rather to provide guidance preventing them from making irrevocable mistakes. Having instilled integrity, openness, and faith, we also want our children to accumulate experiences and enjoy life—really enjoy life, which is why part of our family mission statement is *fun*. Although often undervalued, fun holds immense importance in our household. Is your home fun? How often do you create the joy that flows through the hearts and minds of your children? We're constantly playing, laughing, and joking around because we're innately happy and silly. We roast each other and partake in a myriad of enjoyable activities that cater to having fun. Observing the undeniable sense of closeness that our mission statement has instilled within our children is truly a beautiful thing, made possible through the deliberate and mindful process of conscious cultivation.

> "Is your home fun? How often do you create the joy that flows through the hearts and minds of your children?"

Conscious cultivation can be likened to the meticulous care of a master gardener tending to their prized garden. In this context, the garden represents the family unit, with each member being a unique and vibrant plant requiring tailored attention and nourishment. As the gardener, your role is to remain cognizant of the influence your words and actions exert upon your children, fostering an environment that encourages growth, harmony, and resilience.

As parents, we must be vigilant in nurturing our children's minds and spirits, acknowledging that our words and behaviors are the vital nutrients that shape their characters and worldviews. By actively engaging in conscious cultivation, we demonstrate a commitment to the well-being and flourishing of our family as we thoughtfully and intentionally sow the seeds of love, wisdom, and understanding that will ultimately blossom into a thriving, cohesive, and supportive home environment.

> **"A mission statement transcends the home environment, helping establish lasting habits and objectives that promote your family's well-being."**

When our son Logan was embarking on his way to college, he received acceptance letters from multiple institutions, including his top choice, which he eagerly accepted. This prestigious university, with its exceptional academics and athletic programs, picturesque campus, favorable climate, and competitive acceptance rate, was our first choice for him as well. We encouraged him to examine the school holistically, ensuring that it would allow him to uphold our family mission statement and that, most importantly, he would have fun. A mission statement transcends the home environment, helping establish lasting habits and objectives that promote your family's well-being.

REAL LIFE REFLECTIONS

1. Create a family mission statement.
2. Embrace conscious cultivation.
3. Balance guidance and freedom for children.
4. Support informed decision-making.
5. Evaluate educational institutions.
6. Apply your family mission statement principles beyond the home.

The Reality of What Respect Displays

Respect is a nuanced concept. In our family, it encompasses our children deliberately demonstrating respect toward us, themselves, and one another while also witnessing us treating them with respect. My husband's work schedule is demanding—*incredibly demanding!* RaaShaun may sleep only three hours a night, often juggling numerous responsibilities each day. He carries a lot on his shoulders. The manner in which he balances his career and family life is truly remarkable. Sometimes, RaaShaun is tired and has a lot on his mind. In *Real Life, Real Love*, we touched upon the tendency for parents to reflexively say no to their children's requests. However, there are instances when we might not fully comprehend the rationale or significance behind a child's question. Though I've always been mindful of what I would say before responding to our children, RaaShaun may not always exercise the same caution. Sometimes, he makes a decision and moves on to the next thing he's working on or thinking about. At times, his response may not be warranted. However, the respect we have for each other's opinions prompts us to actively listen and seek understanding. That means RaaShaun always has my ear and I also have his, so it's easy to hold one another accountable.

In response to something Madison asked her father one day, RaaShaun's short answer was *"No."* And from my perspective, Madison was understandably upset because her father didn't pause long enough to hear why or ask her why. Instead, he just said "No" and returned to what he was doing or thinking about. As I said, RaaShaun works hard and constantly has a lot of things on his mind.

When I told RaaShaun, "Babes! You know you're wylin', right? ("Babes" is what I call RaaShaun.) You need to apologize and explain why you responded that way." I sensed that his thoughts were elsewhere and not with our conversation.

But his eyes smiled, and he asked curiously, "Why?"

I replied, "Not only are we teaching them to be respectful, but we're also imparting valuable life lessons. When you don't talk to your children about why you reacted that way, you're inadvertently teaching them the way of the world. Sometimes, people may respond negatively. But keeping respect, trust, and understanding in play when you take a moment to clarify that something's going on with Daddy, not them, is important."

Some are of the mindset that parents don't need to apologize to their children. Why do *we* apologize when it's warranted? RaaShaun and I do it because it teaches our children that apologizing and admitting when you're wrong isn't done out of weakness but, rather, strength and self-assurance. Over the years, our children's behaviors have demonstrated that these lessons in respect have taught them humility and accountability, which they also emulate in their interactions with one another.

"No matter where we go, people often compliment us on the respectful, kind, and polite demeanor of our kids."

No matter where we go, people often compliment us on the respectful, kind, and polite demeanor of our kids. In the process of raising them, we never considered our approach exceptional; it simply seemed normal. Observing the reactions of those outside our home to our children's behavior, we've come to recognize how extraordinary it is when, in truth, it shouldn't be. People hold their children to varying expectations depending on cultural factors. Based on our observations and friends, Black households are often much stricter, demanding more deference, better manners, and a heightened level of civility and accountability over other households. Why? We were slaves. Beaten into submission. We kept those manners and habits out of fear. And sadly, looking at society, that fear still exists. Throughout the annals of history and what today's culture has illustrated, *we* have not been afforded the freedom to go out and challenge the status quo—speaking our minds and expressing our truths. Doing so was and still is a catalyst for harm. The virtue of respect has served as a vital protective mechanism. This sobering reality drove our predecessors to impart upon us the invaluable lesson of respect, a lesson that we've dutifully embraced and propagated through successive generations. We've had, and still have, separate rules that we've sustained to try and protect ourselves and our children.

For generations, our race has faced scrutiny and discrimination, compelling us to be on our best behavior, as if external judgments held the ultimate authority over our worth. However, the emergence of movements like Black Lives Matter and the persistent advocacy of countless individuals have gradually dismantled the monolithic misconceptions and stereotypes that have long overshadowed our existence. Respect, an integral facet of our cultural identity, was initially fostered within the sanctuary of our homes. Although we have nothing to prove, to anyone, this legacy of maintaining our best behavior for the world to see persists. Our initial understanding of respect may have been rooted in the crucible of fear, but it has since evolved into an intrinsic component of our cultural fabric. By embodying and demonstrating respect, we not only honor our families and ourselves but also celebrate the rich tapestry of our shared heritage. How do you accomplish this? Is there anything in your history or culture that causes you to maintain habits or behaviors?

> **"By embodying and demonstrating respect, we not only honor our families and ourselves but also celebrate the rich tapestry of our shared heritage."**

Instilling respect and discipline in children can pose challenges for parents, particularly when both parents must work collaboratively for the welfare and well-being of their kids. Families with divorced or separated parents, in particular, may face heightened difficulties in raising children if they operate under divergent sets of rules and values. At times, parents may oppose each other's disciplinary actions or expectations of respect, driven by lingering resentment or animosity. However, it's crucial to rise above these personal struggles and prioritize the children's best interests. There can be harmony in chaos when you love your children enough to put their well-being first.

Instead of perpetuating a cycle of conflict or toxicity, recognize the beauty and potential in your children and work together to ensure their success. You can accomplish this by finding common ground, establishing consistent expectations, and managing emotional discord effectively. By doing so, you can nurture an environment of love, respect, and unity, allowing your children to thrive and flourish.

In some family structures, particularly those with single parents, the need to instill a deep sense of respect and discipline in children becomes even more critical, as any lapses in discipline may result in particularly challenging consequences. For instance, single parents may lack the flexibility to abandon their professional obligations in order to address a child's behavioral issues at school. Consequently, it's essential to cultivate respect within these families and establish strict guidelines to safeguard their children while also providing a nurturing and supportive atmosphere. The absence of independence and structure within your family dynamic can incite anger and disobedience in children, engendering a dysfunctional environment. When respect is in play, you'll see the difference.

REAL LIFE REFLECTIONS

1. Enhancing family communication is a way of valuing your partner's opinions.

2. Active listening is key to a respectful family environment.

3. Cultural aspects shape norms and expectations about family respect.

4. Societal stereotypes have an impact on your family's respect and discipline focus.

5. Respect as a safeguard has a historical function in communities.

6. Apologizing to your children is a lesson in humility and accountability.

R-E-S-P-E-C-T and the Single Parent

A Real Life Inspiration: RaaShaun and I share a close friendship with Kara, a Black single mother who has devotedly nurtured her three children despite the absence of support from their father or extended family. Residing in a tough neighborhood in New York, Kara has fiercely—and I mean fiercely—protected her children, attentively overseeing their schedules and coordinating a routine that accommodated all their needs. Her kids, now adults, seamlessly formed into a cohesive unit, collaborating on household chores and academic pursuits and attending each other's athletic competitions and events. Kara looks at her status as a single parent not as a detriment but as a testament to her resilience and love for her kids. When we inquired about the secret behind her well-mannered children, Kara attributed their exemplary behavior to the tenet of respect that formed the cornerstone of their family ethos. She told us, "Everything we did was centered on respect. We respected each other's time, personal property, feelings and opinions, our schedules with work and sports, academics, and everything else. For my children, it's innate. They knew I wasn't one to tolerate *disrespect*, and they knew not to leave the house and carry themselves any other way than respectfully. There was no room for error. I demanded respect and self-respect from the onset of parenting because I knew I was doing it on my own. When kids are taught at an early age to respect you, and you consistently reinforce it, everything—no drugs, no drinking, no lying, no talking back, no laziness, no disrespecting yourselves—falls under those guidelines. I discovered early on that fostering self-respect contributed to their personal growth, relationships, happiness—and the outcome was overall success for all of us. Respect was our unspoken mission statement, and it just worked for us."

Kara's kids internalized her intolerance for disrespect, and they were acutely aware of the expectation to conduct themselves with decorum, both within and beyond the confines of their home. Kara emphasized the importance of demanding respect and self-respect from the very inception of her parenting journey, cognizant of her singular role in raising her children.

Kara consciously cultivated a profoundly enriching relationship with her three children, meticulously setting goals that directed their energies toward realizing their purposes, rather than succumbing to the pitfalls that lined the streets. Her two sons and daughter bore witness to their mother's tireless efforts to actualize her dreams for their family. Kara explained that it was vital to demonstrate that her work was an expression of her unwavering commitment to their well-being because her children are her foremost priority. After acquiring her bachelor's degree in marketing and a real estate license, Kara constructed a thriving real estate enterprise, ultimately transitioning from an apartment dweller to a homeowner. Hearing Kara explain how her kids were instrumental in her success, enabling her to concentrate on nurturing them without constant worry, was beautiful. She imparted lessons on financial literacy and encouraged the pursuit of higher education, resulting in the emergence of three college graduates who followed their mother's entrepreneurial spirit. Kara is a strong advocate for self-respect. She believes that it's an essential component in various aspects of life, including personal growth, relationships, happiness, and inner peace. Kara said that self-respect is the cornerstone of her success, empowering her family to make positive choices and create fulfilling lives.

Certain cultures adhere strictly to their established norms, setting lofty expectations and ensuring that reverence for parental figures is passed down through generations. Typically, individuals within these cultures are steered toward prestigious professions such as medicine, law, or politics, and they dutifully follow the counsel of their elders, honoring the bond of respect.

In the context of Black culture, we're working beyond what others must do to get to that point, or we are considered "lesser than." We're viewed differently, which is why for many of us respect is inherent. When we show children respect and guide them to honor themselves, one another, and us, it's paramount to raising children in a somewhat unhealthy society. Why? We lay the foundation for their growth, and they will know what to demand from the rest of the world.

In Kara's family, respect is the keystone supporting a well-designed and sturdy structure. Her emphasis on respect as her family's core value unites her children in their differences, creating a harmonious and resilient family bond. By instilling respect and self-respect from the beginning, Kara's children learn to support one another, value each other's strengths and perspectives, and face the challenges of their environment with unwavering determination.

With respect as the foundation in their lives, Kara's kids are building solid relationships, pursuing their aspirations, and thriving in a society that may otherwise undermine or not recognize their potential. By understanding the crucial role respect plays, you might find inspiration in Kara's approach and utilize it as a blueprint for nurturing a healthy, prosperous, and supportive family environment.

REAL LIFE REFLECTIONS

Six ways to get to respect:

1. Instill respect.
2. Set high expectations.
3. Empower marginalized backgrounds.
4. Be an awesome role model.
5. Balance cultural norms with individuality.
6. Promote healthy relationships.

A Timeless Blueprint

A Real Life Lesson: From our experiences and personal relationships, we are privy to understanding how many unique families—single or dual, blended, culturally diverse, and LGBTQ+—operate. We've found that in numerous households, the dynamics between parents and their children starkly contrast those prevalent in Black families. This may be attributable to the heightened discipline, elevated expectations, or distinctive family structures that characterize Black households. Our observations of the upbringing of children in many—yes, many—of the families we know have revealed a lack of respect for their parents, manifested in the use of profanity, belligerence, or blatant disregard. You know you've seen this! And we've seen too many upsetting public displays of parents struggling to manage their child or children. Now, full disclosure, we never know what kind of mitigating circumstances there are, but from what we witnessed and the way it happened, this one seemed to be an all-out tantrum.

RaaShaun and I were at the Miami airport, and this little boy about five years old threw a monster tantrum. He stood up on his seat and started jumping up and down. His mom said, "Come on, Matthew, don't act like that. Come on. I don't want you to get hurt." But Matthew kept unraveling—jumping from one seat to another and running across the legs of anyone in his way. How much unraveling had to happen until there was no more sweater? That baby kept going! And going! His mother threw her hands up, looked at his father, and nodded for him to stop Matthew, but he angrily shook his head and snapped under his breath, "You spoil him. You let him get away with this shit! You fix it! He's out of control."

With reluctance, his mother got up and scooped her son off the legs of an annoyed gentleman on a call, who threw his hands up and mouthed, "What the f—!"

Matthew kept unraveling—crying and swatting at his mother to put him down, growing louder with every step she took. Finally, when she put him down, he fell on the floor and started rolling around, kicking his feet all over the place. Other observers were locked in on little Matthew, and some were laughing while RaaShaun and I had that nonverbal dialogue going on. Finally, when she sat beside her husband, he looked at his son and spoke one word. Just one firm word. "Enough!" Matthew stopped rolling, screaming, everything! He got up and sat beside his father, quietly folding his arms across his chest. It was like his dad flipped a switch, and Matthew turned it off. We've all seen situations like this at some point or another. When was the last time you witnessed a child acting disrespectfully and questioned the parenting or wondered if their parents would let it persist or stop it?

Witnessing physical aggression among siblings and an absence of gratitude have further underscored this disparity. In certain situations, parents have even appeared intimidated by their own children. Yet, despite seeing and hearing it all, it's still unimaginable. It's not that this behavior is sprinkled here and there. It's consistent in this society, making it increasingly toxic. Can you imagine being afraid of your child? When encountering a child's bad behavior, it might be easy to attribute it to their inherent nature or upbringing, but it is often a combination of both—nature and nurture. However, as parents, we can positively influence their future by laying a strong foundation early in their development. This includes teaching basic principles and maintaining consistency. If problematic behaviors continue and don't align with typical developmental stages, it may be best to consult a specialist. There could be underlying, unseen factors causing this behavior, leading to misunderstandings or mislabeling of the child.

To show we are a close-knit unit and ensure our children feel that they are already a part of something extraordinary, we refer to them as "Choos." It is a nickname their grandmother (my mom) created for them, beginning with Madison. When we refer to them individually, we shorten their first names and add Choo. For instance, Madison is Maddie-Choo. And when referring to our children, we call them the Choo Crew. And truthfully, anything starting or ending with the word "Choo" is fair game. We have a lot of fun with this and expect to be using the nickname Choo until our children have children and they pass it along. This is something that we identify with as a family. It lets our children know they are part of something special—our family unit. Consider creating something for your family and consistently use it with one another.

Our Londy Choo was two and had just started attending school, where she saw other kids throwing tantrums—we saw them too. When she came home, she asked for something. I can't recall what it was, but I know I told her no, and my baby girl threw a full-blown tantrum, rolling around on the floor like little Matthew! I walked over to London, picked her up, and gave her one stern warning: "We—Don't—Do—That." Then, I looked London directly in her pretty little eyes until I saw it click. She recoiled, and when I put her down, she went and sat on the sofa. I sat beside her and told her, "You will never do that again. Okay?" London nodded and fell softly into my lap. I knew it was necessary to stop that behavior early, or it would only continue, whether I was around or not.

Children respect authority. When they don't feel you're worthy of respect, they will run or dominate *you*! Because London got that message early, and my parenting is consistent with that warning, she knew I wouldn't tolerate it. And it worked because I never had a problem with London—*until* seven or eight months later.

As a mom, I have this fear of our children falling down the stairs when they're little. So we've taken precautions, and we're always vigilant; however, we can't control everything like those moments we're not with them. Our children know they can't go up and down the stairs without holding on to the rail. So one particular time, when I came out of our bedroom and saw London walking up the stairs, without using the rail, in a cautionary tone, I advised, "You should know better. Hold on to the railing."

"I'm a big girl. I don't need to hold the railing."

I repeated firmly, "Hold on to the railing so you don't fall please."

London snapped back, "See, that's why I don't like you!"

That's okay because my baby was honest. London expressed her feelings at that moment, so I couldn't get into mine. They're children, and we want to encourage open and honest communication. But what I saw was the perfect teachable moment. Again, when we stop negative behaviors in their tracks, we keep them from manifesting. Don't do it when you're upset or later when they've forgotten what they did.

I said, "London, come here." She came into my bedroom. I paused and took a deep breath before *explaining* why holding the rail is our rule and that "I don't want anything to happen to my little girl because I love you. How do you think Mommy would feel if you fell and hurt yourself?" Her eyes teared up, and she lowered her head. I asked, "Now, if you still feel that way, do you want to say that again and tell Mommy why?" She shook her head from side to side and hugged me. From then until now, I've never had to discipline London for anything.

Our daughter Madison had a little friend, and they often played together with a group of other children. One day, Madison was hanging out with that particular friend at their home. Shortly after she arrived, I received a call from Madison saying, "Mom, I need you to come get me."

"Why? Are you okay?"

"My friend is cursing her mom out."

As I grabbed my car keys, I repeated, "Curse words?"

She said, "Curse words."

Jumping in the car, I told her, "Okay, I'm coming to get you."

When I picked Madison up, I asked her friend's mother what had happened, but her mom casually acknowledged her daughter's behavior as though it was somewhat normal.

Madison explained, "She wanted something and her mother said no, so she cursed her out." Apparently, her friend continued acting out, and her mom just disappeared into another room.

I said, "Let me ask you a question. Do you like that little girl?"

"She's okay," she replied softly.

"Do I have to worry about you hanging out with her?"

"What does that mean?"

"I want to make sure that you are the type of child that doesn't get influenced by other children's behavior. Your friend can be as rude and nasty as she chooses to be to her mother; that's what they permit. But if you enjoy hanging out with her, I don't want to take that privilege away from you. Based on the fact that I don't think you would come home with the same type of behavior, I want you to be responsible enough to experience the world around you, but wise enough to separate yourself from the world around you when necessary. These are all experiences that you will learn. Your friend might be really nice to her mother on a Tuesday and a little terror on Wednesday, but I want you to be very much in control of your own existence."

"Yes, Mommy. I think I can."

Madison understood that no matter what, we must show respect for one another. Take the time to discuss how you can support your children in understanding the importance of respect for one another, even when they witness contrasting behaviors in other households. This also showed Madison that I trusted her. Our children need us to communicate and display trust in them. There are a lot of things we have to do as parents, but pointing out the good in our children is critical!

"Constant communication, especially in teachable moments, is essential. Maintain an open and honest dialogue with your children. Encourage them to share their experiences and feelings and actively listen without judgment."

Our mission statement's timeless blueprint is always in effect. I used that moment with Madison to reinforce its value and, more importantly, *to enforce her value*. RaaShaun and I constantly consider strategies to ensure our children have the ability to separate themselves from negative environments or influences when necessary. It requires a combination of encouraging open communication, providing guidance, and fostering critical thinking skills. Constant communication, especially in teachable moments, is essential. Maintain an open and honest dialogue with your children. Encourage them to share their experiences and feelings and actively listen without judgment. This will help them feel comfortable discussing any negative situations or influences they encounter, and you want them to come to you. This will allow you to help them develop critical thinking skills by asking questions that prompt them to evaluate situations, people, and their own actions. Don't be afraid to encourage them to consider the potential consequences of their decisions and how their choices align with their values.

RaaShaun and I are completely transparent with our children. We share our experiences with adverse environments or influences and explain how we separated ourselves from those situations—even today. We share incredibly funny situations that occur throughout the day with them as well. Doing this can help your children understand that they're not alone and that you're giving them advice because you've navigated some of these situations. Then, give them practical examples to follow. We've established clear guidelines for our children's behavior while further explaining the reasons behind our expectations. And it's helpful to talk with your children to ensure they fully understand the consequences of engaging in potentially harmful activities or associating with negative influences. Give it to them straight.

When you discuss hypothetical situations that involve negative influences or environments, have your children role-play with different scenarios to practice what they would do or say in those situations. This can help them build confidence in their ability to make and communicate the right decisions when faced with challenging circumstances. After teaching them how to handle situations, encourage your children to make their own decisions and trust their instincts. Continue to pay attention to your children's decision-making track record. If they have demonstrated consistently good judgment and responsible choices in the past, it indicates that they're likely to have developed good instincts. In this situation, trusting their judgment and giving them the autonomy to make decisions can benefit their growth and confidence. On the other hand, if your children have a history of making poor decisions or consistently demonstrating poor judgment, like substance abuse or risky behaviors, it may be necessary to step in and provide more guidance and oversight. In this case, you can help them understand the potential consequences of their choices and offer support in making better decisions. Striking a balance between trust and intervention depends on each child's maturity level, past decision-making experiences, and the complexity of the decision. So stay involved, offer guidance when needed, and gradually give your children more independence as they demonstrate responsible decision-making capabilities.

Teach them the importance of standing up for their beliefs, even if it means going against the crowd. We're not saying to send them out to fly solo after doing this. You're the parent, so keep an eye on their activities, friendships, and online presence. Be aware of any changes in behaviors or interests that could indicate they've been exposed to negative influences. And in all of this, trust that your children will learn from you. So, work on any negative behaviors you have that need to change because children model healthy and unhealthy behaviors. Whatever you don't think they see, they see or sense it. Your children will be more likely to follow your lead if they see you consistently making wise choices and handling challenging situations gracefully. These strategies can help your children develop the skills and confidence to separate themselves from negative environments or influences when necessary, and, in this society, they'll encounter plenty.

"By sharing our personal stories of adversity and the strategies we employed to overcome them, we're providing our children with a roadmap for navigating their own challenges."

While negative experiences can be difficult to recount, they can also serve as valuable lessons and cautionary tales for our children. By sharing our personal stories of adversity and the strategies we employed to overcome them, we're providing our children with a roadmap for navigating their own challenges. In doing that, we're evoking a deeper appreciation for the strength and resilience born from the struggle. Additionally, by openly acknowledging the times when we may not have made the best choices or responded optimally to adversity, we demonstrate to our children that vulnerability and self-reflection are vital components of growth and personal development. In doing these things, you are teaching them how to represent your family, grow as a unit, and respect each other. These uplifting, or educational, communications show that you have one another's back because you care about them.

> **REAL LIFE REFLECTIONS**
>
> Five steps to foster respect, confidence, and safety in children:
>
> 1. Teach respect amid negative influences.
> 2. Promote self-confidence and independence.
> 3. Encourage vulnerability and self-reflection.
> 4. Develop risk assessment skills.
> 5. Impart solid decision-making and allow experiences.

The Difference Between Us

Addressing the disparity in parenting styles and family dynamics when your children interact with families from different cultural backgrounds or economic statuses requires understanding, flexibility, and open communication. You can better navigate this difference by educating yourself and investing the time to learn about different cultural practices, beliefs, and values to better understand the diverse perspectives of other families. This will allow you to have informed conversations with your children and teach them to respect and appreciate these differences.

Promoting acceptance, kindness, compassion, and empathy is essential for the well-being of all members within a family unit, as well as the broader community. It may be a good addition to your mission statement because in blended families or families with diverse backgrounds or disabilities, these values are especially important as they can help bridge gaps and facilitate understanding between people with different experiences and perspectives. RaaShaun and I support encouraging positive behaviors that create stronger family bonds and contribute to a more united and supportive society.

As we've explained regarding Madison and Logan, they've faced exclusionary treatment; however, we firmly believe in promoting an inclusive and accepting environment for everyone rather than subscribing to negative behaviors. Take the time to correct your children in moments that can teach them to be empathetic and respectful of others, regardless of their cultural background or economic status. Help them understand that families can have different values, beliefs, and practices that are equally valid and deserving of respect. And talk openly with your children about their experiences with other families and encourage them to share their thoughts, feelings, and any concerns about the differences they observe. When you encourage unbiased dialogue, it can help your children to accept and understand those differences. We encourage you to use these conversations to discuss embracing diversity and learning from others rather than passing judgment.

With Madison, I established clear expectations for her behavior when interacting with other families, taking into account the different cultural norms she may encounter. Be open to adjusting your own expectations as needed to accommodate these differences.

Given we live in a culturally diverse world, a good way to help your children accept and understand differences is, when possible, develop relationships with the parents of your children's friends from diverse backgrounds. Engage in open and respectful conversations about your different parenting styles and family dynamics and work together to find common ground and support one another. This can help your children learn how to adapt and be flexible when faced with different family dynamics or cultural practices. Encourage them to be open-minded and willing to learn from others while staying true to their own values.

Demonstrate tolerance, acceptance, and curiosity about other cultures and lifestyles in your own behavior. Your children are more likely to follow your example if they see you embracing and celebrating diversity rather than showing disrespect. Instead, address common stereotypes and prejudices by discussing them with your children. When you teach them to challenge these assumptions, you're encouraging them to be critical thinkers and to form their own opinions based on their experiences and interactions with others.

While society is often quick to acknowledge and disrespect differences, we must discourage that attitude and behavior by focusing on the commonalities that bring people together. Help your children see that, despite someone's differences, most families share similar values such as love, respect, and support for one another. Incorporating these strategies into a mission statement allows you to address the disparities in parenting styles and family dynamics, fostering an environment where children can develop meaningful relationships with others from diverse backgrounds and learn the value of embracing cultural and societal differences.

REAL LIFE REFLECTIONS

1. What are ways you can educate yourself about different cultural practices, beliefs, and values in order to better understand and appreciate diverse perspectives?

2. What are some ways to teach your children empathy and respect for families with different values, beliefs, and practices, regardless of their cultural background or economic status?

3. How can you maintain open communication with your children about their experiences with other families and use these conversations to discuss the importance of embracing diversity?

4. What strategies can you implement to establish and adjust clear expectations for your children's behavior when interacting with families from diverse backgrounds?

___

___

___

5. How can you model tolerance, acceptance, and curiosity about other cultures and lifestyles to encourage your children to embrace and celebrate diversity?

___

___

___

A Part of Something Special

Helping our children feel secure and interconnected within their family unit requires parents to make a concerted effort to create and sustain a supportive, nurturing, and inclusive environment. There's strength in solidarity. We see it daily with our children and other families with solid values and cohesiveness. To achieve this, fostering open communication, demonstrating unconditional love, and establishing a shared sense of identity and belonging within the family *is* necessary. As a family, when we say we are our own unit and have each other's backs, we show it in an empowering way that engenders confidence. From my husband to our beautiful baby girl Peyton, within the heart of our family, there's a greater purpose. We make sure that our children know and feel that they're part of something special. Understanding the power of a close family, we love how beautifully our children embrace one another as a unit.

"There's strength in solidarity."

During my childhood, I formed a small club where its members, my girls, united under a shared password, fostering a sense of exclusivity and importance. I wanted to create something special, and it was. Unfortunately, this camaraderie is also reminiscent of the allure that gangs hold for inner-city youth seeking identity and belonging. If we don't want to continue losing our children in a society ridden with bias, racism, discrimination, loss of faith, and lack of identity and confidence, we must cultivate an environment where our entire unit feels safe, heard, respected, accepted, loved, and acknowledged so they don't go searching for it. Offer a sense of belonging that every child deserves.

Helping your children understand there's a greater purpose for being part of your family unit and feel that they are a part of something special—it isn't work. It's beautiful. Complimenting one another and being generous with your positive thoughts are easy ways to build self-worth and closeness. With the quote "I am my brother's keeper" in mind, it's the job of everyone in the family to uphold and reinforce one another's self-esteem. We're challenging you and your family members to increase the affection shown to one another. Constructing this loving environment provides two main benefits. Children who experience a sense of love and worthiness perceive themselves as valuable contributors to the world, which in turn fosters self-esteem and confidence. Growing up with this inherent sense of love and belonging helps to safeguard them from searching for external sources of approval, validation, or affection outside the family environment.

> **"Children who experience a sense of love and worthiness perceive themselves as valuable contributors to the world, which in turn fosters self-esteem and confidence."**

We need to normalize taking the time to regularly engage in family discussions and allow children to freely express their thoughts and feelings without fear of judgment. We must promote open communication because, if we don't, we shut children down and eventually off. When we bring our children close enough to *feel* what they are feeling and can sense they need to talk, we can help create a sense of trust and understanding among the entire family unit because we can strengthen our bond and alleviate unnecessary conflicts—conflicts born out of hurt, pain, and being invisible.

Go out of your way to make your children feel unconditional love by entrenching love at the core of your family. Our role as parents is to provide unwavering support and reassurance, ensuring that our children feel valued and cherished for who they are, regardless of their achievements, setbacks, or anything else. This makes the possibility of overcoming adversities possible. They are *our* children. We're the ones they need acceptance from, and when they don't receive it, we can only pray they find healthy acceptance elsewhere. In real life—the harsh reality is that they'll find something else to be a part of that could be detrimental to their overall well-being.

Establishing shared family values, traditions, and rituals is paramount. It can help create a sense of belonging and unity. In addition, these shared experiences contribute to a collective identity that reinforces the idea that the family is a safe and supportive space. To go a little further, shared values serve as the guiding principles that govern family interactions and decision-making processes. They represent the moral compass that directs your family's trajectory, helping to ensure that it operates in harmony and with mutual respect. We continually work to cultivate the harmony within our home and between our children and ourselves. When your family unit embraces your values, they can gain a deeper understanding of their role within your family and contribute to the overall well-being and stability of your unit.

Traditions and rituals are the tangible manifestations of these shared values. They allow opportunities for your unit to form an incredible bond, create memories, and celebrate its unique identity. For example, we celebrate the twelve days of Christmas. Every Christmas Eve, Santa flies to our house and leaves a gift for each kid because they are so deserving. We have a family friend come to ring the doorbell when everyone's ready for bed, and by the time they get there, Santa's gone. They swear that they see Santa Claus flying away. The power of suggestion is fun! The kids usually find a toy or something they want, and they're taught and shown that they are so deserving that Santa singles them out. Madison and Logan are now in on it and wondered how we pulled it off for so long with them.

We also celebrate the hell out of Halloween because it's fun. We take it the extra mile by imparting creativity to the kids, and they weigh in on what they want to see, and we make it happen. But on a daily basis, we pray before meals, and we have dinner together every night. When you think about how having traditions and rituals affects a child, it gives them that sense of security and home and that they are a part of something special. Do things for your children that are fun. This is your chance to be imaginative and do all the fun things you would have wanted to do as a child or have done for you. Life is serious enough. Let your children feel safe and happy at home.

Find value in family members developing a sense of continuity that transcends generations and reinforces their interconnectedness. These shared experiences foster a sense of belonging, enabling each individual to feel valued and supported within your unique family structure, which you are not to compare to your friends' or anyone else's family structure—just make sure it's healthy and beneficial and you're happy. Give your family permission to be unique, amazing, and fun. Be vigilant that acceptance of one another *must* be given, and you know what that means in your family. Remember, your children will seek acceptance when they don't get it from you.

Our confidence in how we raise our children is so strong that our focus is not on the opinions of others unless our actions warrant negative judgment or adversely affect those around us. This, too, makes our children feel we're a unit, connected, supportive, and a part of something special. But unfortunately, so many people worry about the thoughts and opinions of others—social media is full of them. We don't. We can't. There are too many, and if we spend time worrying about them, we're not focused on what's most important. However, in instances where conduct is morally or inherently objectionable, causing harm to ourselves or others, the perspectives of others may serve as valuable catalysts for self-improvement and the betterment of our environment. Confidence in our decisions and lifestyle enables us to acknowledge differing views without permitting them to encroach upon our lives. By instilling this self-assurance in our actions, we shield our family unit from the weight of external judgment, nurturing an awareness of our place within a larger, meaningful collective. Addressing these questions and taking proactive steps to foster a safe and connected family environment can help your children feel secure and supported, ultimately contributing to their overall well-being and sense of belonging within the family unit. With that being said, if one of you falls behind, together, as a family, pick them up. Move together with love and compassion as a unit.

> **REAL LIFE REFLECTIONS**
>
> 1. Regularly facilitate meaningful conversations with family members.
>
> 2. Continuously show unconditional love and support to your children and partner.
>
> 3. Develop shared family values and traditions for unity and belonging.
>
> 4. Adopt healthy methods for resolving family conflicts.
>
> 5. Actively participate and show interest in your children's passions and pursuits.

Remove the Need to Fit In as an Option

Embodying a united family doesn't imply an insular existence devoid of morals or values in a happy bubble. Instead, it entails embracing our identity with pride and cherishing how we raise our children. And we *love* how we raise our children, especially with values and beliefs deeply rooted in fun, family, and faith. We've invested in creating a unit characterized by positive habits and affirmations that counteract the negativity pervading the world. Not only do RaaShaun and I consistently celebrate one another, but we also celebrate our children's unique qualities and strengths, fostering a strong sense of self-worth. We are confident they feel safe and understood because our children know they are part of something exceptional and substantial. We don't want them to feel they need to fit in—*anywhere*. RaaShaun and I keep that off the table as an option. We've got them! We want you to ensure your children are confident you have them too!

When children are exposed to good values at a young age and feel special and part of something good, it can help lay the foundation for healthy social and emotional development, equipping them to navigate the complexities of life with resilience and grace. The core of who you are highlights your values, strength, and exemplary nature, signifying that they are a strong foundation for guiding your beliefs and actions. Feeling connected to a close-knit, fun-loving family with good values can help establish a lasting family bond.

Brooklyn is our kind and loving seven-year-old. She was at a soccer game when she came and told me, "Mommy, I spoke to that little girl over there," she said, with her eyes sadly drifting in the girl's direction, "and she told me she didn't want to be my friend."

"When dealing with conflict, especially with another parent, it's important to be mindful of the setting and to think before reacting."

When I saw my baby's wistful expression, rather than focus on the rude little girl, I focused on the boost of confidence my Brooky-Choo needed at that moment and replied enthusiastically, "Who cares! You're the amazing one! You shouldn't be knocking down anyone's door to be your friend." The more I spoke these powerful affirmations, the brighter the spark in Brooklyn's beautiful little eyes became. "You don't need to do any more work than normal to be someone's friend. Okay? You are the special one! You are thoughtful. You are kind. You are funny. You try to help people all the time. You don't run after anyone, never ever! Do you understand?"

When dealing with conflict, especially with another parent, it's important to be mindful of the setting and to think before reacting. For example, in a repeated conflict scenario at school, there may be an opportunity to involve a mediator to help resolve the issue. This provides a structured and potentially more controlled environment for conflict resolution. On the other hand, addressing conflicts in public places like parks can be riskier, as it may be hard to gauge the other person's true emotions and state of mind at that moment. In such cases, it might be wiser to focus on your child and avoid potential confrontations, recognizing that the setting plays a crucial role in approaching and managing conflicts.

Brooklyn's eyes grew even wider as she released the biggest, brightest smile and said, "Mommy, I understand."

Those words had settled into her soul.

This was similar to a seed being planted in the soil and finally blooming into a resplendent flower. Bearing witness to such a transformative moment is an immensely gratifying experience. We want you to cultivate these profound connections within your family, instilling an unwavering certainty that every member, both parent and child, supports one another unequivocally. It is essential to prioritize self-awareness, healthy self-esteem, and a strong family support system. In doing so, children will be better equipped to navigate societal pressures and remain true to their core values. This helps dispel the notion of needing to conform and demonstrates that you stand firmly by their side.

You can help your children build a strong sense of self-worth by celebrating their unique qualities and reinforcing the idea that they don't need to conform to others' expectations. This will make them feel more secure in their identity and less inclined to seek approval from others or succumb to negative influences. Create a nurturing and supportive home environment where your children feel loved, valued, and understood. When children know they have a safe space to return to and a loving family to rely on, they are more likely to feel secure in their own identity and less likely to seek validation elsewhere.

We must remember that our children need guidance and support in making informed decisions, just as we did, especially in today's environment. Maintain open and honest communication about their experiences and feelings. When they have already experienced something, whether traumatic, hurtful, or that they didn't fully understand, this is not the time to judge them. Be supportive and teach them with love.

Encourage them to share their thoughts on fitting in, peer pressure, societal norms, and personal experiences. If you don't know what's going on with your children, you can't help them navigate these situations as greater concerns arise; they may have pulled away from communicating these issues with you. When both parents can be made aware and involved with what's going on with their children, it shows a unified front—that you are working together for their benefit. That alone speaks volumes. If you are a single parent, these conversations can offer the necessary guidance and reassurance, helping children navigate complex situations while staying true to themselves. Embed critical lessons such as emphasizing the importance of treating others with kindness and understanding within these conversations. Trusting your guidance and being accepted and respected by you will help your children gain the confidence to understand that they don't need to fit in to be accepted and respected. In today's ever-evolving society, teach them that they can adapt to different situations without compromising their values or trying to fit in. We often hear as parents "that's the way it is," but teach them the stronger, more resilient way to handle situations. Teach them your way, or the lessons you've learned.

By exhibiting tolerance and empathy, and embracing diversity, you are the best person to instill in your children the values necessary to thrive in a diverse world without feeling the need to conform. *Teach them to trust your family as a whole!* Your children are more likely to adopt these values themselves and feel less pressure to fit in. By incorporating these strategies, you can teach them that they always have the support of their family unit, which is priceless.

REAL LIFE REFLECTIONS

1. Cultivate a family environment that encourages self-identity.
2. Promote strong values for healthy child development.
3. Boost your children's confidence in response to rejection or exclusion.

> 4. Foster unity, support, and a sense of value within the family.
>
> 5. Show consistent support, negating the need for external validation.

Unfaltering Assuredness

Faith is extraordinarily significant to our family, and conversations about our beliefs and God permeate our daily lives. That said, feel free to adapt our insights to align with your own convictions.

Faith instills a sense of purpose and direction and a foundation of your core values. It encourages us to strive toward our highest selves. Without a clear set of guiding principles, whether it be from a higher power or within, you may be misguided.

"Faith instills a sense of purpose and direction and a foundation of your core values. It encourages us to strive toward our highest selves."

RaaShaun and I are acquainted with numerous individuals who question or disavow the existence of God, yet we refrain from judgment. That isn't our role in their lives. On the other hand, when asked, I've had many wonderful and deep conversations about faith with people because we're resolute in what we believe. Some want to know about our relationship with God. Others have tried to challenge it. But I tell them God's teachings are in the Bible, which serves as a beacon for all of us.

Faith transcends mere adherence to religious texts or attendance at places of worship; it involves deriving meaning from these sources and integrating the virtues they espouse into your family's foundation through trust, assurance, and confidence in God. Regardless of whether you agree that God exists or believe in the Bible, one thing that's widely accepted is that the Bible is rooted in goodness. And for our family, goodness is the goal!

When it comes to your morals and values, your purpose for your family, and the long-term success that you want, consider what you believe in and how those beliefs have shaped and impacted your life. Encourage your children to embrace their identity and not feel the need to fit in with others by creating a safe and nurturing environment at home. Celebrate your family's faith and cultural practices, and help your children understand the importance of their beliefs in shaping their identity. Share stories, rituals, and values associated with your faith, emphasizing their significance in building character and unfaltering assuredness.

Make no mistake, strong values play a crucial role in promoting healthy social and emotional development in children. To instill these values from a young age, you can model the behaviors you want your children to learn, be it honesty, kindness, or empathy. Incorporate faith-based teachings and principles into daily life and conversations, providing opportunities for children to practice and internalize these values. They won't know how to do this if they don't see you do it.

When your children experience rejection or exclusion, you can effectively respond by actively listening, then offering empathy and understanding. Help them recognize that these situations don't define their self-worth. Encourage them to draw strength from their faith and values, knowing that they have an inherent worth that cannot be diminished by the opinions of others. You can reinforce their confidence by reminding them of their unique qualities, talents, and the support they have from their family and faith community.

We've found it's possible to foster a sense of unity and support within the family by prioritizing quality time together, engaging in shared activities—*known as fun*—and maintaining open lines of communication and expression. Be deliberate in encouraging family discussions and reflections on faith-related topics, and celebrate milestones and achievements together. You can create opportunities to support and uplift one another, emphasizing the importance of a strong family unit grounded in faith and love. It's not too late to begin, but you must be genuine and consistent.

One way to consistently demonstrate unwavering support for your children is to actively listen to their concerns and feelings, validate their emotions, and offer guidance rooted in their faith and values. Understand that it's necessary to continually remind children of their unique strengths and the importance of staying true to their beliefs. You don't tell them once and let them figure it out. Be consistent in displaying and communicating examples. By providing a strong foundation of faith and family support, your children will be better equipped to navigate life's challenges without feeling the pressure to conform or seek external validation.

REAL LIFE REFLECTIONS

1. How does faith influence your family's daily life, conversations, and interactions with one another?

   _____
   _____
   _____

2. What guiding principles or values do you want to instill in your children to help them become their best selves and navigate life's challenges?

   _____
   _____
   _____

3. How can you respectfully engage in conversations about faith with individuals who may have different beliefs, while remaining firm in your own convictions?

   _____
   _____
   _____

4. In what ways can you integrate the virtues and teachings from your faith into your family's foundation, fostering trust, assurance, and confidence in your beliefs?

   _____

   _____

   _____

5. How have your beliefs shaped and impacted your lives, and how can you use these experiences to guide your children toward long-term success and a strong sense of purpose?

   _____

   _____

   _____

A Soft Place to Land + A Safe Space = Emotional Security and Confidence

Creating a soft place to land and a safe space for children carries numerous benefits that contribute to their overall well-being, emotional stability, and developmental growth. We love seeing parents do this *no—matter—what*. What RaaShaun and I have created is emotional security. A safe and soft space gives children the reassurance they need to express their feelings openly without fear of judgment or reprisal. They're more likely to share their thoughts, fears, and hopes when they feel their emotions are validated and accepted. And having a "consistently safe" environment helps your children develop trust with you and in their own judgment. It builds their confidence in knowing that they have a unique and unmatched support system they can rely on, especially during the most challenging times. When you have a safe place, you promote self-expression, and your kids will feel more comfortable expressing themselves. We've noticed that ours explore different facets of their personalities, experiment with new ideas, and freely communicate their thoughts and feelings. Everything they say is with confidence. Even the questions they ask.

"A safe and soft space gives children the reassurance they need to express their feelings openly without fear of judgment or reprisal."

When your children feel they have a soft place to land in a safe space, you've done a wonderful job in helping alleviate anxiety. We don't want our children to be uncomfortable anywhere, especially at home, in an environment we can manage. Knowing they have a soft place to land can significantly reduce anxiety and stress in children. As parents, we provide stability and continuity, which is particularly important when life becomes chaotic and, as we've witnessed, unpredictable.

A great way to encourage your children to take healthy risks is when they are taught to do it in a safe place where they can step out of their comfort zones and be imaginative, creative, or just themselves. That alone can elevate their confidence and self-esteem. This is critical for their development and learning. Learning that mistakes are a part of life in a safe place with a secure place to land when things don't go as planned can help them become more resilient. And we want our children to try again—and again in a nonjudgmental space. When your children feel safe, you're building a healthy relationship with them, which can help them learn how to foster and maintain their relationships as they grow.

In essence, a soft place to land in a safe space is a nurturing environment where children can grow and develop into emotionally healthy, confident, and resilient individuals. It's essential to help them navigate the peaks and valleys.

(RaaShaun)
Reframe the Picture

Our family mission statement was born from a collaborative effort between Gia and me. It solidifies the family as a unit, and we always act as one. Sometimes we need a set of rules to anchor us or to stand by, to clarify our objectives and shape the family's identity. And although these rules and objectives may be implicitly understood, often, they aren't posted on a wall. Instead, we hear statements about things we can and cannot do, yet these precepts exist. A well-crafted mission statement can serve as a compass for navigating life's challenges and ensuring that each family member is aware of their purpose and responsibilities.

"Our family loves having fun, laughing, and playing games."

Our family loves having fun, laughing, and playing games. When we play games, there are a set of rules that are in place to help keep the game fair and fun. By following the rules we can maintain a level playing field and help the game flow more smoothly. Our family's mission statement communicates how we should treat each other, and how we should go about our lives and operate in the world. That statement allows us to reset to zero each time, and it's a powerful way to refocus on what's important to us.

In several aspects of life, mission statements outline behavioral expectations and define a shared purpose. For instance, in kindergarten, children are taught to be nice. That's what's in the kindergarten mission statement, so kids know they're going to be nice all day long. In sports, coaches and teams have mission statements addressing behavioral and academic expectations. Companies define their expectations and purpose in the form of mission statements. With our mission statement, we, as a unit, know what our family is about, so there is never a question of are we this or that. It's something that Gia and I can live by and our kids can live by. It provides a reference point for the family's values and aspirations. We talk about it so much that it's become innate.

Our mission statement is not an authoritarian decree demanding compliance, saying, "You'd better do this!" And no one wants to create a mission statement that the kids will perceive as negative. Many times, when you hear the words "mission statement," you think of "restrictive rules," and it automatically has a negative connotation. Who wants that? Explain to your family that sometimes, those guidelines are put in place to safeguard against harm and potential adverse consequences. Our intent isn't to have rules because we want to be the bad guy or the fun police. The mission statement should also be designed to help keep your family organized and functioning smoothly. Frame it so that it's positive, focusing on the values, principles, and goals that your family wants to embody.

> "The mission statement should also be designed to help keep your family organized and functioning smoothly. Frame it so that it's positive, focusing on the values, principles, and goals that your family wants to embody."

Let's reframe the picture. For example, our radio broadcast, *The Breakfast Club*, adheres to a set of rules and regulations from the FCC designed to preserve our licenses and ensure proper conduct—and we follow them. In a similar vein, our family mission statement serves as the standard clearly articulating our purpose. By establishing a clear set of values and goals, parents can create an environment where each family member feels supported and encouraged to grow, learn, and thrive together.

A family mission statement can create direction, purpose, and balance in your home. Passionately articulating these goals to your children is essential for fostering their understanding and commitment, and regardless of schedules, or other obligations, everyone must be equally invested in adhering to them.

REAL LIFE REFLECTIONS

1. Reflect on the goals you have for your family and consider how creating a family mission statement can help clarify your family's objectives, values, and goals, leading to a stronger sense of unity and purpose.

   _____

   _____

   _____

2. Consider what's missing. What aspects of your family life do you want to emphasize and prioritize in your mission statement, such as having more fun, showing greater respect for one another, building your faith, improving communication, spending time together, or instilling the values of community service, compassion, kindness, and sharing in the responsibilities at home?

   _____

   _____

   _____

3. How can you frame your family mission statement in a positive and empowering way, rather than as a set of restrictive rules, to encourage all family members to embrace it willingly so it becomes authentic?

   _____

   _____

   _____

4. What are ways to build that closeness as a unit and consistently reinforce and live by your family mission statement, making its values and principles an innate part of your daily lives?

   _____

   _____

   _____

5. Discuss ideas you would like incorporated into your mission statement and why they are significant.

   _____

   _____

   _____

PART 1: THE FAMILY UNIT

6. Where will you place the family mission statement so everyone can see it daily?

_____

_____

_____

2. Constructing an Unshakable Foundation

In the construction of a house, the foundation constitutes the base upon which the entire structure rests. Without it, the house would have nothing to support it. As the initial component to be laid, the foundation is essential for preventing the home from collapsing, shifting, or succumbing to external damage. Unfortunately, some foundations falter due to inadequate structural design, improper supports, or other overlooked factors, ultimately revealing a lack of foresight and planning in the building process. To erect a resilient home that can withstand inclement weather and time, the goal is to construct an unbreakable foundation out of the strongest elements so that it will hold everything you put on top of it. You must be intentional about what you create and *build it to last*.

> "A structurally sound foundation will serve as a safeguard against the most damaging storms that may come your way."

When you reflect on how you were raised consciously and subconsciously, you'll see that elements from your upbringing were adapted, which can bolster or undermine the integrity of the foundation you build for your family. To construct an unshakable foundation, it's necessary to discern the origins of those elements, and determine whether they serve to fortify or weaken the base. Did these elements contribute positively to your upbringing, or did they cause fragmentation and deterioration? Next, consider the critical constituents of your foundation: integrity, respect, love, honesty, humility, joy, compassion, trust, and faith. A structurally sound foundation will serve as a safeguard against the most damaging storms that may come your way. If your foundation isn't what it should be, know it's never too late to reinforce and solidify it.

(RaaShaun)
Taking What Has Proven to Work and Adding to It

My father was a military veteran and a retired police officer. In that era, Dad single-handedly laid the foundation of our home, and his word was law. When he poured that concrete, it could support anything! Our house was built according to Dad's rule, and yes, there was only one—his way or the highway. For example, when he told me not to do something, I didn't challenge him. I didn't even *think* about disregarding his authority. My father would always warn me, "Let me know when you're coming into this house. I don't want to shoot you. Make some noise. I want to hear you coming in!" So I did. Every time.

As a kid, I didn't understand his rationale on many occasions, but because of our environment and what my father did for a living, *he did*—and that was all that mattered. I didn't question how our foundation was built because there was no asking my father why this or that, and my father didn't have the time to explain. But respecting and trusting his authority was innate. Mom and I were certain that he had our backs, and we always felt safe. I wanted our kids to feel that way too. I knew what it was like to grow up with a structurally sound foundation because we had one, and I'm grateful. It's unfortunate that, in today's society, some kids don't honor their parents with that type of respect and obedience. Why is that? Because we leave room for debate, defiance, and disrespect. Too much room—and we need to close that gap!

"As a father, I've seen the importance of achieving balance between upholding parental authority and being an emotionally accessible and engaging parent. It's a delicate balance but incredibly helpful."

Learning from past experiences and adopting proven strategies from childhood or what you've seen work in other family units can be useful in creating a resilient family foundation. Drawing from my father's unwavering authority and sense of security, I adapted these principles to today's changing family dynamics while preserving Gia's essence of actively listening to build upon that security, trust, and respect. Flexibility and adaptability as a parent will allow you to navigate life's challenges with less stress and thrive as a cohesive unit. As a DJ, I constantly have to adjust to the music and trends—imagine if I wasn't flexible.

As a father, I've seen the importance of achieving balance between upholding parental authority and being an emotionally accessible and engaging parent. It's a delicate balance but incredibly helpful. If you actualize this, do it in a way that works for your environment. It might take a minute to find balance, but you can. Gia is good at sustaining respect and open communication within our family. As fathers and parents, we may occasionally recognize that we have time constraints, and believe me, I have them; however, we need to prioritize these moments because the strength of our bond with our children depends on it.

REAL LIFE REFLECTIONS

1. How can you adapt the principles of respect and obedience to your family's unique circumstances while maintaining a healthy parent–child relationship?

   _____

   _____

   _____

2. What methods can you employ to foster open communication without compromising your authority as parents?

   _____

   _____

   _____

3. How can you create an environment where your children feel safe, supported, and confident in your ability to protect and guide them?

_____

_____

_____

4. In what ways can you involve our children in decision-making processes to ensure they feel valued and respected while still upholding your role as parents?

_____

_____

_____

5. How can you reinforce the importance of trust and respect within the family dynamic, and what steps can you take to close the gap that may arise due to today's changing societal norms?

_____

_____

_____

Infusing Values and Beliefs

Explanations were scarce in our home, and "because I said so" came from a man who was a police officer. Dad saw things I didn't see and that he didn't want me to ever see. My father saw the drug era differently. It was from a vantage point that he didn't want me exposed to, so he made sure I didn't go down the same path as some of my friends. Growing up, *my father's authority* protected me, just as your authority can be a protective measure for your children. I might have taken it on the chin and had moments where I was angry with him—okay, I hated him in those moments—but when I was an adult and found myself building a foundation with Gia for our family, I loved and respected what my father built. It never faltered.

A testament to solidity is my parents' marriage for fifty-four years. It demonstrates the strength of the foundation they built. Admittedly, I embraced many of their practices and left the things that weren't fitting or that didn't translate to me. But as I grew older, with time and wisdom and through my experiences, I gained a deeper understanding of their logic, some of which became components of creating our foundation.

The foundation for your adult life will often be shaped by elements of your childhood, regardless of whether you come from a single-parent, two-parent, or grandparent(s) household. Adapting or disregarding certain aspects will depend on respecting or rejecting those beliefs and rules. Incorporate positive values and beliefs that have demonstrated their efficacy. The problem is when your foundation is built on the only thing you know, and it's largely negative, and you don't do anything to change it.

Embedding core values and beliefs in your family forms the bedrock of a strong and resilient foundation. There are always positive aspects of your upbringing that you can draw on, but pay attention to the negative because they matter as much as the positive attributes—so you don't repeat them. Adopting the positive aspects of your upbringing and incorporating new values that resonate with your family's needs can create a solid foundation for fostering a supportive environment for your kids. Your upbringing isn't always indicative of the type of parent you become.

I talk to people for a living. The things that are common knowledge or that I'm privy to are constant reminders that no family's perfect. And I hear about all kinds of difficult or sad situations. But even under some challenging conditions, I admire the parents who keep going. They continue striving to do the best they can or know how to do. They keep trying to improve their relationships with their children, spouses, or significant others and infuse what they know worked best for them into their families. Many times, in my culture, relying on faith is definitely at the top of the list, along with discipline and spending time with our kids. When parents see the struggles their kids are going through, they use everything they've seen their parents do and more to guide *or* save them. But even if something wasn't deliberately shown or taught, there are always some good values that we've learned consciously or subconsciously. Whether helping your child overcome addiction or other adverse situations, you're most likely doing what you know how to do or what you've seen your parents do—or not. But trying something is better than not trying.

In *this* society, kids are different. I said it. They just are. Society's different. Peer pressure's more intense, and it's causing countless more kids to take their lives. Rules and laws are different. There's a long list of what's different. And part of the problem is that kids aren't raised to be resilient. They need more guidance from a healthy parental mindset. But by the same token, they have access to more damaging elements than we did as children. So, when we look at how we were raised versus how we're raising our kids—we can't do it the same way and let that be enough. Our parenting styles have to be different from the previous generations', and we need to be more aware and involved in our children's lives.

We have six kids, so parents constantly ask Gia and me about parenting. Sometimes, when I tell them what worked for us, with Logan, Maddie, London, Jaxson, Brooklyn, or Peyton, I hear myself saying something that worked from Gia's upbringing or mine and what we've added to it to meet today's needs. We see kids falling by the wayside who are struggling to survive. Some are completely disrespectful to their parents and everyone else. Others have been emotionally abandoned. And it causes me to consider the type of foundation they came from, reinforcing the need to create a strong and reliable foundation for your family that can withstand tough times and keep everyone connected and supportive of each other.

We see and hear about some really bad situations. But within those narratives, we're also hearing from, witnessing, and know of parents, whether single or together, who continually strive to keep their family intact. They try to prevent their kids from veering off into self-sabotage, addiction, self-loathing, depression, identity crises, or one of the many other crises they can fall or be pushed into. If they don't know what to do or how to establish specific values, these parents ask someone. They'll find help. Sometimes, however, people are prideful and don't want anyone in their business. Understandable. But not when it keeps your kids at risk. Having strong foundational values can help you when these moments arise.

I applaud parents who don't give up and let the kids run the household, disrespect them, or go down the wrong path. If there's a problem they don't know how to solve, they're persistently seeking answers online, reading books, joining a parenting forum, or talking to a professional, demonstrating their commitment to finding solutions. People who say they don't have the resources need to know they're available. Google. Call social services and ask them for ideas. There are many community resources and programs that can help. Either we can always focus on what we don't have—or we can go out there and find a solution. Having an unshakable foundation doesn't mean adversity won't strike. It means your family won't break apart when it does.

It's crucial to continually insert your family's values and beliefs into your actions and behaviors as your children grow. Then, as your circumstances change, stick with what's working and add other values, disciplines, activities, or what you feel is needed. If you become stronger in your faith or beliefs, your foundation may need to be restructured to work better for your family unit. For example, if you marry someone with their own values and cultural beliefs, you might add some of them to your foundation. Whatever you strive to be as a unit and want your children to embrace, build a foundation to support it.

Constructing Success

If you want stability for your family, invest in learning and adapting the most effective techniques for laying a structurally sound foundation. This will help you identify what's necessary to ensure its longevity. You don't want your foundation collapsing in the event of a minor earthquake that registers 3.2 on the Richter scale, especially when it's preventable. If you haven't lived in a home with a strong foundation, before building something you don't know how to make, ask someone who has weathered tumultuous times, and despite their foundation being shaken, it hasn't collapsed. Talking with your parents, successful couples, a therapist, or a pastor, or researching on the internet can offer valuable insights. Don't just wing it at the expense of your family—the stakes are too high.

Create a concise understanding of who you are and the guidelines needed to construct a healthy and happy base for your family. Make sure you're laying a foundation that can sustain *all of you*. Contemplate your beliefs, boundaries, delineated roles, mutual respect, partnership, affection, commitment, safety, significant traditions, faith, philanthropy, education, trust, and nurturing attributes. And then pose any relevant questions to yourself, bearing in mind that the paramount inquiry is whether your family perpetually takes precedence. *Does your family come first?*

"Create a concise understanding of who you are and the guidelines needed to construct a healthy and happy base for your family. Make sure you're laying a foundation that can sustain *all of you*."

REAL LIFE REFLECTIONS

1. How do you actively demonstrate your commitment(s) to the well-being and happiness of your family?

   _____

   _____

   _____

2. In what ways can you foster open communication and vulnerability within your family dynamic?

   _____

   _____

   _____

3. How might you ensure that the values and principles you espouse are effectively transmitted to your children and integrated into your family culture?

_____

_____

_____

4. How do you nurture and sustain the emotional bonds between all family members, promoting unity and cohesion?

_____

_____

_____

5. How can you establish a continuous learning and growth mindset within your family, encouraging adaptation and resilience in the face of adversity?

_____

_____

_____

It's Not Personal—It's Parenting

Gia and I grew up together, and having matured side by side, we were able to extract some priceless wisdom from our parents. While my parents had one style, Gia's had another. Despite the differing approaches, as we matured, we developed a clear understanding of *our* own identities. Though Gia was raised differently, we were able to merge the lessons from our respective upbringings and figured it out from there, creating a unique foundation for our family based on our beliefs. The foundation for your family is built with what you believe.

PART 1: THE FAMILY UNIT

One of many vital lessons—a foundational value, among many—we learned and adapted from Gia's upbringing was the effectiveness of clear explanations when communicating with our children. Gia excels in this domain, patiently elucidating her reasoning, which, in turn, fosters understanding and respect from our children. And they take that demand for respect everywhere they go. We see it and hear about it all the time. Contrarily, I initially emulated my father's terse, unelaborated refusals, giving them a straight-up "No." However, Gia illuminated the importance of evolving my communication style to resonate with the present generation—in today's society. Parenting the way our parents did, some of it works, and some of it doesn't. Kids today pretty much demand an explanation, or they will ignore, disrespect, debate, or hate you when a simple and concise explanation could have sufficed.

Gia's patience, evident in her interactions with our children and me, has underscored the value of this approach. Observing my wife's communication style has taught me to listen more attentively, process information, engage in thoughtful discussions, and make informed decisions while *explaining* the rationale behind them. This way, it's not personal—it's parenting.

As our family expanded—and with the evolution of society—we continually refined our core values, and I developed a profound appreciation for the foundation on which my upbringing was constructed. My experiences growing up in Queens, combined with the deliberate, conscious cultivation of our values, have contributed to shaping the person I am today, where I am, and our family.

Our kids have the privilege of not growing up in Queens and having the harsh realities and experiences where they can get shot, drugs are prevalent, or they're subjected to some of the things that Gia and I endured. Given the foundation we've built, it alleviates many concerns for their safety and well-being, allowing us to trust in their judgment and decision-making. I've explained to our children that I don't have to worry about Logan's safety when he's going to a store to buy shoes or my daughter hanging out at clubs. When Madison stepped out, she didn't have to worry about "the gunman," someone selling drugs on the corner, or getting into a car with someone under the influence. We have more control and input into our kids' lives than we choose to exercise.

> **REAL LIFE REFLECTIONS**
>
> 1. Adapt parenting techniques to better suit your children's needs.
> 2. Foster open, honest, and respectful communication with your children.
> 3. Demonstrate decisions that are in your children's best interests.
> 4. Model patience, understanding, and empathy in interactions.
> 5. Impart relevant, adaptable values and principles to your children.
> 6. Cultivate a strong family foundation while nurturing your children's independence and resilience.

Foundational Roles

Gia and I have crafted and preserved a blueprint for our lives, and we work to conform to it as closely as possible. The most crucial component of our foundation is *God*. Then, it's our *love bond* and the mutual understanding of our identities. We even have discussed our roles in the relationship transcending traditional gender expectations, enabling us to complement one another's strengths and circumvent our limitations. We've learned to respect one another's perspectives. In doing this, everyone is respected and feels important. It's not that I hold the door as a man or Gia cooks. Gia's warm and intrinsic maternal nature and extraordinary nurturing abilities have been instrumental in fostering our children's development and fortifying our family bond. Her proficiency to actively listen allows her to create an environment of comfort and understanding while discerning the subtle little nuances of body language and possessing the ability to accurately assess the emotional landscape of anyone around her. *Anyone.*

Honoring and valuing each voice within our family unit is an integral part of our foundation. My wife's instincts are crucial to sustaining the family bond. As parents, it's our responsibility to know what our children and our family need most and give it to them. Okay, so you're thinking this is where money comes into play, but actually it doesn't. While financial resources may play a role in meeting some of their needs, the truth is that most of the things your family needs are intangible—your time and for you to listen, offer advice, and provide affection and unconditional love. My wife and kids know they're loved. They know why I work the way I do. And they understand that my priorities are each of them. So I do what it takes to make sure we work well as a unit and they have everything I can give them. That's my best. If you're doing your best, be proud of yourself but keep striving. Continue providing those priceless intangibles because they matter the most.

"Honoring and valuing each voice within our family unit is an integral part of our foundation."

Initially, when we had Maddie, I was an awkward dad. I didn't know how to change the diaper. I was uncomfortable making the baby uncomfortable. When we understood our respective roles, we became increasingly aware of the unique strengths and limitations we brought to the table and what we would and would not do. Working with one another ensures we complete things efficiently and effectively, which keeps things operating smoothly.

The short version of this message is that when Maddie was a year old, she was crawling around between Gia and me, all cute and stuff, and she inadvertently scooped up a penny and swallowed it like an M&M. And yes, I was crying and hyperventilating because I was distraught. Seriously distraught! We called 911, and they assured us our daughter wasn't in immediate danger. He said the penny would eventually emerge, but we needed to make sure it came out through poop or puke and watch her closely for the next thirty-six hours. I stayed right by her side and didn't take my eyes off her. I assumed the responsibility of monitoring our daughter's diapers because while Gia adored Madison, my wife wasn't digging for a penny in a diaper full of poop—that was my job.

At the time, I was Fabolous's tour DJ. Between those first two days and going back on tour, the penny hadn't come out. When I returned home, Gia had several smelly little Pampers lined up, waiting for me to dig in and find that penny. In an unspoken agreement, I was the poop-and-puke person, and there was no debate or discussion. That's what I do. And it's done and appreciated without scorekeeping. Identifying roles right down to the "little shit" can keep the environment operating seamlessly. It creates a peaceful and respectful environment. By managing our foundational roles, both large and small, without the need for scorekeeping or keeping tabs, we allow ourselves the freedom to give and receive in equal measure and to truly appreciate one another's contributions. This approach fosters a peaceful environment and mutual respect. By embracing this mindset, we unlock the true potential of our relationships, allowing us to thrive individually and as a collective unit, enabling us to enjoy a sense of fulfillment and contentment that transcends any individual accomplishment or recognition.

REAL LIFE REFLECTIONS

1. How can you collaboratively create a blueprint for your family's foundation that embodies your values, beliefs, and aspirations?

   _____

   _____

   _____

2. What roles and responsibilities can you define within your family that best utilize your individual strengths and contribute to the overall well-being of your unit?

   _____

   _____

   _____

PART 1: THE FAMILY UNIT

3. How can you promote a supportive and nurturing environment that values each family member's unique voice and perspectives?

_____

_____

_____

4. In what ways can you maintain a balance between the tangible and intangible needs of your family, prioritizing both financial stability and emotional connection?

_____

_____

_____

5. How can you cultivate an atmosphere of mutual appreciation and respect, free from scorekeeping, that enables your family to thrive?

_____

_____

_____

6. What strategies can you implement to continually refine your roles within the family, ensuring your edifice remains healthy and resilient through the years?

_____

_____

_____

The Delicate Equilibrium Between Nurture and Structure

Real-Life Applications: The foundation of our family thrives on balance. It's not exactly a tightrope walk, but we have a good balance. As previously stated, Gia is the nurturer and has primarily created and maintained the structure with our children. There's definitely a delicate equilibrium between nurture and structure in raising children. My wife takes the kids to the numerous activities they're involved in and is in tune with every aspect of their day. She knows where they are, and trust me when I say they know where she is pretty much—all the time. I can trust her to make sure our kids have everything they need, are happy, and have the best experiences ever, and Gia can trust me to work and pay for all of them. We want everyone to be happy, doing what they love and what will help them grow personally. But when it comes to our foundation and roles, Gia is the caring one they can count on for anything, and I'm the disciplinarian. The mean guy. It works great in our situation.

Parents and partners need to have a balance between the scales of nurture and structure, and single parents really need a delicate balance of good cop, bad cop. You can't be such a bad cop that your children hate you. Then your parenting is likely to be less effective, if at all. Admittedly, sometimes, I have to go over the edge to make a point, and I can do it knowing Gia is there to balance it out. That is a benefit of working together. If you have sons—at some point, they get to the age where they puff their chests out, and you have to correct them when necessary. While Logan never tried that with me, he'd try it with his mom.

> **"Parents and partners need to have a balance between the scales of nurture and structure, and single parents really need a delicate balance of good cop, bad cop."**

When Logan was seventeen, the boy got an attitude with Gia *in my presence.* I was minding my business cooking when he said something smart to his mother. I'm not going to let him talk to my wife or his mother that way, especially when it can set an example for the others. So naturally, I responded. And when I did, the first person he called was—*Mom!* I didn't have a problem with the boy, but I knew he had that respect for me to correct his communication with his mom once he got my attention. That's enforcing and maintaining that balance.

Now, the same thing goes for dads. You can't be an asshole dad where your daughter hates you. You have to find balance there too. If you pay attention, you can often identify the girl whose dad isn't in her life or actively there, and we need to be better as fathers being present and raising them. Many times women feen for that male in their life and his acceptance. It's our responsibility as fathers to make sure that doesn't happen, even if you're not married or operate in dual households. You can demonstrate love and respect for your daughter and still have a balance where you can educate her and have serious conversations. Show her that no one can treat her better than her dad and set the bar so high that she won't settle for anything less. I make it a point to continually show my daughters how much I love them, but it's playing that line so they respect, understand, and trust you.

You find balance and achieve trust and respect by being transparent. No lies. No excuses. Be honest so you can build a healthy relationship with your children. If your daughters can learn from you and have consistent and honest conversations, they won't need to solicit or take unsolicited advice from others. They'll know what Dad would say, which comes from being one hundred percent reliable. When you are, they won't need to search for that father figure or another man in their life that could misguide them. If you're a single mom, you can still build that relationship with your sons and daughters by being trustworthy, honest, and reliable so they don't *need* anyone else. We've seen some phenomenal single mothers like Kara build that relationship. You don't want your children to leave the house looking for love, respect, trust, and all the things your foundation should have been built on. Pour that concrete and fill in the cracks so that no one else needs to pour anything onto your foundation.

When my daughter comes to me about anything, it makes me feel that her mom and I did well. I have a lot of real conversations with Logan and Madison—with all our kids. Well, I talk to Peyton, but I have a little time yet with her. We don't keep anything from them, and they don't keep anything from us. And when they need something, there aren't any boundaries where they feel awkward talking to their mom or me. One day Mom wasn't home, and I was the one who went to 7-Eleven to pick up something for Madison. The guy running the store saw me in the feminine hygiene section and said, "I have a daughter too." The fact that Madison can say, "Dad, can you go to the store and get something for me?" demonstrates our bond and the value of our relationship.

Just as a house requires a sturdy foundation to ensure its structural integrity and longevity, a strong family bond depends upon a well-balanced and supportive parental dynamic. You can create more stability by attending to each relationship within the family unit and balancing your respective roles as parents.

> **REAL LIFE REFLECTIONS**
>
> 1. How can you maintain a healthy balance between being nurturing and setting boundaries, ensuring that your children grow up feeling both loved and disciplined?
>
> 2. What strategies can you implement to ensure open, honest communication between you and your children, promoting trust and understanding within the family?

PART 1: THE FAMILY UNIT

3. How can you work together as parents, either in the same household or in separate homes, to provide a unified front for your children, fostering a sense of stability and continuity?

_____

_____

_____

4. How can you create an environment in which your children feel comfortable approaching either parent with their concerns, needs, and questions, ensuring they always have a support system to turn to?

_____

_____

_____

5. How can you continually assess and adjust your parenting styles, ensuring that you maintain a well-balanced approach that evolves with your children's changing needs and circumstances?

_____

_____

_____

(GIA)
Family First

People often say "Family first," which sounds powerful and loving, but society shows that many fail to actualize this belief. The foundations that families have created or have settled on are no longer sustaining them in the way it's required today. If you want to create an unshakable foundation, you'll want to learn and embrace the art of cultivating resilience and unity in a world of uncertainty and rapid change. You will want to use the materials that are not readily available in society yet vital to the success of your family.

When you deliberately create an unshakable foundation, you are positioning your family as a priority. And the need has never been more vital. In *Real Life, Real Family*, we want you to embrace love, communication, and togetherness, foster a growth mindset, practice empathy and understanding, set clear boundaries and expectations, and celebrate one another.

> **"Putting your family first means you'll continually nurture your family's roots with the fundamental elements that create a solid and unwavering foundation."**

Creating a strong and stable foundation for your family or blended family is like planting a thriving, deep-rooted tree in fertile soil. Imagine your family as a tree, with its branches representing the individual members, each reaching out in its own unique direction. The tree's roots symbolize the collective values, love, and support that anchor your family firmly in place. You ensure the tree's growth, strength, and resilience by nurturing the soil and providing the essential nutrients. In the same vein, placing your children and immediate family at the forefront of your priorities fosters an environment where they can flourish, feel loved, and thrive. Putting your family first means you'll continually nurture your family's roots with the fundamental elements that create a solid and unwavering foundation.

REAL LIFE REFLECTIONS

Ten ways to build a strong family foundation:

1. Center life around family.
2. Cultivate resilience and unity.

3. Adopt a growth mindset.
4. Practice empathy and understanding.
5. Set clear boundaries and expectations.
6. Celebrate each other.
7. Seek outside support when necessary.
8. Understand your family's roots.
9. Nurture family roots.
10. Prioritize your family's well-being.

3. Echoes of Wisdom

Parenting is similar to casting a stone into a pond, creating ripples that extend far beyond the point of initial impact. Our behaviors, attitudes, and actions reverberate through the lives of our children, shaping their thoughts, beliefs, and perspectives in ways both subtle and profound. As such, it's vital that we lead by example, embodying values and principles that we want to instill in our children. By doing so, we can create a lasting legacy of love, respect, and understanding that will empower our children to navigate the complexities of life with wisdom and grace. Teaching our children everything they need to be successful can provide generational guidance from the roots of wisdom.

(GIA)
Sowing Seeds of Insight

My parents were the center of my world for twenty-six years until they passed away. They were my role models, and I held them in the highest esteem. Their love and guidance were invaluable. Over time, I learned how to harness lessons from my childhood to forge an even brighter future for our family.

Though my mom was a bit more complicated, in a really positive way, my father, in particular, embodied a simple yet effortlessly cool persona. I admired Daddy. He was straightforward: a good car, a solid pair of shoes, and a quality timepiece were the only material possessions he truly needed. It was clear to me that my father was a man of great intelligence and intuition, and I savored the opportunity to engage in lengthy conversations with him, often settling in his den, soaking up his insights and perspectives on the world. Daddy served in the military as a radar and sonar operator in security-controlled areas and became a computer scientist and business owner, with a sharp analytical mind complemented by his ability to think critically and outside anybody's box. Despite his formidable intellect, my father also had a gift for simplifying complex ideas and presenting them in a way that was accessible to everyone. Where I might overanalyze something, he'd say, "If it ain't right, don't do it." End of story. And those few words kept me from doing a whole lot of nonsense in my life because his words carried a lot of weight with me. When he'd say, "You are your daddy's daughter," it was the biggest compliment! My father was my best friend. I could tell him anything. It didn't matter how bad it was; Dad would tell me I was wrong and all the reasons why. But at the end of the day I learned he had my back. With certainty, I had loyalty from both of my parents. Though I lived in a world where there was the possibility of being disciplined, I never hid anything from my parents. Having their guidance kept me from doing things I shouldn't. We had trust, which is something RaaShaun and I have built with our children.

"Through my close relationship with my parents, I gleaned valuable insights into the type of parent I aspired to be."

RaaShaun and I started dating in September 1994, and he loved joking around and having fun. The following year, when I was fifteen, RaaShaun went to Spencer Gifts and bought a gag gift. The envelope read "Pregnancy Test," and he sent it to my house thinking it was funny. Dad got the mail, and when I came home from school, he called me into his office, which was downstairs. He pulled out a yellow envelope underneath his keyboard with my name on it and handed it to me. I stared at it, but it took a good ten seconds to process.

"Dad! This is crazy! I'm still a virgin," I told him. Even though I was telling the truth, I looked like a whole liar!

Daddy insisted calmly, "Okay, open it."

I pulled out a piece of paper that said, "Gotcha."

Daddy smiled and said, "You were sweating bullets, though."

Dad was the ultimate sidekick. The foundation of our house was built on trust and having one another's back. At that moment, Dad demonstrated that if this is what's going on, we have to figure out what we're going to do. I love that RaaShaun and I are like that with our children. They can trust us with everything in their lives; when we teach them something, our words are echoes of wisdom.

Through my close relationship with my parents, I gleaned valuable insights into the type of parent I aspired to be. My father, in particular, made a lasting impact on me through the time he devoted to engaging in meaningful conversations, pouring his wisdom and insights into my receptive mind. In many ways, I owe a significant portion of my personality and outlook on life to my father's influence. When RaaShaun and I took core values from our respective upbringings, we built our future on them, ensuring that our family unit remained firmly grounded in purpose, shared vision, and mutual respect. *It has worked amazingly!* By embracing these timeless principles, we created a foundation of strength and stability to carry us through the inevitable challenges and triumphs of family life. As a couple and as a single parent, you're going to have them, and reflecting on those lessons, the words of wisdom can be helpful and comforting.

REAL LIFE REFLECTIONS

1. Adapt parenting techniques to better suit your children's needs.
2. Foster open, honest, and respectful communication with your children.
3. Demonstrate parenting decisions are in your children's best interests.
4. Model patience, understanding, and empathy in interactions.
5. Impart relevant, adaptable values and principles to your children.
6. Cultivate a strong family foundation while nurturing your children's independence and resilience.

PART 1: THE FAMILY UNIT

Positive Transformations Through Behavior Refinement

Real Life Perspectives: Regarding roles, Mom was the disciplinarian, and though we were close, sometimes I'd challenge her. Admittedly, I was rude and disrespectful at times because I had an inflated sense of self, thinking I knew more than she did. It only happened here and there, and it was not the nature of our environment because I loved and adored my mother. For the most part, I was very respectful. More accurately, I was a teen, and it wasn't until I started dating RaaShaun that I'd take opportunities to show off like I had the power and could talk like that to my mom.

One day, RaaShaun looked at me and said bluntly, "The way you talk to your mom is crazy!"

"What do you mean?"

Watching RaaShaun shake his head in disappointment, it became clear that even the thought of disrespecting his mother would never happen. Never! His deep respect for his mother was a testament to their powerful bond, mutual love, trust, and unwavering support and respect—values that RaaShaun had internalized and embodied in his everyday life.

"If I ever spoke to my mom that way, she would yoke me up by my neck and Dad would come behind her."

One day RaaShaun and I went to the movies. Cell phones were like big, huge bricks, and I was sitting in the movie theater with a brick on my lap. When it rang, it was Mom.

She said, "You bring your little ass home, you wretch!"

"Why?"

Mom didn't say.

I said, "Since you won't tell me why, I'll be home after the movie."

RaaShaun cut his eyes at me and said, "You're wylin'!"

"No, I'm not," I said dismissively. "I'm sitting here, and without any reason, she wants me to uproot myself and ruin the movie for us. I'm not doing that."

This time, I was the one shaking my head.

When RaaShaun took me home, I swear, the car might have been rolling when I got out because he didn't want any part of that.

Mom pulled a black leather jacket off the couch when I walked through the door. She reached inside the pocket and pulled a condom out, and—I started laughing!

I said, "What are you talking about? That's not my jacket. It's Roman's jacket. The one I borrow occasionally. You should know. You paid for it. Ask my brother why he's using it."

From my perspective, I had that kind of positive reinforcement from time to time that made me believe in my actions.

I called RaaShaun and told him I knew it was nonsense and a misunderstanding. That was my mentality *until* RaaShaun corrected my disrespectful behavior by sowing seeds of insight. He told me I could *"never"* talk to Mom that way. I'd *never* even think to show that kind of disrespect to my mom, and if I did, I'd have one chance to try it, and that would be my last.

RaaShaun said his father wouldn't allow it. But more importantly, he never considered disrespecting the person who loved him the most. It was beautiful the way he showed his mom respect—and I don't mean sometimes. He did that all the time. Now, I was snarky and somewhat condescending, cutting things down with logic. Though I never cursed her out or yelled or screamed at Mom, the bottom line is that RaaShaun was right: I needed to change and honor my mother with the respect that she deserved.

That day, it clicked for me, causing a seismic shift in my perspective and behavior. Everything changed, and I never did that again. What I thought was cute wasn't. I knew I was wrong, but it wasn't until someone I loved and respected spoke those words that their truth reverberated through my soul. It was then that I resolved to never again speak to my mother in a manner that belied my true feelings of respect and adoration for her. I knew I would *never* raise a daughter who would talk to me like I had spoken to my mother. This experience underscored the pivotal importance of respect as a cornerstone of our foundation. By reflecting on our personal histories and using them as guideposts, we can chart positive transformations through behavior refinement before negative behaviors become personality traits and get out of hand. Even small modifications can yield significant transformative outcomes.

"Our behavior, much like a butterfly flapping its wings, can have far-reaching consequences, setting off a chain reaction of events and emotions."

Our behavior, much like a butterfly flapping its wings, can have far-reaching consequences, setting off a chain reaction of events and emotions. In the same way that a butterfly's tiny wings can create a storm across the world, our words and actions can have lasting impacts on our children, relationships, and personal development. Just as I experienced a powerful transformation in my relationship with my mother, we must be willing to examine our behavior, identify areas for growth, and embrace change in order to create congruent and respectful relationships with our loved ones. In doing so, we can set the stage for a more balanced and nurturing family environment, where every member feels valued and respected because they matter.

REAL LIFE REFLECTIONS

Six ways to improve behaviors:

1. Cultivate a respectful environment.
2. Share personal experiences to aid in understanding.
3. Address negative behaviors early.
4. Promote open communication.

> 5. Model healthy behaviors.
>
> 6. Promote growth and accountability.

You've Got to Have a Hard Baseline

When we're talking about raising children, it's good to have a standard or starting point, and our role as parents is to establish it. When considering the wisdom we have acquired as parents, those echoes, positive or negative, come from the past. RaaShaun and I observed how our parents treated one another, and we've chosen to mirror some of those behaviors. In some cases, we strive to do better. Praying, cooking, and cleaning together have given us structure; families need that. However you do it, do it. You need a baseline that brings your family back to their roots so they understand who they are, where they come from, the power of their name and all that it encompasses.

As stated previously, when building a foundation, we often mirror behaviors we observed from our parents, drawing inspiration and making improvements where necessary. Shared activities such as praying, cooking, and cleaning are essential pillars, grounding the structure and connecting us to our heritage. Over time, and with repetition, these activities become more than routines; they symbolize a link to our past and help cultivate a more profound connection within the family. Spending time together in these pursuits reinforces these bonds, creating stability and a framework that resonates with our cultural legacy. In this case, the baseline is the blueprint, guiding the construction process and reminding us of our roots, heritage, and the power of our family name. No matter how the house evolves or expands over time, it always rests on this blueprint, which embodies who we are and where we come from.

As a young woman, mother, wife, husband, or partner, you may wonder if you deserve to be treated with kindness, compassion, respect, and dignity; if your opinions matter; and whether you should establish boundaries. The answer is yes. Absolutely. And it's beneficial for you to teach your children that they deserve to be treated in that same respectful and positive way. Those around you should be empathetic to your needs, feelings, and experiences and make an effort to understand and support you. When you teach your kids these values, they'll carry them out into the world. Teach them not to allow anyone to force them to do anything that makes them uncomfortable or that violates their values, and then constantly remind them of this. Let them know it's okay to take the space to express themselves freely and make their own choices; however, that comes with accountability for their actions and behaviors.

"As a young woman, mother, wife, husband, or partner, you may wonder if you deserve to be treated with kindness, compassion, respect, and dignity; if your opinions matter; and whether you should establish boundaries. The answer is yes. Absolutely."

It's also important for your family and those around you to understand and appreciate their roots and cultural identity. This means acknowledging the power and significance of your name and heritage and embracing it as a part of who you are. Show them how to have a deep appreciation for their unique identity and background and to sustain self-acceptance.

Teach your children to be respected, appreciated, a priority, and that they should be continually shown all of those things. So, be that example, and ensure your interactions with others support this. Your children may never know their value if you don't have a standard of how you want to live and how you allow people to treat you.

My parents raised me with a hard baseline that included clearly established nonnegotiable boundaries and rules to provide structure and expectations without room for deviation. That baseline protected me from losing myself—who I innately am—and I never lost it. In fact, it evolved. When those positive behaviors are rich in your life, your kids will see that as a reference point. You're showing them how to have a healthy and hard baseline too. That's how our children are raised. If I have a baseline, RaaShaun definitely has one—each of our children has a baseline. And that baseline means that you draw a line as to how you will allow yourself to be treated at home, school, and work and in life.

From an early age, I was really engaged in science, immersing myself in teams and projects that captivated my curiosity. I recognized that it seemed as though my every desire was met and encouraged by my mother. She was incredibly proud of me and was always buying things or doing something for me, which was her way of reinforcing her beliefs and setting that standard. In essence, Mom taught me that I deserved a wonderful life.

Everything is based on love, care, and respect in our household, and it's working well because I have an amazing life. We have an amazing life! My life isn't hard. RaaShaun is even thoughtful in calling to ask, "What can I do to improve your day?" What we talk about and share with others is how we are in real life. We're very loving and affectionate toward each other and try to lighten each other's load any way we can. Knowing how much my husband works, he deserves to come home to a comfortable and happy home, and it is. Everything in our house is about having fun—laughing, joking, and playing pranks. That's our existence. We lie in bed and cuddle as often as possible, and we do for one another the things that have value to each other. I'm not talking about monetary value. They're things that exist only between us, and there are a thousand things that RaaShaun does for me and I do for him. This doesn't make life void of challenges, but it means we can weather storms, and we know who we are to one another. We're complete and utter soul mates. I can't imagine life without him. We're two whole individuals who make each other happy, and we do the same with our children. At any given moment, we can see their faces go from dim to bright because of the way we love them.

> **"Everything is based on love, care, and respect in our household, and it's working well because I have an amazing life. We have an amazing life!"**

RaaShaun and I will do anything we think will make one another happy and our children happy, well-adjusted, confident, and passionate about life. It doesn't mean you have to give your children everything you think they want, but it does mean that you will work within your capabilities without putting unnecessary stress on yourself. RaaShaun and I expose our children to as much as we can so that they want these things for themselves and are willing to work for them. We know they'll have a hard baseline. Naturally, you want them to have the drive, passion, and work ethic for their own benefit, but if you don't teach your children what they deserve, they may never know their true value. What my parents showed me was to have a hard baseline not only for my value—but for the way I live.

As a parent, you can design what normal is for your children. We do that with Madison (really, all of our children) by giving her a particular lifestyle even while she's in college. We have carefully helped set the standard with enriching experiences like travel, fine dining, exposure to culture and arts, and other opportunities. We want our children to recognize this standard and one day continue in their own way. It's not about tangible items but about instilling values and aspirations. The goal is for the standards we set to inspire our children to seek these similar standards and continue elevating them for themselves and future generations. And this is something individualized to each household. Whatever you can comfortably accommodate, give it to your children. When we discussed what Madison wants to do with her education and as a career, we've set her up to have a hard baseline for what that will look like. I've explained that this gravy train, benefiting from our opportunities and circumstances without putting in much effort, will stop because we have put her in a position to be independent and successful without us. Madison is aware that if this is the lifestyle she wants to continue living, she will have to understand the work that it entails.

With Madison, we taught her what a person's average income would need to be to eat at STK, Philippe, or Mr. Chow in New York, and we explained what a bill at a restaurant like that actually meant. That's three days of working minimum wage. Most people will work those three days and won't turn around and spend that money on a meal. If you don't explain it, you'll have children detached from reality. Seriously detached. But you have to teach them what it takes to achieve these things. You don't want them to sit around and wait for someone to give it to them. I've explained, "What you see your father do, honey, that is not the norm. He works entirely too much and wants us to have anything we desire."

We want all our children to experience greatness, so that is their mindset. Life is about living your best life. You deserve it, and your children deserve it too. Can you be happy in a small apartment, with great love in your life? Absolutely—but that isn't your ceiling. Even if you can't provide everything you want for your children, you can still expose them to more than they have now so they know that there's more to dream about and aspire to. Teach them to look beyond their immediate surroundings and circumstances. If they live in an underprivileged area where other options and opportunities are concealed, they may not know what else exists beyond what they see. Encourage curiosity, ambition, and seeking fresh experiences and potential opportunities. Whether through books, conversations, or community involvement, help them see that there are diverse paths they can pursue. Inspire them to envision a future where they aren't limited by their current environment but empowered by their dreams and the determination to achieve them. Take them to museums to see magnificent art. Enroll them in a course that teaches them how to invest. Visit a career fair. Advocate for education beyond what is acceptable, and broaden their horizons. Help them find the resources to attend college. Teach them to believe in themselves and that they can be the first to accomplish a goal or innovation. Whatever you do, please encourage your children to seek the best in life and to have the passion and work ethic to achieve their dreams.

If I couldn't give something to my children, I'd set them on a pathway to attain things I couldn't access. People feel guilty for investing in self-care and personal happiness. If you don't teach your children to do these things—who will? Do you want them to learn how to work to survive or to thrive?

People have asked if I expected this amazing life with RaaShaun, and I always say, "No. I had no idea how our life was going to go." I never considered his salary, potential earnings, or different roads it would take. Every day, it was one foot in front of the other toward our dreams. If RaaShaun faltered and couldn't get a grip on his career, I had my education and drive intact, so I would have done what was needed. My education, passion, and drive are vital components of my resilience, ensuring that I could support and uplift our family if that was our path. This understanding was pivotal as I walked alongside RaaShaun on our shared journey. I recognized that our success was not defined by his career or material wealth but rather by the depth of our love and the strength of our partnership.

"Resilience is a quality that allows children to adapt to change and cope with the inevitable challenges that life will present."

Resilience is a quality that allows children to adapt to change and cope with the inevitable challenges that life will present. It allowed me to overcome that attack with a razor in high school, as explained in *Real Life, Real Love*, and continue my journey without a diminishing passion for my purpose and life. Nothing could remove from me what my parents had instilled in me at an early age. I remained determined to pursue my goals. By encouraging our children to embrace setbacks as opportunities for growth, we equip them with the ability to persevere and emerge stronger than before. In my own life, I learned that no matter the path RaaShaun and I might have taken, I had the inner strength and adaptability to face any obstacle head-on.

As parents, we must teach our children to have a baseline when approaching the world with kindness and open-mindedness. By nurturing empathy, we help our children forge deep, meaningful relationships and contribute to a more compassionate society. The role of parents extends far beyond providing material comforts and verbal praise. Our responsibility is to instill a strong sense of self-worth, resilience, and empathy in our children. By nurturing these qualities, we empower our children to navigate the world with confidence, adaptability, and kindness. And in doing so, we prepare them to lead lives of true fulfillment, regardless of the unpredictable twists and turns that their futures may hold. These traits are invaluable tools in the face of adversity and encourage the fostering of meaningful and healthy connections with others.

RaaShaun does beautiful things that are unprovoked. As mentioned earlier, we celebrate the twelve days of Christmas, and the special things my husband does for me also show his daughters how they need to be treated. The way Madison, Brooklyn, and London see their father treat me gives them a baseline for how they want to be treated, and it provides the same baseline for our sons, Logan and Jaxson—in time, Peyton will see it too. Quality time and attention affect a child, giving them that sense of security and what a home environment and family unit should feel like—it sets a baseline for how they want to live their lives. For us, we're constantly playing games together and interacting with one another on a high level, often finding ourselves laughing from the depths of our souls until it hurts! The more you pour into them, the more you fill up your child's love tank, which comes back in the most beautiful ways. So, don't deviate from your baseline. Hold yourself to a standard and teach your children to do the same.

REAL LIFE REFLECTIONS

1. Establish a baseline of love, respect, and appreciation in family interactions.

2. Maintain this baseline amid life's challenges for a harmonious family function.

3. Model healthy, respectful relationships for your children.

4. Involve your children in your family baseline creation and maintenance.

5. Reinforce your children's self-worth and high relationship standards.

6. Nurture security and belonging within your family environment.

Your Behaviors Are the Example, Not Your Words

As a parent, I'm particularly aware of the ways in which our children can challenge us and try our patience, specifically when they possess traits that are all too familiar to us. In the case of our son Logan, I recognized in him *many* of the same qualities that I had as a child. His unwavering self-assuredness and unshakable "I know I'm right" logic remind me of my own past tendencies toward stubbornness and an unwillingness to admit fault. I've told Logan there is no room for two stubborn people in this house. He's very stubborn and feels as though he's right, and in the way my husband's words broke me down causing me to be more respectful to my mother—Logan needed to be corrected. But in all fairness, I understand how he comes to his conclusions; *he is me.*

When I was growing up, my parents always made sure to explain their reasoning when telling me no. Looking back, I realize they were often considering factors beyond my understanding. As a parent, I've taken the same approach with my kids. With Madison, it worked seamlessly. However, with Logan, I quickly realized I needed to adjust my approach. I knew that for him to truly understand and accept my decisions, I needed to have a deeper conversation, showing Logan the same grace and thoughtfulness I expected in return.

Despite the challenges that come with parenting, I firmly believe that I am the parent, and it's my responsibility to make thoughtful decisions that are in the best interest of my children. While Logan's nature and DNA may dictate that things have to make sense to him, I understand that there are times when I need to step in as the parent and make decisions that may not necessarily make sense to him at the moment. Ultimately, my goal is to foster open and respectful communication with my kids, even when we may not see eye to eye. By showing them grace and explaining my reasoning, I am raising thoughtful and compassionate individuals who will make a positive impact in the world.

It was important to me to impart upon my children the wisdom that comes with acknowledging one's own limitations and the possibility that one's beliefs may be flawed. I endeavored to teach them the value of accountability, open-mindedness, and humility, all of which are essential components of respectful and productive discourse.

Conversely, I soon realized that my words alone were not sufficient to impart these crucial lessons to Logan. Instead, I had to lead by example, demonstrating to him the very same behaviors and attitudes that I was advising him to adopt. I made a concerted effort to be even more mindful of the messages I was sending, both implicitly and explicitly, through my words and actions. By shining a light on examples of my errors and mistakes and showing Logan that I was receptive to alternative perspectives, I was able to help him develop a deeper sense of humility and an appreciation for the value of listening and learning from others.

As parents, it is incumbent upon us to continually reevaluate and refine our approaches to parenting, especially as our children grow and develop their own unique personalities and perspectives. Consider that sometimes children do bad things because they want your attention. They want you to correct, teach, and hear them—do it!

Children are constantly seeking attention and validation from their parents. Unfortunately, in some cases, children may engage in negative or destructive behavior as a means of getting your attention. It may be particularly true when children feel ignored, undervalued, or neglected by you.

> **"It's important to remember that your children are still learning and growing, and mistakes are a natural part of that process."**

By acknowledging and addressing these behaviors, parents can help their children feel heard and valued. You can accomplish this through open and honest communication, setting clear boundaries and expectations, and reinforcing positive behavior. Providing your children with positive attention and reinforcement for good behavior can help prevent negative behavior from becoming a means of seeking attention.

It's important to remember that your children are still learning and growing, and mistakes are a natural part of that process. So, rather than reacting with anger or frustration, take the opportunity to teach and guide your children in a positive and supportive manner. Doing so can help them grow into responsible, well-adjusted individuals equipped to handle life's challenges.

By cultivating a foundation rooted in respect, accountability, and humility, we can help our children to thrive and succeed in a complex and challenging world. It is our responsibility to let our behaviors be the example and to build something truly special, a foundation that will stand the test of time and serve as a beacon of hope and inspiration for generations to come.

REAL LIFE REFLECTIONS

1. Are there any specific behaviors or attitudes you recognize in yourself that you want to change in order to provide a better example for your children?

   _____
   _____
   _____

2. How can you ensure that your actions consistently align with the values and principles you aim to teach your children, even during times of stress or conflict?

   _____
   _____
   _____

3. In what ways can you promote self-awareness and self-reflection in your children, encouraging them to consider the impact of their actions and behaviors on others?

   _____
   _____
   _____

4. How can you cultivate an environment of trust, openness, and vulnerability, allowing your children to feel comfortable admitting mistakes and seeking guidance?

_____

_____

_____

5. What strategies can you employ to model empathy, compassion, and understanding, both within your family unit and in your interactions with the wider world?

_____

_____

_____

(RAASHAUN)
Parenting for Life Success Beyond Materialistic Pursuits

Most parents work hard to take care of their kids. Mine did. But Gia and I always talk about being happy when doing anything and making moves for our kids. If I want to do something that makes them happy, I will teach them how to make it a business. I want them to do what they love because, at the end of the day, money means nothing if you are not happy. So I tell my kids to be happy.

People ask, "Why do you work so hard?" It's because I want my kids to start at zero. When Gia and I graduated college, we had student loans, which meant we started our lives in debt. My parents' only investment was purchasing a home. But I had to figure out how to buy a house and a lot of other things on my own. As Gia and I figured it out, we wanted to help other parents do the same, and an example of us doing that is by writing this book and sharing what we've learned. You may not use everything in this book, but perhaps some variations of it to fit your needs will be beneficial. You have to teach your kids and your community how to be happy and wise with their time and money.

When Logan was in high school, I was impressed that he came to me and said, "Dad, we should invest in this stock. I hear there's going to be a merger." I looked over his shoulder as he explained the stocks he was interested in and saw him making great decisions. But more importantly, he was happy and excited about it. My daughter Madison is going to school for real estate. She's always asking questions about real estate, investing, and finances. Maddie knows how she wants to live and will work to make that lifestyle happen. I never in a million years asked my parents how much something cost, but these are lessons that I've learned we need to teach our kids. We need to be open and educate them so they can make solid decisions that will help prepare them for their futures so they will be happy.

"My parents taught me the same thing we teach our kids—sneakers, jewelry, cars, and anything can come and go at any moment."

My parents ensured I got my education. My life, how my family lives, and what we can do resulted from learning the skills to take care of my family. I learned how to think and make critical decisions. My parents taught me the same thing we teach our kids—sneakers, jewelry, cars, and anything can come and go at any moment. It's nice to have the things you want—but that's not happiness. Happiness is inside you.

REAL LIFE REFLECTIONS

1. Guide your children toward career-aligned passions.

2. Endeavor for a debt-free start for your children.

3. Impart lessons on financial literacy and time management.

4. Encourage your children's interest in finance and investing.

5. Maintain transparency in discussing money with your children.

6. Emphasize that happiness isn't tied to material possessions.

4. Architects of Unconditional Love

While RaaShaun and I understand that expressing affection may not come naturally to everyone, in our household, affection serves as a vital tool that lays the emotional groundwork and fosters the growth of relationships among family members. Affection can manifest as warm hugs, celebratory high-fives, or tender kisses that convey love and closeness. We make a conscious effort to be extraordinarily affectionate with our children, which in turn has taught them to reciprocate this warmth with us and their siblings. Healthy attachment and connectedness can create a sense of belonging and security, and it can enhance emotional intelligence.

What has always struck us is that even as our older children transitioned into young adulthood, they never outgrew this affectionate behavior or felt embarrassed to express their love in the presence of others. This approach cultivates a loving home environment and fortifies our family bond. Additionally, affection can be communicated nonverbally through endearing terms for your children. While seemingly effortless, these simple expressions of love carry significant emotional weight. They offer immediate reassurance and, when used consistently, remind us of the deep love and adoration that defines our family.

In our family, unconditional love represents an unbreakable bond. It's given freely, effortlessly, without the condition of action or circumstance, and it's limitless. When you experience this type of love, you can offer your children security and a soft place to land when disappointment looms. However, love includes consistently showing respect within our family unit.

RaaShaun and I find ourselves shrouded in heartwarming expressions of affection and displays of love for each other and our children because we've become architects of unconditional love. It's what we've built. We construct with love, give with love, educate with love, discipline with love, and love—with genuine, unadulterated love. Within the pages of this book, you'll discover that a significant portion of our message revolves around building. Whether it pertains to our foundation, mission statement, home, healthy habits, or family, our approach to building is always intentional. We work to build. We invest to build. We speak to educate, which is building. We discipline to build character and awareness. We continually laugh and joke around with our Choo Crew to build and strengthen our bond. Everything we do has the element of building to it. And we've built a family whose foundation is love. Love serves as the cornerstone of our family. We have tirelessly labored to create and maintain an environment brimming with love, devoid of the negative emotions that could invade our hearts and minds and remove the magic in our home.

"We construct with love, give with love, educate with love, discipline with love, and love—with genuine, unadulterated love."

Architects produce a blueprint, a scaled plan, or a technical drawing describing a building or construction project's design, structure, and specifications. Now, the blueprint allows architects, engineers, and builders to identify potential issues or conflicts during construction. Basically, the blueprint ensures accuracy, efficiency, and seamless execution in the design and construction process, and our goal is to achieve the same in executing *real* unconditional love for our family. I say "real" unconditional love because, as a society, the "real" aspect seems to go away as soon as someone does something you don't like. Our family is not about that. Real is one hundred percent authentic. It's irrevocable. Permanent. There are no conditions to it. If your children make mistakes or poor choices, your love for them must always be there. Some parents have children that get into drugs, or they disappoint the family, and they don't love them the same. They discover their child is LGBTQ+, and they don't accept them. The child loses faith or is an atheist, and they tell them they're going to hell. They have a child with a disability, and they no longer want that child. So, how is this love? It's not. It's a conditional relationship.

There's no other feeling like the feeling of knowing that someone is always in your corner. Feeling supported can be the driving force that makes all the difference between failure and success. These two facts mean that no matter what obstacles are thrown our way, we can overcome them together through our unconditional love for one another, which is something we actively practice on a daily basis. Our job as parents is to love our children unconditionally. If they mess up, help them through it. That's unconditional. If you have a child and *you* can't help their situation, you can find a professional who can help them. But what you don't do is stop loving your child.

An *architect of unconditional love* is a parent who meticulously designs and constructs the intricate framework that fosters an environment of warmth, compassion, and understanding within personal relationships. Just as an architect conceives and creates the blueprint for a building, an architect of love crafts a plan to nurture the emotional and psychological well-being of those they care for, fostering deep and lasting connections. If each of us worked to build within our families, we would ultimately construct a society that's not trying to tear everything down.

In developing the blueprint, an architect of love considers each individual's unique characteristics and aspirations, carefully considering the diverse facets of their personalities, experiences, and desires. This allows the architect to craft a tailored approach that caters to the specific needs and preferences of the relationship, laying a solid foundation upon which mutual trust, respect, and love can flourish.

They also acknowledge the importance of adaptability and flexibility in the blueprint, as the ever-evolving nature of human relationships demands continuous reevaluation and adjustment. By incorporating a growth mindset, the architect actively seeks opportunities to learn, grow, and enhance the relationship, ensuring it remains resilient in the face of change and adversity. You don't do something once and expect it to last forever without nurturing it. So, yes, while I am the nurturer in our family, it doesn't mean that my husband doesn't have to foster a relationship of unconditional love within the family. It's a lifetime commitment. Children need unconditional but healthy love; your spouse or partner needs it too. If you're a single parent, divorced, or at odds with the other parent, step aside and put your children first. Allow the other parent to unconditionally love their children because it will create a healthier child, and that's what matters.

When two parents are involved, providing your children with love and support has to be the goal. Of course, there are situations where one parent isn't willing or able to fulfill this responsibility. Under these circumstances, don't bash the other parent. At times, forcing the other parent to be involved can do more harm than good. Emphasize putting your children first by working together to find practical solutions and strategies to effectively co-parent. Consider involving a family counselor or mediator to facilitate a healthy conversation and lead to a resolution. Put your energy into creating a stable, loving, and nurturing environment for your children because their happiness and healthy development come above all else.

As parents, we want you to be an architect and craft your blueprint. Employ a combination of empathy, active listening, and effective communication to create open and honest dialogue between all parties. This helps to identify potential challenges and opportunities for growth and to develop shared goals that unite and strengthen the bond between your entire unit—such as in a mission statement. Through a balance of reflection and collaboration, continually refine your blueprint, solidify the structure of your relationships, and create a refuge of love, support, and mutual growth for all involved.

(Gia)
Results of a Phenomenal Blueprint

Real Life Examples: Unconditional love does not dictate the relationship title nor does it mean you accept the negative or disrespectful things because you love someone. It means you strive to make people better. When I think about unconditional love, I think about RaaShaun. I think about loving him through his greatness and all of what's in between. There is nothing my children or husband can do to make me stop loving them, but there is always that caveat: I can forgive and release that burden, but you don't have to be a part of my life.

Love has different aspects—romantic, family, brotherly, and God's divine love. I can have affection for you. I can have a friend I love, but then I might decide there is no place in my life for that person anymore. Unconditional love is harder to get from me as I interact with people and see how and who they are. *Unconditional love* means I will love you to the ends of the earth, protect you, and move mountains for you to have everything you need—and it's reserved for RaaShaun and our children. Besides our children, my love isn't easy to access as it means there is always a place for you, no matter what you do. And there is the ultimate: God's divine love.

In regard to parenting, unconditional love is innate because many people don't know what love is to begin with, let alone the unconditional version. It starts in your own household with your children—your family unit. Some parents provide food on the table, clothes on their children's backs, and a roof over their heads; therefore, that must mean "I love you." Untrue.

Look at societal problems, social media, and your relationship with your children. Showing unconditional love needs a revised definition. It must be accompanied by a phenomenal blueprint outlining consistent actions that give the word—"love"—meaning.

If you don't actively engage with your children, focus on their well-being, happiness, personal growth, and progress, and provide them with opportunities for success, it's time to reevaluate how you parent. Your upbringing, which may be shaped by generational or cultural factors, influences your identity and how you express love. The absence of a nurturing environment can be a significant obstacle.

Some individuals may grow up in challenging circumstances, such as having an absent father or a mother struggling with addiction, and might inadvertently perpetuate the cycle. On the other hand, a child from a similar background may consciously choose to break away from adverse circumstances. For example, they may enroll in educational programs, participate in organizations like the YMCA, seek stable employment, and intentionally pursue a different path than the one they were exposed to, highlighting the ongoing debate between nature and nurture.

RaaShaun was raised in a home where he felt he didn't receive a lot of affection, but his parents have always displayed an unspoken unconditional love for him. The sun rises and sets with RaaShaun. As their only child, he is their everything. However, RaaShaun has never woken up and gone and jumped in his parents' bed. He's never gone to them for advice or had the physical warmth and hugs from his parents. But again, pulling from both of our foundations, he saw that affection in my household, took it, and processed it in a way meaningful to him. My husband is the single most affectionate father *imaginable*.

"Our children don't walk into and out of a room without hearing 'I love you.' That's how we communicate."

My mom wasn't directly affectionate, and I still don't know why. She never said, "Gia, I love you." I don't know if my mother ever hugged me. But somehow, I knew growing up that there wasn't a mother who loved their child as much as my mother loved me. *Everything* she did and showed me let me know I was number one.

Our children don't walk into and out of a room without hearing "I love you." That's how we communicate. I hadn't processed that I never heard it from my mother until I was nineteen, and Mom came to visit me at college. Sitting in my kitchen, I told her, "Mom, you know what I realized?"

"What's that?"

"You've never told me you love me."

"What?"

I could see it hit her like a ton of bricks, and she became emotional. I got up and warmly wrapped my arms around her, and I could tell she was uncomfortable. It was like hugging a stiff little pencil.

"Give me a hug," I joked. "Look me in the eyes and tell me you love me."

And she did.

That day, I realized that my mother wouldn't hold my hand and wasn't affectionate with Dad, but Mom was warm and loving in her own special way. My mother would jump through hoops to give me what I wanted. I have never wanted something and not received it in life, and that started when I was a kid. Like Mom, I knew I'd want my children to know that no mother loved their children as much as I love them.

One beautiful afternoon, I arrived at London, Brooklyn, and Jaxson's school to collect them at the end of their day. Right on schedule, I observed a procession of delightful little children emerging from the doors, making their way toward their parents, older siblings, caregivers, or designated guardians. I stepped out of the car and walked toward the school so my darlings would know my whereabouts since they exit from three separate doors. First, I spotted Jaxson, his endearing smile radiating from his face as he waved his hand without inhibition. He was unconcerned with who might be watching or whether his nine-year-old friends witnessed his excitement upon seeing his mother. When Brooky appeared, she dashed toward me with the most adorable stride, leaped into my arms effortlessly, and greeted me with an exuberant kiss. As for London—our eyes meeting felt as if the world couldn't be more perfect.

I cherish the moments when my children leap into my arms or express their love for me in their own unique ways. If the other parents didn't witness me picking them up regularly, they might assume I had just returned from a long vacation. But this heartwarming display is simply their typical way of conveying how much they missed me during the part of the day we spent apart. This is merely one of the many ways they demonstrate their love. We have observed how being architects of love has nurtured our children to become architects of love themselves.

RaaShaun and I crafted the blueprint for how we would express love to our children, and they witness this love manifested in our actions and communication with one another. They understand what innate and profound affection looks like, but more importantly, they experience the deep resonance of our love. Despite any adversity, they remain confident that our love is unwavering and unconditional.

From the moment of their birth, our children have been embraced with kisses, warm hugs, love, and affectionate communication. Affection is a form of communication. They snuggle up with us in our bed talking and laughing, forming the most tender bonds, and they are constantly treated with respect. Demonstrating respect for your children is the most effective way to convey love. We also demonstrate that love without respect is hollow. Love and respect are intertwined, and when that respect is compromised, it is crucial to mend it swiftly rather than allow distrust and dysfunction to seep into our relationships. A sturdy foundation can help withstand these adversities.

> **"The art of parenting, much like the work of an architect, is a careful balance of designing a plan and bringing it to life."**

The love and respect that RaaShaun and I have deliberately built into our family's foundation reinforces the bond between us and creates a harmonious sanctuary of affection, understanding, and trust. Likewise, our children, nurtured within this structure, are naturally inclined to develop their pillars of love and respect, ensuring that this magnificent sanctuary continues to evolve and thrive. It's just magic!

The art of parenting, much like the work of an architect, is a careful balance of designing a plan and bringing it to life. As architects carefully lay the foundation and construct the framework for their structures, parents, too, must lay a solid foundation of love and support for their children, constructing the framework of their relationships with intention and care. The final result is a beautiful, strong, and harmonious family structure that stands the test of time and withstands the challenges that life may bring.

REAL LIFE REFLECTIONS

Building a loving family means:
1. Strengthening love and respect.

2. Modeling healthy communication.

3. Providing an example of a loving partnership.

4. Encouraging expressions of love.

5. Repairing family relationships.

6. Empowering children to foster love.

7. Identifying and addressing misalignments.

Navigating Absence in Parent–Child Relationships

In today's society, we are seeing more of the disappearing embrace between parent and child, and we often recognize children who are not comfortable with or used to hugging their parents. They won't dare hold their hands or be caught showing affection, especially in public. Why? Is it nurture, nature, or both? Let's unravel the mystery of affection's absence in parent–child relationships.

In the ever-evolving landscape of a child's journey into adolescence, the art of affection undergoes a metamorphosis similar to that of a caterpillar transforming into a beautiful butterfly. This change, however, can sometimes take on a less conventional path, where the display of affection may retreat into the cocoon of their developing persona.

As children and teens navigate the labyrinth of emotions, social dynamics, and self-discovery, they may experience a temporary eclipse of their innate ability to express affection. In addition, there may be developmental conditions, such as autism spectrum disorders, that can affect a child's ability or inclination to express affection, which may have nothing to do with their parent. Sometimes, children just want autonomy, and that's their way of expressing it. As young individuals strive for independence, they may perceive affection as a tether to their childhood and view affectional withdrawal as a way to break free. Their desire for autonomy can manifest as a temporary retreat from open displays of tenderness and warmth or become permanent but continue to nurture it without growing frustrated. Give love, hugs, kisses, and your time. Let your children hear you profess your love for and pride in them. You're the parent. You set the example. Don't allow societal norms, peer pressure, or mental health concerns to cause you to pull back.

The emotional spectrum of children and teens can be as vibrant and complex as the patterns of a kaleidoscope. As they explore this mosaic, they might find it challenging to articulate or express their feelings, leading to a temporary ebb in their affectionate nature. That's okay. Talk to them and help normalize expressing their feelings. Give them examples of others' or your experiences. And tell them why you want to be able to show your affection.

Remember that the social court of peer pressure and the desire most children have to fit in can make children and teens hesitant to exhibit affection, especially in public. They may worry about judgment or ridicule from their peers, resulting in the concealment of their affectionate sides, but it doesn't mean they don't love you. Invest in teaching them to be confident and comfortable in their thoughts and behaviors and be consistent.

As adolescents venture into the uncharted waters of their emotions, they may erect walls around their hearts to protect themselves from potential pain or rejection. We've maintained being vigilant in preventing our children from needing to construct walls because of us or others by staying involved in their lives and prioritizing in-depth communication. We are entirely in tune with our children. Even more importantly, they are in tune with RaaShaun and me. Their affections aren't limited to me. All of the Choo Crew show their love and affection to both of us. Madison and Logan haven't lessened their incredible bond with us. In fact, it's stronger. And as a twentysomething, Logan doesn't care what his peers think of his bond with us. He's the same in any room he's in.

There may be many reasons or one significant one that you aren't aware of, regardless of the strength of your bond. Sometimes, children withdraw, which has nothing to do with you or your bond. You may be incredibly close with your children; however, open communication and active listening without judgment are beneficial. If you can't get to the root of their withdrawal, seeking therapy to delve deeper can help. Your child may have endured something that's causing them to protect their vulnerability, which can temporarily enclose their capacity to express affection. Pay attention to this, as there could be painful reasons that affection is absent, such as sexual or physical abuse or depression.

As you discern the emergence of barriers, try dismantling them, gently dislodging each brick while assisting your child in navigating these complex emotions. Again, it's worth noting that there may be substantial reasons driving this behavior, which your child might be reluctant to discuss directly with you. If your efforts to penetrate this emotional fortress prove unsuccessful, consider enlisting the aid of a qualified therapist or psychologist to explore the underlying motives for their withdrawal and self-protection before the wall reaches completion. However, with a loving, compassionate, informed approach, you can help your child confront and overcome these challenges, fostering emotional growth and resilience.

While it may seem like children and teens have shed their affectionate layers, this phase is often just a process in their journey. With patience, understanding, and gentle guidance, they can be equipped with the wisdom and emotional strength to take the wall down and embrace the world with newfound love and affection.

As diverse as this world is, people are still learning to accept their children as they are, or are not, not as they want them to be, and we're doing our children a disservice if we don't teach them to wholly love themselves and show it. If they don't show self-love, that may also make it difficult for them to show you love.

For children who are averse to touch, or have cultural norms that are absent of affection, let them have their safe space—*their body*. Don't push past those boundaries. There are alternative ways to show affection other than physical touch—quality time, eye contact, and verbal expressions of emotions that are congruent with your behaviors. Respect them and continue communicating your love for them so they know how you feel.

In these situations, consider yourself an *architect of emotional connections*, and you're building a lasting and meaningful bond with your child—one that can stand strong amid the ever-changing landscape of their emotional development. So, with that said, now you need to design a bridge, and this bridge will represent the emotional connection between you and your child.

> **REAL LIFE REFLECTIONS**
>
> 1. Provide a safe space for your child to express emotions.
> 2. Maintain a strong emotional connection while supporting your child's autonomy.
> 3. Encourage your child to express their thoughts and feelings confidently.
> 4. Be alert to behavioral or emotional changes in your child that may need professional attention.
> 5. Foster open communication and trust to address your child's underlying emotional issues.
> 6. Employ strategies to guide your child empathetically through emotional challenges, fostering wisdom and resilience for healthy relationships.

(RAASHAUN)
Create That Type of World

Unconditional love—this is a difficult point to discuss regarding this generation of young people because outside of our children, I don't often see unconditional love the way I had it growing up. Our kids are overly affectionate and caring. You'd think they set an alarm to give us love and kisses, but Gia and I know it's because of how we've nurtured and loved them. And loving your kids, making them feel important, happy, healthy, well-adjusted, heard, special, and intelligent—none of that has anything to do with how much or how little money you have. If Jaxson sees me, he will run and jump into my arms and knock me or Mommy down. Logan says, "Dad, I love you," all the time, and he doesn't care who's around. Madison, London, Brooklyn—the same—and Peyton, she's being nurtured to be the same. If you want unconditional love, you've got to earn it. Love them often, express your love even more, and let them grow up so they never know what it's like not to have your unconditional love. Peyton has been loved, hugged, and kissed so much that, like our other kids, we know she can feel it. And she won't ever be without it. When we see other parents and even people we don't know, the way they compliment us for our natural expressions of love, we can't make it up. They can see our love, but I think they can feel it too.

Our kids went to a new school a couple of years ago. One of the teachers stopped me and said, "It's such a blessing to have your kids in this school. When your kids pass each other in the halls, they hug each other." Some parents and kids are afraid to or don't want to, or they don't know how to express healthy love and affection. I'll give my sons a hug and a kiss because I want them to know I love them. I want them to know I see them. Our kids want to be loved. *Kids want to be loved.* In fact, I don't know a single kid who doesn't want to be loved. Our kids want us to feel what they feel. All of them jump in our bed and snuggle with us. We love it! And by comparison, I never wanted to be in the bed with my parents. Although my parents showed love in the way they took care of me, they didn't show love that way. Holding hands or kissing me didn't happen. But it doesn't mean we shouldn't express that type of affection with appropriateness.

As society continues to evolve, there's a growing concern about the increasing prevalence of coldness, rigidity, and hostility within interpersonal relationships. These negative influences have the potential to adversely impact a child's mental health by fostering feelings of loneliness and isolation. It's necessary for parents to counteract these effects by emphasizing the importance of providing our children with an abundance of love, affection, and emotional support to nurture their psychological well-being and foster their resilience in the face of these societal challenges. Imagine a world where in everything your children do, they know they are loved by you in a way that is completely unmatched by anything else or anyone else—other than God. Our children live in that world. Create that type of world for your children.

My wife has persistently shown that type of love and affection, and it's definitely helped shape our foundation and environment. I wasn't the cat's meow growing up. I was a nerd with glasses and braces, and I was a scrawny little man. When I met Gia, I started to grow. I fell in love with a girl that didn't care about all of that; she just wanted to be my friend. Gia was very affectionate. She did all the things that made me feel good, and it had nothing to do with sex. She knows how to display love and make you see and feel what it is on the healthiest and most amazing level. I learned how to do that from Gia, and it made me do those things instinctively with my kids. Their responses have taught me, it's one of the best things about the Choo Crew!

"Real unconditional love is misrepresented because of the vast issues and diverse individuals, perspectives, and judgments that exist in society."

Real unconditional love is misrepresented because of the vast issues and diverse individuals, perspectives, and judgments that exist in society. And as for today's younger generation, they can't handle things the way we may have. Today, a fight could lead your child to a higher risk of getting shot, stabbed, or killed. Issues that were sometimes settled between kids have a greater proclivity to create more violence and hate because we really never know what is going on in someone's head, and we need to teach them how to deal with these issues. Admittedly, numerous factors have weakened our kids. Don't get me wrong, we know kids that are wise beyond their years and mentally tough, confident, and secure in who they are. But the manifestation of issues such as cyberbullying, academic pressure, exposure to media and advertising that causes distorted body image and diminished self-esteem, family dynamics with higher percentages of divorce and conflict, the stigma of mental health, trauma that's gone unresolved, and less quality time with their parents, to name just a few, has weakened their sense of belonging and love. Many of the kids Gia and I have encountered, or watched grow up, aren't equipped to handle these issues.

As shared in *Real Life, Real Love*, something happened to Gia when she was a junior at St. Francis Preparatory School in Queens. They had early dismissal that day, and Gia and her friend Dahlia took public transportation to a McDonald's on their way home. A girl Gia didn't know and had never seen before commented about Gia's complexion. At that time, like Gia said, "Skin color and privilege made enemies." The taunting grew worse, and the girl's crew, two boys and four girls, joined in, but Gia didn't retaliate. Security kicked the girl out of the McDonald's, and the police were called, but when they all went their separate ways, the girl and her crew returned. When the girl went to cut Dahlia, Gia grabbed the girl and threw her on the ground. The rest of the crew jumped in kicking, punching, and stomping on Gia. The girl used a razor and sliced Gia's face and thigh. This permanently scarred Gia, but she didn't break or become depressed. I don't know anyone that would respond the way Gia did. I don't. She understood and internalized some things, and it didn't mean it didn't hurt or bother her, but for the most part, she knew she had to keep moving forward in life. That wasn't the end for Gia. It was traumatic and something significant to overcome, but Gia had the full support of her parents.

Today, parents and society are moving so fast that parents aren't sitting with their kids long enough to teach them how to address issues head-on. They don't know. The skills aren't there. Fighting isn't the same. Some kids carry guns or other weapons to school; they kill people because of hate, racism, or other issues. Your kids need your support. They need honest conversations, unconditional love, and consistent guidance even if you do it over the phone. If you don't give it to them, they can sink into depression when they encounter issues. Some kids are out there looking for love in the wrong places, or they try to find ways to fill the absence of love by getting into drugs. Sometimes they do bad things because they want your attention. They want you to correct them, teach them, and hear them. And some parents know, but countless others aren't aware, their child is planning an exit strategy out of life. None of these are the solutions we want as parents, and imagine if you could help shape their life into something better if you gave them—you. You can work and have objectives and goals you want to accomplish, but you can also make your kids feel loved and important at the same time.

I know people who've lost their children to suicide or gun violence, which may have been prevented. And we see LGBTQ+ kids who don't know if their parents love them unconditionally because they aren't accepted or supported through difficult times. In some of our radio interviews with guests and friends who have problems with their kids, I can tell they're disconnected. Some admit they don't have the time or energy to deal with whatever their kids are going through. In summary, kids are struggling, and their parents are tired.

When parents don't know what to do, they let their kids fall by the wayside. Do you love your children unconditionally, or are there conditions to that love? And if there are conditions, do your kids know it? If there are conditions, you're taking a risky stance. Kids do not thrive when your love is conditional. They are not innately happy when your love is conditional. They will hit a wall when they realize that the person or people who gave them life also give them conditional love.

Look out into the real world. Every day, there's evidence that parents aren't giving their kids the degree of love and attention they need today. There is hard evidence that it's conditional. Watch the news, read the paper, peruse social media, and talk to your family, friends, or co-workers about their kids. One day they're fine, and the following week, things have evolved; something has happened. We have to be more committed to talking with our kids and connecting to their world without judging them. That's how you begin. If there was this unconditional love for our children, the rising mental health concerns and suicide attempts and suicides—would be substantially less. Ask your child who is struggling with suicidal ideation, at what point did it become an option? Ask them when things changed and this thought entered their mind. Care enough to ask. Why do so many children experience depression and anxiety? Let them be able to admit to you that things suck or are difficult. That's okay. But listen. Really listen. If you know what's going on with your children, you can create a timeline and determine when things changed even when they can't. You can detect—when they went on a trip for spring break, they were happy, but when they came home, something had changed. Unconditional love can prevent suicide. Knowing they have people who unconditionally care about them can save their lives. Love isn't a magic emotion that automatically prevents mental health issues or suicide because some kids have a genetic predisposition, biological or chronic issues, substance abuse, or other mitigating factors. But loving your kids enough to be in tune with them can trigger warnings and let you know they need you—or help.

Today kids deal with a lot of peer pressure to fit in, and there's a whole list of reasons they need our unconditional love. Just to name one: body image issues, like weight or self-esteem. Your kids may perceive your comments or actions as judgmental or conditional rather than supportive and loving. Kids who exhibit personality traits that contrast with their parents' values or preferences may feel they aren't entirely accepted or loved for who they are: for example, if you were a star athlete but your kids don't play sports and have no desire to play. If you disapprove of your kid's friends, they may think your love is conditional upon their choice of friends or social affiliations. Kids who experience mental health challenges, such as anxiety or depression, may think your attempts to help or support them are conditional love. Kids from multicultural or biracial backgrounds may struggle to feel a sense of belonging within their family or community, leading to a perception that their parents don't accept or understand their unique cultural identity. Other examples: Kids who adopt spiritual beliefs that are different from yours. Kids with physical disabilities. Kids who pursue academic or career paths that deviate from their parents' expectations. Kids who express themselves in unconventional ways. And kids in blended families who don't feel accepted and loved because they aren't both parents' biological child. The point is that we as parents can't misinterpret or adjust what real love is when it's not working the way we envision, and we must do better. This—what we've shared—is the short list. Think about how your children may feel that your love is "conditional" and work to correct it.

> ### "When your children know you love them unconditionally and you're consistent, what others think won't matter as much."

In elementary school, I was bullied. Though my feelings weren't exactly crushed the way kids are affected today, I knew I had to stand up to the bullies. So one day, I told Dad about all the bullying I was dealing with and that I had to fight him. All he said was, "Alright. I'll be there." I didn't think he'd show up, but I went to school the next day, and my father was there. I fought the bully. Fighting with my dad standing there gave me the heart to overcome bullying. My father's presence let me know I had everything I needed at home from him and my mom.

When your children know you love them unconditionally and you're consistent, what others think won't matter as much. That day my father showed up at school was a display of unconditional love. It wouldn't have mattered to Dad if I had lost. He was there to support me. That was his way of showing his love. Knowing Dad was there, I beat that kid's ass. But today, we have to show unconditional love and teach lessons of overcoming adversity and support differently. We have to show unconditional love when it's easy and, more importantly, when it seems hard. We won't always love the circumstances, but we can always display love for our kids.

While I don't encourage fighting in today's culture, my dad's being there displayed his love. However you need to show love to your kids, show it. Today kids, society, parenting, how things are handled, and the consequences are different. Vastly different. Peer pressure is different. There is spoken, unspoken, direct, indirect, negative, and positive peer pressure. Social media contributes to bullying. Sometimes, that can hurt kids more than anything because when people know what bothers someone the most, they will attack that. Some of those kids found joy in using my weakness, the fear of being bullied, against me. I grew tired of giving them that. Nowadays, children empower others with knowledge of their insecurities, and parents do the same, so some of these kids adopt that weakness from their parents. They see us hand our insecurities to people, and we have to learn how not to let our children do the same. We need to teach them unconditional self-love and how to exude confidence.

I have a friend who was always walking behind his ten-year-old son and pulling his shoulders back, correcting his posture to display confidence. And when he spoke, he'd say, "Put some bass in your voice, son. Speak up. Let your presence be heard." His son, now twenty-three, walks into a room like he owns the building. Chin up, shoulders back, and he speaks with complete confidence. He makes decisions with confidence and authority too. Regardless of their identity, you can do the same with any of your children because we need them to be confident.

Someone's identity, history, economic status, dual-parent or single-parent household, or culture does not preclude them from teaching confidence. Gia and I have consistently been the example for our kids. We even taught them how to snap back, speak up when necessary, communicate their thoughts and ideas, display empathy even when others don't, and always display confidence because Mom and Dad have their backs no matter what!

When Madison was little, she was bullied on the bus, and kids were making fun of her and cracking jokes. When Madison and Logan got home, they told their mother and me what had happened. The whole family got together and went back and forth, teaching Maddie to "snap back" at those kids. We had all types of silly comebacks, and we had her practice on us, instantly giving her confidence because they would shut down anybody. Something that little helped lift her in a way that may have seemed insignificant to some, but it was necessary to address at that moment. That's how we show our kids unconditional love. We taught Logan if anyone says something bad about his sister, he better say something. My dad taught me that. We display unconditional love for one another by supporting one another. But times have changed.

"The tragedies of suicide, gun violence, and mental health struggles among children aren't just societal problems; they are symptoms of an underlying crisis within our families."

There seems to be a disconnection between parents and children growing up in today's rapidly evolving society that has led to severe consequences. We must provide unconditional love, consistent guidance, and more genuine open communication with our children. The lack of connection leaves them vulnerable to depression, hate, racism, seeking love in the wrong places, or even contemplating an exit strategy from life itself. Even seemingly insignificant acts can shape your child's confidence and self-esteem. Taking the time to role-play and teach them how to respond to bullying and instilling self-assurance are a few ways our children need us to engage.

The tragedies of suicide, gun violence, and mental health struggles among children aren't just societal problems; they are symptoms of an underlying crisis within our families. These issues can sometimes arise from miscommunication, misinterpretation, or the pressure to conform. Regardless of what it is, our support shouldn't be conditional. Our children need a consistent and unequivocal demonstration of love. We have to commit to understanding and connecting with their world, setting aside judgments, and embracing their unique identities. The support encompasses everything from physical disabilities, mental health challenges, academic pursuits, unconventional expressions, cultural identities, and a lot more.

Examples of our personal experience provide a more relatable testament to the transformative power of our support and understanding. What we're seeing, reading, or hearing about has contributed to the need for this book. As mentioned above, there is a disconnection between children and parents today. It's no longer just a family matter to be kept behind closed doors. The doors have been broken down so that it has become a significant societal crisis. Unconditional love, understanding, and support can aid in healing a child's pain and build resilience and confidence, equipping them to face the complexities of modern life. We're seeing a call for better parenting and an urgent plea for a more compassionate and connected society. It's a call to action that recognizes love, consistency, and awareness as essential tools to foster healthy, thriving children.

REAL LIFE REFLECTIONS

1. How can you recognize and address the unique challenges that this generation faces, such as cyberbullying, academic pressure, and mental health stigma, in order to better support your children?

2. How can you help your children build resilience and healthy coping mechanisms when faced with adversity or difficult situations?

_____

_____

_____

3. Are there any instances where you may have inadvertently given your child the impression that your love is conditional? If so, how can you address these instances and reassure them of your unconditional love?

_____

_____

_____

4. How can you better understand and support your child's unique personality traits, interests, and values, even if they differ from your own?

_____

_____

_____

5. How can you help your child develop self-confidence and a strong sense of self-love?

_____

_____

_____

5. Strengthening the Foundation of Self-Esteem

Observing the skilled craftsmanship of a master watchmaker, carefully assembling a timepiece with precision, attention to detail, and a deep understanding of the delicate balance between form and function, reminds me that as parents we have to complete our family's structure with the same level of care, awareness, and intention. And building healthy self-esteem with all members of your family unit is a significant contribution to your family's success.

Self-esteem refers to the way individuals perceive and value themselves. It's an essential aspect of mental and emotional well-being that influences how children, teens, and young adults of diverse cultures navigate their lives. Healthy self-esteem helps your kids face challenges, make confident decisions, and maintain positive relationships. In today's society, where pressures from social media, peer comparison, and high expectations are widespread, developing and maintaining self-esteem is crucial for individuals of all backgrounds and ages. The ubiquitous nature of technology and social media presents new risks for children and adolescents. Educate yourself on digital safety to mitigate these concerns and engage in open dialogues with your children about appropriate online behavior and potential dangers. The earlier you teach your kids how to have healthy self-esteem, the stronger it will become.

"The ubiquitous nature of technology and social media presents new risks for children and adolescents."

Without healthy self-esteem, your children may struggle with self-doubt, anxiety, and depression. Since mental health concerns are rising in this country, that's an indication that self-esteem is declining. Consider what you see in your children and how they carry themselves. They may be more susceptible to peer pressure and negative influences that can lead to poor decision-making and risky behaviors. Additionally, low self-esteem can negatively impact academic and career performance, interpersonal relationships, and, as we're seeing, overall mental health. The demand for high achievement in academics can cause significant stress for children, teens, and young adults. However, you can support your children's academic success by encouraging a balanced approach to education, emphasizing the importance of effort over achievement, and providing resources, such as tutors, mentors, and therapists, when needed.

As parents, we're responsible for encouraging open communication with our children to discuss their feelings, concerns, and experiences related to self-esteem and to help develop their unique strengths, talents, and interests without imposing unrealistic expectations. We can do that by showing it in our own lives, which can help our children cope with setbacks, failures, and criticisms constructively. Help them develop a strong cultural identity and pride by recognizing and appreciating their own diverse backgrounds. And teach your children to set healthy boundaries and develop assertiveness skills to protect their self-esteem in social situations.

(RAASHAUN)
Social Media's Contribution to Killing Self-Esteem

I'm revisiting the topic of social media because of our concerns with self-esteem. Suicide is a huge issue, and we need to discuss it instead of just mentioning it. Too many children have suicidal tendencies, and social media is a significant contributor. When we were younger, we looked at billboards and saw them feed insecurities we didn't know we had. Today it's amplified. Every day we're losing children to suicide because of mental health disorders, substance abuse, bullying and cyberbullying, relationship and family issues, and exposure to ways to self-harm. Next year and the year after, other things will be added to the list. Doing the things in this book, and seeking professional help as soon as you see or think it's needed, can help prevent our kids from getting to this desperate cry for help or life-ending stage.

When kids spend hours on social media, what they see isn't complete reality. There are filters and body-editing tools. Some kids are conditioned to think they need plastic surgery to achieve perfection or be accepted, and when girls have a baby, they think they're supposed to snap back to their pre-pregnancy body in six weeks. Children are making fun of each other, and how it lands on any given day can be the difference between life and death. The number of likes on social media are critical to them. If they don't get a lot, it's devastating, or they buy likes to look important. They see people looking as if they have perfect lives on social media when many are just as inadequate, if not more than, those looking at their pages. Children and adults are searching for validation from what? Smoke and mirrors. After everything they see, they sit there wondering, *Is something wrong with me?*

Social media magnifies the small things we go through and negatively feeds insecurities. Insecurities hit any age, contributing to many young people's mental health crises. We didn't have social media, and we didn't have the escalating volume of mental health concerns that exist today, and social media is a direct cause of them. Toxicity has access to your kids via social media. You don't know everything they're taking in, but you need to discuss social media, reality, peer pressure, and *consumer pressure*. We must be more responsible in preventing our kids from using unrealistic measures as their standards.

REAL LIFE REFLECTIONS

1. Foster open dialogue with your child about social media and its mental health impacts.

2. Encourage a realistic and healthy perspective on body image and self-worth in the social media context.

3. Teach your child about the distinction between online personas and real life, emphasizing not to compare themselves with others on social media.

4. Support your child in developing a balanced, responsible relationship with social media, including setting boundaries and managing online time.

5. Create a safe space for your child to share thoughts and feelings about social media pressures.

6. Participate in your child's online world without infringing on their privacy, offering guidance when needed.

7. Implement strategies encouraging offline activities and social interactions, counteracting the potential negative effects of social media.

Build Their Self-Esteem So No One Can Remove It

In this complex society, we must be deliberate in elevating our game as parents because what was working before is no longer working. Self-esteem contributes to who you are as a person and can guide you in this world. Knowing this, we try to give our kids so much love and attention, tell them we love them, and keep them off social media until we feel they're ready to face the world on their own—just like we let them learn to cross the street safely before putting them on a school bus. Unfortunately, some parents buy phones for their kids and give them access to things when they aren't ready. Instead, we should watch the news and learn about the dangers. Pay attention to the damage to their self-esteem social media is causing and assess the world as a whole—there are people out there who get joy out of hurting others by attacking their self-esteem. Giving them easy access to your children without parental controls, monitoring, or having your children's passwords can be dangerous, especially if your children do not understand the dangers.

When Brooklyn was six she came home and told us that she had a problem with another kid at school. Jaxson, who was eight, looked at me and said, "Dad, it's okay. I handled it. I made him apologize." I nodded, and the grin on my face grew wider because that's how we raised our kids. If Mommy and Daddy aren't here, they have their siblings to rely on. Self-esteem sets the groundwork for their whole existence. If we told them enough, they would believe they could fly. I think that it's these things that plant those seeds of self-esteem. We talk to our kids and teach them because we want our kids to want to come back to us for any love, support, encouragement, or anything else they need. We want them to know they have what they need in us. That confidence in knowing that we've got them supports healthy self-esteem.

"It's important to do what you can to make your kids feel beautiful and have unwavering self-esteem that they can take out into the world and accomplish whatever they want, with or without the support of others."

If you or your children don't have high self-esteem, you have to figure out why. Is it because your parents didn't compliment you and show love? Did you come from a place where you were thrown into a school, community, activity, or with other kids, but you weren't accepted and didn't feel you belonged? Growing up, that didn't happen to me, and my parents never made me feel less than others. What we had, we had. We danced and had family get-togethers. When I saw people who had something nice, I was never jealous because I was always taught to focus on myself. Here I am, confident in myself, and I pour all of that confidence and a little extra into our kids. My wife does the same. It's important to do what you can to make your kids feel beautiful and have unwavering self-esteem that they can take out into the world and accomplish whatever they want, with or without the support of others. If you never felt that way, that's even more of a reason to do all you can to build your kids' self-esteem.

We love doing photo shoots with our kids. It's fun, and we're about having fun. We were getting ready for one, and my daughter Brooklyn came in wearing black eyeliner, but she looked like she had a black eye instead. What did I do? I told her she looked beautiful and did the photoshoot with her. Especially since she's young, that could have been a moment where I damaged my daughter's self-esteem. I understood why Gia thinks before she speaks up about something. Sometimes, we don't see it, but that's an example of how it happens. When Brooklyn was younger, I called her a beautiful brown-skinned girl. Brooklyn isn't surrounded by other little girls who look like her in our community that often. So, we've made it a priority to instill a strong sense of confidence that she can carry both inside and outside our home. We want her to feel self-assured and proud of who she is, regardless of the reflections she sees around her.

I recall my own experiences growing up when people would notice that my parents and I weren't the same shade. Some would even ask if I was adopted. These encounters were reminders of how appearances can shape perceptions and impact my approach to parenting.

My goal has been to equip Brooklyn with the understanding and self-esteem needed to navigate a world where she may stand out because of her appearance. It's not about shielding her from potential misunderstandings or judgments—it's about building a resilient self-identity. We want her to know her worth, embrace her uniqueness, and move through life with the assurance that she is loved, valued, and capable of anything she sets her mind to. Our children rely on us to help create a sense of self-esteem so solid that they can navigate life's challenges, remaining unaffected by obstacles and setbacks that might otherwise hinder them.

You don't need a lot of money to teach your kids to have high self-esteem. It will come from your words and actions and the exposure you give them. Take your kids everywhere. Take them to nice restaurants, and visit different places. If I leave the country, I take our kids to give them exposure so they never feel less than anyone in any room. It doesn't matter where we go; money doesn't impress our children. My intention for our children is to provide them with diverse experiences, exposing them to various cultures, cuisines, and environments. This will enable them to make well-informed decisions about their preferences and dislikes with confidence.

> **"My intention for our children is to provide them with diverse experiences, exposing them to various cultures, cuisines, and environments."**

When I was a kid, it was a lot different. I didn't care about self-esteem or think about insecurity. It wasn't on my mind. My parents didn't show the same amount of love that I show my kids; however, they made me feel I could do or accomplish anything I wanted. My parents poured love into me and told me "I could" accomplish anything I wanted, so I didn't care what anybody else said. Why would I?

Watching Logan and Madison adjust to where Gia and I lived was the hardest. They had no idea how hard we've worked or how far we've come. It was difficult because life was different fifteen to eighteen years ago. After we left Queens, there weren't too many Black kids in our area, and we were viewed as "the Black people in the music industry." We weren't accepted, and it trickled down to my kids. I know my daughters are beautiful and kind, but I never thought Maddie received the love, respect, and appreciation that she deserved in our new neighborhood given she is so loving and kind to others. Even with Logan, I felt he wasn't accepted by kids either. Like Maddie, Logan wasn't invited to the playdates, and he dealt with a lot of situations like that. To counteract these experiences, and knowing Logan had an interest in what I do as a DJ, I took him to concerts and introduced him to prominent artists like Jay-Z. I sought to instill a resilient sense of self-esteem into my son. My goal was to develop a self-esteem so solid that no one could undermine it—one that reminded him of his identity, roots, and family. It allowed my son to see what I do, how I interact, communicate with confidence, and learn from me. Kids need to see us in action.

When our children struggle to fit in, it's our responsibility as parents to offer them love and encouragement that's so profound they need nothing else to boost their self-esteem. Gia and I became our kids' best friends, filling the void left by their school experiences. We did this to ensure they never settled for less than they deserved. As parents, we can all do this for our children, regardless of our circumstances.

REAL LIFE REFLECTIONS

1. How can you identify the root cause of low self-esteem in yourself or your child and address it effectively?

2. In what ways can you instill a strong sense of self-worth in your child, regardless of your financial situation or background?

3. How can you expose your child to diverse experiences and cultures and teach them to appreciate and confidently navigate different environments?

4. How can you create a supportive and nurturing home environment where your child feels valued and empowered to achieve their goals?

5. What can you do to help your child build resilience and cope with feelings of exclusion or non-acceptance from their peers or community?

   _____
   _____
   _____

6. How can you foster a strong parent–child relationship that makes your child feel loved and supported, even when they face challenges in their social lives?

   _____
   _____
   _____

7. What activities or experiences can you introduce to your child that will help them develop their interests and passions and feel confident in their choices and preferences?

   _____
   _____
   _____

Offering Emotional Restoration

As a parent, it's sometimes difficult for me to shut down and listen. Meanwhile, Gia has a brilliant skill—she listens to learn, whereas I listen to pass. I listen to get out of that situation. I didn't understand what school was—I went to school to pass. I wish I'd gone to learn and take it seriously. But the truth is that I memorized to pass the test. I had to learn how to actively listen.

Gia will say something, and I'll say, "Yeah. Uh-huh. Uh-huh."

But Gia will stop me and say, "No. No. What did I say? What point am I making?"

Then it's, "I'm not your child. I don't have to tell you that I heard what you said," but I really didn't.

Besides Gia being late, our biggest point of contention is when I'm not actively listening. When Gia's talking, she wants me to be present. She doesn't want me to talk *at* her. She knows I'm listening when I summarize what she said, ask questions for clarity, and give my undivided attention with proper body language. In a relationship, with your kids, in business, that's a reasonable expectation because we need to be present and care about what's being communicated. I'm still learning to do this. Gia wants me to respond to what she said, not pass. Being in tune and correcting all of us as needed so we can be our best versions of ourselves—as previously explained, we have roles in a two-parent household; that's Gia's role, and she executes it well. Gia's not going to cut the grass, take out the trash, and things like that—I'm going to do them.

There are specific roles we will take on, and our responsibilities actually play to our strengths. For example, when there's a problem, Gia will round up the posse and say, "This is the problem we're having, and we need to address this." Then we get everyone together and discuss it as a family. The impressive aspect is that conversation brings diverse perspectives from each parent and child, and everybody feels heard. We take different angles from each kid and actively listen and care about what they say. That way, our kids aren't saying, "Well, you're the mom. You're supposed to feel that way." If there's something Jaxson has an issue with, we get perspectives that may support or oppose the point. But we talk through it and come up with solutions that everybody can accept and understand. We'll get Jaxson's nine-year-old perspective and also seek Logan's twenty-year-old point of view, which could add valuable insight for Jaxson. This keeps us learning from each other, and it's an excellent way to acknowledge Jaxson's and Logan's feelings.

When it comes to parenting, Gia and I don't disagree in front of the kids. We ride with each other that way and usually go with who's more passionate. Even if I don't necessarily agree, I rock with her and vice versa. We have a united front.

Sometimes, our kids are mad at me for something, and Gia explains things to them and breaks down the situation. They still might be a little angry, but they understood when she was done explaining. I do the same with the kids. We don't throw one another under the bus trying to be the better or more loved parent. We balance each other out for the good of our kids and each other. Sometimes, I get in my feelings. If Gia does something and doesn't tell me, I'll say, "Don't forget, I'm Dad!" But we don't do that in front of the kids either. We can give each other a look and stay on a united front.

Because of Gia and the impact she has on our kids, I'm learning to not shut down and to actively listen so I'm not passing on critical information they've shared where I could have communicated a life lesson, given valuable advice, cautioned them, or laughed about a funny situation.

The point is that we want you to make your kids a priority. If you can sit down for meals or carve out time to stay connected and have family discussions about what's going on in your lives, their experiences on social media, and the changes they see in close friends and peers—engage in those conversations regularly. Remember that being judgmental can discourage open communication. They'll stop talking and shut down. Consider how you felt when your parents judged you. If you listen and understand the scope of the situation, then delicately offer suggestions on approaching and addressing concerns, they'll be more likely and willing to learn from you. Just talking to your kids can be a way to soothe some of their stress and alleviate anxiety, offering a sort of emotional restoration. And join in by telling them what you see.

"Show genuine interest and ask how they did and what happened. Show pride in them when you're actively listening."

As a single parent, and even in a dual-parent household, attending your kid's school events and extracurricular activities can be difficult and, sometimes, impossible, especially when you have more than one child. Although Gia does attend, unfortunately, I can't make all of my kids' events due to travel and my schedule. And for many other parents, it's not possible. But when I can't make it, my kids know *why* I'm not there. I let them see and understand what Daddy does and how much I travel from their experiences with me. But I am always in tune with their lives, friends, activities, everything. Show your unwavering support and love for their interests and achievements whenever possible.

Make your time with your kids more important than grabbing dinner or a drink or going on social outings with your friends. We're not saying don't practice self-care and make yourself a priority, but ensure your kids are in a healthy and happy space. Then, when you walk through your door, prioritize your kids. Show genuine interest and ask how they did and what happened. Show pride in them when you're actively listening. Gia and I talk to our kids. I might be on the road, at the office, or tired, and our kids are expressive and want to talk. London will tell me about her ten-year-old problems and what she doesn't like, what she loves, or what she is learning. What do I do? I sit through the whole thing and listen.

When a child wants to talk, listen. Gia and I know everything—yes, I said it, *everything*—going on with our kids, because it's important, they know we care to know, and, more importantly, we've cultivated an environment and relationship where they want to tell us. By intentionally creating space for open communication and being present in your children's lives, you can foster an environment where your kids feel loved, supported, and empowered to face life's challenges head-on.

REAL LIFE REFLECTIONS

Seven steps to foster open communication and support in your family:

1. Establish a family discussion routine.
2. Foster a nonjudgmental environment.
3. Balance personal and professional responsibilities.
4. Demonstrate unwavering support.
5. Cultivate an open environment.

> 6. Show genuine interest and active listening.
> 7. Encourage resilience and problem-solving skills.

(Gia)
The First Line of Defense Is Being Heard

Though, as parents, we need to become skilled at actively listening to our spouse, partner, significant other, and children, it's not about sitting there *like* you're listening. It's genuinely being present. While they're talking, actively listen by nodding your head and asking probing questions to ensure you're invested in the conversation, and they are too. It feels good when someone's curious about what's going on in your life, with a situation, or even something small they want to share. When someone's actively listening to a child, it can make them feel on top of the world. I don't want RaaShaun or our children ever to feel rushed or hurried in their communication or that I'm prodding them to say what they need to so I can move on. The things they want to say are important to them, and they need to feel important to me. If I can't actively listen because I'm in the middle of something or rushing out the door, I'll tell them and make it a priority the first moment I have, and I don't forget about them.

"When you actively listen, you acknowledge the value of their time and communications. You are showing them they are important to you. They matter."

Imagine how you feel when you make a joke and no one laughs. Was anyone listening? Even with friends, I don't surround myself with people I'm not interested in. When my friends are talking, I'm generally engrossed. I'm personally conscious of the way people around me feel, and it's essential for me to feel comfortable. I've been at a restaurant with friends, and when others talk, some appear to be the least interested in what they're saying. It's a human being thing—people want to feel important. When you actively listen, you acknowledge the value of their time and communications. You are showing them they are important to you. They matter. You care about what they have to say.

The first line of defense *is* being heard, which means that the best way to address and prevent problems is by actively listening and paying attention to the concerns and needs of others. When someone feels that their voice is being heard and their concerns are being taken seriously, they are more likely to feel valued, respected, and supported. This can help to prevent problems from escalating and can help to build stronger, more positive relationships.

Show genuine interest in the individuals you interact with and demonstrate empathy toward their concerns and interests. Too many parents are not interested in what their kids have to say. You are under the assumption that you know them because they are your children, but you don't. Unless they share what happens throughout their days, their feelings, adversities, and emotional ups and downs, you don't know enough to guide or protect them. You can change this by training yourself to really be interested in your children the way RaaShaun has learned to actively listen and respond accordingly.

When I pick our children up from school, as soon as they get in the car or when they get home, I'll say, "Now, each of you, one by one, tell me about your day. Tell me about the best part of your day and the worst part of your day. And if you could change anything, what would it be?" And then we have a conversation based around that, which causes them to engage in critical thinking. They love when I ask questions of them and show genuine interest. Many times we may say something to be polite, but we aren't listening to the responses. We don't want our children to think we're not listening.

Our son Logan will come into our room, lie down on the bed, and start talking. Madison and I talk about her boyfriend, college, and where she's going for lunch. All these things let you know you are important to your child and they are heard. When your children are in social settings, they'll have the confidence and conviction to speak up and ensure they are acknowledged and heard because they are used to that respect from you.

The emphasis on active listening within the family dynamic is an urgent plea to be genuinely present in our relationships with our spouse, partner, children, and friends. Active listening isn't a physical presence but an emotional engagement that recognizes and validates the individual's feelings and thoughts. By nodding, looking into their eyes when they talk, asking open-ended questions, and showing curiosity, we're acknowledging the value of their communication, reinforcing their self-worth, and strengthening our relationship. Doing this encourages positive relationships and builds trust, respect, and empathy. Simply asking your children or partner about their day and taking the time to actively listen and respond appropriately—with interest—can lead to deeper connections and prevent problems from escalating. Ultimately, this underscores the need for people to feel important and cared for. It challenges us to be more compassionate and attentive in our daily interactions.

REAL LIFE REFLECTIONS

1. What strategies can you use to cultivate a habit of asking thoughtful and open-ended questions that encourage your children to share their thoughts and feelings more deeply?

2. How can you recognize when your child feels unheard or undervalued in a conversation and take steps to address those feelings?

3. In what ways can you model active listening and communication skills to encourage your children to practice these skills with others?

_____

_____

_____

4. How can you balance your need to provide guidance and protection to your children while giving them the space to express their own feelings, adversities, and emotional ups and downs?

_____

_____

_____

5. How can you encourage your child to openly share their experiences and emotions, and make it clear that their thoughts and feelings are valued and respected within your family?

_____

_____

_____

6. Creating Healthy Habits from the Ground Up

In today's fast-paced and demanding society, nurturing healthy habits within the family unit is essential for promoting happiness, well-being, and a well-functioning family dynamic. Embracing these habits is particularly important given the widespread prevalence of sedentary lifestyles, poor dietary choices, and stress. By exercising and participating in activities together, families can release endorphins, strengthen their bonds, and encourage the adoption of healthy routines that children can carry with them into adulthood.

Fostering healthy habits in our current society is necessary because of nearly everything! Let's begin with combatting obesity and chronic diseases. With the rise of sedentary lifestyles and processed foods, paying attention to what you're putting in your body and allowing your children to eat is crucial. Instead, instill healthy habits that counteract these trends and reduce the risk of obesity, diabetes, and other chronic illnesses. Even with budgetary restrictions, you can replace unhealthy foods with fresh vegetables as snacks as the new normal. If you aren't aware of how to do this, consult with your doctor or a dietician or research online from reliable sources.

"We try to be intentional and do things for one another that have value to each other."

We're constantly seeing the breakdown of mental health in society, and we must be more vigilant about what's happening at home with our children. Regular physical activity, proper nutrition, and spending quality time with family members can help alleviate stress, anxiety, and depressive symptoms, contributing to better overall mental health. Making the environment more relaxing, having fun, playing games, and doing enjoyable things can cause a shift in a stressful environment and in everyone's mindset. Laugh, joke, and watch shows that make you laugh. Learn how to lighten a stressful atmosphere or just increase the humor in a fun home environment. We try to fill our house with laughs, jokes, and fun—it's a big part of our existence. We try to be intentional and do things for one another that have value to each other. There are a thousand things that RaaShaun does for our children and me. We are two individuals who make each other happy, and we do the same with our children. Together, as a unit, every day, we aspire to do the same for RaaShaun. We live an active and healthy lifestyle as a whole.

Deliberately cultivating a positive self-image and encouraging self-awareness and body appreciation from an early age can help children develop a positive self-image and boost their self-confidence, impacting their success in various aspects of life. When they see you do it, that reinforcement is significant.

One of the beautiful things is that RaaShaun and I have strengthened our family bond by participating in activities as a unit. Our trips and outdoor adventures foster camaraderie, teamwork, and open communication, ultimately reinforcing family bonds and creating lasting memories. We love doing things together. We love just being together. Creating strong family ties will do that. By teaching healthy habits early in life or correcting and replacing unhealthy habits, we have laid the groundwork for creating healthy habits from the ground up that can serve our children well throughout their lives. Is that important to you?

(RAASHAUN)
Warning Signs Reveal Something

I'm a father. A man who loves my family more than anything in life, and my kids know it. They're acknowledged, heard, loved, and provided for, but even that can't protect kids from mental health crises. Some kids are more susceptible than others, and negative experiences can strike at any time. While I'm not giving advice as a mental health professional, I am speaking as a concerned father because we need to be more vigilant in this society. We cannot take our relationships with our children for granted. Mental health crises have become increasingly common as though normalized.

While parents, unless they are mental health professionals, are not qualified to handle or manage these behaviors, we have to be aware of them and take action when something's not feeling or seeming right with our child. If they exhibit any of these behaviors, don't wait to see what comes next. Sometimes, your love may not be enough because there are other contributing factors. In *Real Life, Real Family*, their mental health concerns are a priority. Contact a professional to get your child the help they need if the following are present:

- Expressing thoughts of self-harm or suicide.
- Engaging in dangerous or reckless behavior.
- Experiencing hallucinations, delusions, or a loss of touch with reality.
- Extreme mood swings or emotional outbursts.
- A sudden or significant increase in feelings of anxiety, depression, or hopelessness.
- Withdrawal from social interactions or previously enjoyed activities.
- An inability to cope with daily tasks or responsibilities.

Keep in mind that each case is unique, and the severity of symptoms can vary greatly. It's crucial to consult with a mental health professional for a proper assessment and support when dealing with any of these issues.

"A mental health professional can be an essential ally in identifying the root of the problem, overcoming challenges, and achieving emotional balance."

When you engage the help of a mental health professional, your kids can gain a deeper understanding of their emotions, learn effective coping strategies, and receive support in their journey toward mental wellness. A mental health professional can be an essential ally in identifying the root of the problem, overcoming challenges, and achieving emotional balance. There are accessible community mental health services and university counselors, representing a positive shift toward prioritizing mental well-being. You can give your kids everything, but more than anything, you want them to be healthy, happy, and well-adjusted.

> **REAL LIFE REFLECTIONS**
>
> 1. How do you strike a balance between providing love and support while also recognizing when your child may require professional mental health assistance?
>
> 2. What are some strategies you can employ to remain vigilant about your children's mental health in today's fast-paced society?
>
> 3. How can you ensure you are fostering an environment in which your children feel comfortable discussing their mental health concerns?
>
> 4. In what ways can you educate yourself about potential warning signs of a mental health crisis in your children?

5. How can you maintain open communication with your children about mental health issues, reducing the stigma surrounding these conversations?

   _____
   _____
   _____

6. How can you effectively differentiate between typical adolescent behavior and potential mental health concerns that require intervention?

   _____
   _____
   _____

7. What resources or support networks are available to seek guidance on how to help your children navigate mental health challenges?

   _____
   _____
   _____

Integrating Fitness and Emotional Well-Being for a Happier Home

Regardless of how busy you get, engaging in physical activity stimulates both the mind and body, establishing a foundation for a healthy and active lifestyle. We encourage this with our children and take care of ourselves because the advantages of such a lifestyle are immeasurable, as it discourages complacency and fosters a commitment to fitness. Eat healthy, drink plenty of water, get your sleep, and exercise. It doesn't matter what you do, but do something. If you're under the care of a physician, ask what you can do to exercise or remain active if your health allows.

Health also encompasses mental and emotional well-being. For example, spending quality time together can substantially benefit the entire family. Consistent care and attention to your family's emotional health can help everyone flourish. To facilitate this, we host a regular family meeting on the first Sunday of each month. These gatherings allow us to take stock of what is happening within our family unit. We express ourselves and share updates on our individual lives and take the time to check in on each other's well-being. Holding each other accountable is one of the most effective ways to ensure we stay on track toward reaching our goals and becoming our best selves.

REAL LIFE REFLECTIONS

1. How do you encourage physical activity and healthy habits within your family to lay the foundation for an active lifestyle?

   _____

   _____

   _____

2. How often do you spend quality time with your family, and what activities do you enjoy together?

   _____

   _____

   _____

3. What strategies do you use to hold yourself and your family members accountable for personal growth and goal achievement regarding your health and wellness?

_____

_____

_____

4. How can you create a nurturing environment that supports the emotional and physical health of each family member?

_____

_____

_____

5. What steps can you take to strengthen the bond within your family, fostering a sense of unity and mutual support?

_____

_____

_____

(GIA)
Interpreting and Processing the World Around You

We must be mindful that seeing our children doesn't mean we're aware of what they're doing, thinking, and feeling. Some parents can look directly at their children and have a conversation without knowing they are abusing a substance, have been bullied, or have been sexually, emotionally, or physically abused. Just as parents know how to mask problems, so do our kids. And again, our responsibility is to be aware of what's going on so we can help them correct negative behaviors before they become habits or bigger problems.

Children may unknowingly disrespect themselves in many ways, and if we're in tune, we can catch and address them. And it's better to approach it with a short conversation, a soft place to land, in a safe space, giving them an alternative rather than a lecture or demand. We want our children to be receptive because we want to help them. As RaaShaun stated, the negative influence that social media and peer pressure have is apparent. Several things children see can lead to them adopting self-deprecating behavior to fit in or gain acceptance. On social media, the tone of what children are drawn to is perfection. They want to be perfect, but they're unaware of the impact seeking perfection can have. The pursuit of being perfect can lead anyone down a rabbit hole. The world our children inhabit is filled with confusing and sometimes harmful messages. Setting unrealistic expectations for themselves can create a cycle of self-disapproval when they fail to meet these standards. Discussions about pursuing perfection and its dangers can help reframe their perspectives and redirect their decisions. Children are impressionable, and they're counting on us to lift the veil on those deceptive communications, practices, and people.

The way people present themselves, particularly on social media, is something many parents don't see, and some of the things being shared can pose a danger to your child's mental health. The way children dress, their behaviors, and the language they use can attract an element of individuals that can harm your children. We've heard this over and over again, and we've seen it in the media. We see young girls being trafficked, yet we still act as though it won't or can't happen to our children. It's happening more because we are not listening!

We know of a beautiful fourteen-year-old girl (we'll call her Reece). Reece was a great student and always polite and radiant. She seemed close to her mother. Her parents were going through challenges, and Reece didn't seem to have the same degree of support that she once had. A little over a year passed before I saw Reece again. I was coming out of a shop, and she said hello. She was still sweet as ever, but her appearance had changed. She looked thirty. Her natural beauty had been concealed nearly in every way. This young girl appeared to be a friend of her mother's rather than her daughter.

A few months after that, I'd heard the unimaginable had happened. Through a social media app, Reece attracted the attention of an older man whom she went to meet after talking with him for a few weeks. Today, that baby is gone. It's devastating. Her parents don't know if she's being trafficked or worse. Reece is considered a runaway because she left on her own, which is repeatedly happening. The statistics for missing girls are startling and growing. We can't protect them if we don't know what they're doing. And this is one reason why RaaShaun and I have such a handle on our children's whereabouts—at all times. It's why we are aware of what's going on with them. And another reason we love them the way we do.

Sometimes, children internalize negative situations in the home or in their personal lives. For example, if our children are bullied, endure constant criticism, or are abused, it can cause them to undermine their own self-worth and capabilities.

Paying close attention to the way our children interact with others is paramount. We not only see our children; we also acknowledge what we see in them. We talk to them and ask questions to ensure that we always understand them. As parents, naturally, we want our children to understand us. But it's equally important to reciprocate and, in the process, learn to understand their language and needs in today's world. They may be exhibiting overly submissive behavior, forgoing personal boundaries to please others, taking on an image that doesn't represent their true essence, and their eating or sleeping habits may have changed. By being vigilant of these subtle signs, we can better support our children's emotional well-being and help them foster and sustain healthy self-respect.

In today's society, we often see children disrespect themselves, even in how they interact with others or communicate. We are not sending young people into the world with the tools to express themselves articulately and confidently, so they concede to the ways of their peers or what they see in daily interactions, the media, and in movies. We've seen the lack of emotional intelligence fostered. When children are upset, the first thing they do is yell, scream, and swear, and it can escalate, or they can become violent.

I was in the heart of elementary-age girls with Brooklyn and London at a dance competition, and they kicked butt! In the belly of the beast, I was witnessing the nastiest display of disrespect. One girl was preparing for her performance, and her mom was trying to help her. She pulled an item from her bag and threw it at her mom. Aware of my presence, the mom lowered her eyes with shame and embarrassment, which turned to sadness. The little girl, aware I had observed her ugly little behavior, looked at me, and I gave her the nastiest look, letting her know she should be ashamed of how she was treating her mother. Perhaps I thought of RaaShaun's advice to me regarding my mother. The mom looked as though she just had to take it. More like she'd been conditioned to take it. I wondered how she could let a small child, with little life experience, run her and talk down to her. From what we have seen, some of the parents treat each other this way. If one parent or partner talks down to the other, children will emulate the behaviors they see and hear, and RaaShaun and I have seen this occur far too often, which prompted us to address it in *Real Love, Real Family*. Sometimes, children model the behavior they observe, and some of these children show indications of being abused. Parents need to be mindful of what they allow their children to witness. It can give children permission to model the behavior.

Children don't know how to interpret the world around them or process it. It's vital for us to model respectful and healthy communication within the home to foster emotional intelligence in our children. Teaching them to express themselves articulately and confidently can have a lasting impact on their interactions with the world around them.

Encouraging children to explore interests outside of the home and engage in hobbies is an excellent way to foster their mental and physical development. Our children participate in a wide range of activities, including baseball/softball, basketball, tennis, soccer, gymnastics, swimming, tae kwon do, piano, and acting lessons. Of course, they may not continue all these activities long-term. However, exposure to various interests enables them to discover what truly excites them. Once they identify their passions, they can focus on developing their skills.

Sometimes, parents try to live vicariously through their children to compensate for their unfulfilled ambitions. This can be detrimental to their children's well-being, as it undermines their ability to exercise free will. It's important to remember that children will naturally excel at the activities they enjoy the most.

Our children aren't puppets; they can be raised in a way that allows them to be independent and confident thinkers. Teach them that you can agree to disagree instead of taking opposition as an attack or making them feel ignorant or stupid. Teach them to communicate healthily and articulately. How our children carry themselves often indicates what is taught at home. Ask questions that challenge them to sustain their composure and manage their emotions when communicating. While some will know what buttons to press to trigger them and set them off, we have focused on raising children to be confident in their beliefs and behaviors. They know how to refrain from reacting, which is rooted in how they were taught.

REAL LIFE REFLECTIONS

1. What signs should you be looking for to recognize if your child is experiencing bullying, abuse, or other negative situations that could impact their self-worth and well-being?

   _____

   _____

   _____

2. How well are you understanding and respecting your children's boundaries, and are you teaching them to maintain their own boundaries with others?

   _____

   _____

   _____

3. Are you setting a positive example for your children in the way you communicate and interact with others, including your spouse or partner?

   _____

   _____

   _____

4. How can you support your children in developing independent and confident thinking, while still maintaining a respectful and open line of communication?

   _____

   _____

   _____

5. How can you teach your children to manage their emotions effectively and respond calmly when faced with challenging situations or disagreements?

   _____

   _____

   _____

PART 2

Raising Children to Be Resilient to Stress

7. Manifesting Patience

As parents, we all want our children to be their best selves, and we do everything in our power to help them achieve their goals. However, it's crucial to remember that children continue to learn and grow and will inevitably make mistakes along the way. This is where patience comes into play.

Patience is the ability to tolerate delays, mistakes, and difficulties in your children without displaying anger or frustration toward them. Sure, you may get frustrated or be impatient—this is real life, they're real situations, and you're human. But try to take a breather before responding. That's not only to the benefit of your children; it's to your benefit too. Your health and well-being is important.

Practice mindfulness by staying present in the moment rather than worrying about the future or dwelling on the past. This can help you to stay calm and focused, making it easier to deal with challenging situations with your child in a patient and thoughtful way.

Take a moment to serenely breathe if you find yourself becoming frustrated or impatient. Take a few deep breaths or a brief moment of solitude to regain your composure to help prevent an immediate reaction that you might regret later.

Empathize with your child and try to see the situation from their perspective. This can help you to understand their feelings and behavior better so you can respond with more patience and understanding. Remember, they're learning and growing, and this process takes time.

Being patient with your children doesn't mean accepting bad behavior or poor choices. Instead, it's about understanding that they're still learning and mistakes are a natural part of the learning process. When they make poor decisions, exercising patience and understanding, instead of rushing to judgment or punishment, will help them learn from their mistakes. A lack of patience can make children feel undervalued and unimportant, leading to low self-esteem and self-worth, affecting their relationships and overall well-being.

It's essential to remain mindful of our behavior and strive to be patient, loving, and understanding with our children, even during the most challenging moments. We cannot take back our words, anger, or actions, and our children will remember those moments long after we've forgotten. Patience fosters relationships—a brief moment of frustration can destroy them. Deliberately practicing patience, we teach our children one of the most valuable lessons: We don't expect them to be perfect.

(GIA)
A Patient Parent Cultivates Compassion and Emotional Intelligence

Ever since Madison and Logan were young, people have often commented on my patience. Now with six children, I receive more comments. But RaaShaun is sometimes surprised by my ability to maintain composure and a soothing tone during frustrating situations without becoming flustered. It's learning to be calm in the storm because managing the impact of patience on your children's well-being is critical. Patience is essential, and it significantly contributes to raising children who are resilient to stress. However, when we lose control and become impatient with our children, we may unintentionally teach them to internalize negative behaviors and attitudes with lasting effects. This can lead to a pattern where your children believe aggression is the only way to have their needs met, resulting in negative consequences in their relationships and overall quality of life.

A patient parent helps to cultivate compassion and emotional intelligence. Losing control teaches children that impulsive reactions are acceptable when they get frustrated or upset. Imagine the repercussions of such behavior in a classroom setting, during sports activities, or when they struggle to understand a new concept. The behaviors modeled at home will eventually manifest outside the home, potentially at the worst possible moment. Children are incredibly perceptive, picking up on our behaviors and attitudes. They're more likely to emulate that behavior when they witness us losing control and reacting out of anger or frustration.

Displaying impatience with your children teaches them that mistakes and failures are unacceptable. Reacting with anger or punishment can make them feel ashamed or embarrassed, causing them to believe that making mistakes is not okay. This can be extremely damaging to their self-esteem and may discourage them from trying new things or taking risks. And this is why the things I do and say are natural and deliberate.

> **"When I say we communicate, we over-communicate—I know the vast things that happen in our children's lives, their conflicts, and everything."**

By not showing patience, respect, or consideration, you're essentially conveying that your child's feelings or needs don't matter. This can be incredibly hurtful for a child and can damage the trust and bond between parent and child. In other words, when you don't exercise patience with your children and you lose control, you teach them negative lessons about behavior, mistakes, and self-worth. Remember that you're their role model. When conversing with my husband or children, I think before I speak, especially if I'm passionate about something. I don't shoot from the hip. I never scream—though I may raise my voice occasionally, but I work against that. When I say something, I've already thought about what that means. I raise our children the same way, and this ties into raising low-stress children; it's more difficult to get them flustered because they have been taught to have an internal dialogue before they get upset or agitated.

When I say we communicate, we over-communicate—I know the vast things that happen in our children's lives, their conflicts, and everything. Every time they come to me with a situation, if needed, I explain how to handle it and give them examples of how to better manage the situation. I then ask them to repeat it to ensure they got it. Sometimes, you may talk to your kids, and they've already checked out, or they really don't understand your messaging, so make sure they do.

Exhibiting patience doesn't mean I don't get overwhelmed—I have a lot on my plate. I know that my actions and attitudes profoundly impact our children's development, just as yours do with your children. However, we've made their well-being our priority.

Countless children suffer physical and emotional abuse because their parents don't exercise patience. As we approached the entrance to the stadium for Logan's football game, I noticed an adorable little girl, no older than seven, with curly brown hair. She stood beside her father, her eyes wide and earnest, asking him for something to drink. He was on the phone and could have been handling a crisis, but that doesn't matter. We need to exercise emotional intelligence.

"Daddy. Daddy," this little girl repeated before saying it again, simultaneously tugging at his arm to grab at his phone to get his attention.

With annoyance, her father put his finger to his mouth, attempting to quiet her and stop her from jumping at his phone.

Her expression went from hopeful to dejected, but she tried again.

He covered the phone and shook her while giving her a few stern words, and she started crying in a very sad way. I breathed a sigh of relief when I saw her mother coming toward her—I thought she was coming to intervene and calm the situation, but she grabbed the little girl's arm, literally dragged her away, and shoved her in the back seat of their car, mirroring the same behavior as the father. But then something else happened—a gentleman that recognized him walked up, within seconds of the little girl being dragged away, and patted him on the back. While still on his phone, he paused his call, gave the guy a hug and a high-five, and spoke to him briefly. When the guy walked away, the father continued his call.

By modeling patience, understanding, and compassion, you're better equipped to help your children become confident, resilient, and emotionally intelligent adults. When Brooklyn, London, or any of my precious babies ask me a question when I'm on the phone, I ask the person I'm on the call with to hold. Then I ask my child if it is something important they need to tell me right now or if it can wait until Mommy's off the phone. If they say it can wait, I let them know when I'll be available. If they say it's important and start talking, I listen. Period.

Being patient with our children has helped them feel safe and loved, which are interrelated and important. And when they want to tell us something, we listen because it's important to them. Full disclosure—it's not always important, but to them it is. It allows them to grow and learn at their own pace. Part of building a strong foundation is making your home a safe place. If you're not patient, it isn't. A lack of patience creates a stressful environment, and children don't thrive in unhealthy environments. When we're patient, we create a nurturing, low-stress environment.

Think about something valuable to you. A computer, car, clothing, or anything else. Let's say your child accidentally damages it, and, at that moment, you have underlying, unaddressed issues, and your anger is unintentionally directed toward them. Is it necessary to be angry when that material item can be replaced? What if your child comes through the door, seeking your time? Whatever they have to say may seem unimportant because you're working, preparing a meal, or resting after a stressful day. Perhaps you don't feel well or are tired. When you hear your child begin sharing with you whatever they want to say, and you stop them and send them away or snap out of frustration, what do you think happens? That was an opportunity for you to hear what they want to "share" and strengthen the bond of trust. They're coming to you because they trust you. It's an honor to have your child want to "share" their thoughts, feelings, or experiences.

REAL LIFE REFLECTIONS

1. How can you recognize and manage your emotions to better exercise patience with your children?

   _____

   _____

   _____

2. In what ways can practicing patience with your children improve your overall relationship and create a healthier and calmer home environment?

   _____

   _____

   _____

3. How can you demonstrate patience when your child makes a mistake while still guiding them toward better choices in the future?

   _____

   _____

   _____

4. What strategies can you implement to remain patient and understanding during particularly challenging moments with your children?

   _____

   _____

   _____

5. How might your childhood experiences and upbringing influence your patience as a parent, and what can you learn from those experiences to be more patient with your own children?

_____

_____

_____

6. What are some examples of everyday situations where practicing patience can help your child develop emotional intelligence and resilience?

_____

_____

_____

7. How can you balance the need for patience with setting appropriate boundaries and expectations for your children's behavior?

_____

_____

_____

Patience and Emotional Regulation

In today's fast-paced society, it can be easy to get caught up in the whirlwind of daily activities and inadvertently overlook the importance of truly connecting with our children. To practice patience, embrace the power of mindfulness and active listening. Set aside dedicated time each day to engage in meaningful conversations with your children, free from distractions like electronic devices or household chores. Actively listen to their thoughts, feelings, and concerns, responding with empathy and understanding. By cultivating a genuine interest in their lives and fostering open communication, you demonstrate patience and strengthen your bond with your children.

Practicing patience can be particularly challenging in a world where instant gratification has become the norm. Reframe your perspective on time by valuing the process rather than just the end result to counteract this mindset. Encourage your children to embrace learning and growing, recognizing that mistakes and setbacks are natural and essential to personal development. By shifting your focus from immediate success to long-term growth, you can cultivate a more patient and supportive environment for your children to flourish.

Understanding and managing our emotions is a critical yet often overlooked aspect of practicing patience. In moments of frustration or impatience with our children, practicing self-awareness and emotional regulation is essential. When you find yourself becoming impatient, pause and take a few deep breaths to regain your composure. Then reflect on the underlying emotions fueling your impatience, and consider whether external factors, such as stress or exhaustion, influence your reaction. By developing a deeper understanding of your emotional landscape, you can better regulate your responses and cultivate a more patient and nurturing relationship with your children. Healthy activities such as journaling, taking time to consider negative thoughts surrounding your emotions, exercising, and even getting adequate sleep promote patience and emotional regulation.

REAL LIFE REFLECTIONS

Cultivate patience and mindfulness in parenting:

1. Incorporate mindfulness practices.
2. Create a routine that prioritizes communication.
3. Cultivate a growth mindset in your children.
4. Improve self-awareness and emotional regulation.
5. Identify and address external factors.
6. Understand the role of instant gratification.
7. Create dedicated, distraction-free time.

(RAASHAUN)
Where There's Love, There's Patience

There are many ways to learn patience, but the lessons come from experience and seeing what having patience can do and what it can cost us. I learned from Gia to be patient. Gia's example that encourages me to be patient is "Hey, look at our relationship. What if I had given up on you because of your situation?" (*Real Life, Real Love* fully explains this narrative.) Gia has a patient heart, and forgiveness and understanding have paved the way for us to have a stronger family. We want our spouse, significant other, or others to be patient with us, and we need to extend that respect to our children. I could be a little more patient, but I feel like I have to move and shake because of my work. Gia likes to break down conversations and interpret them to make sure everything's understood. That's not me. With Gia, I had to learn to be more of a listener and a good conversationalist. Although it is my profession, I am not a huge talker outside of radio.

Gia wants to know the science behind things. I don't care. For the most part, I'm firm but fair, which came from my father. But I know she's right when it comes to our kids. They need us to be patient with them. That's another critical way to show them we love them. Then, in the process of listening, we can learn from them.

I'm working on becoming more patient and a better listener with my children. Many parents struggle with actively listening to their kids. One day, I came home after having a colonoscopy, and I went straight to bed. In preparation for it, I hadn't eaten in two days, and I was exhausted from the anesthesia. My son Jaxson came into my room and said, "Dad, I want to play *FIFA*. I want to play *FIFA* together." Full disclosure, I was tired, and I didn't want to play a damn video game. But I could hear it in his voice that it wasn't about playing a video game. It was about hanging out with Dad.

Despite my fatigue, I dragged my ass out of bed, and instead of playing video games, we opted for a game of UNO so his sister could join in as well. I did that because I knew that's what he wanted. Something about how he asked indicated that Jaxson needed that time with me. It was his tone of voice, eye contact, and persistence. As Gia has explained, "Don't just hear them. Actively listen to what they say." Whatever it was, maybe his friends weren't playing with him at that time, but I've learned to recognize the difference between "Dad, I'm bored" and "Dad, I want to spend quality time with you." It involved sacrificing my rest and sleep, but those precious moments with my children that require my patience are invaluable.

The understanding that childhood and our children's needs can be fleeting is enough for me to prioritize time with Jaxson over rest and sleep. If they need something or are dealing with a problem we don't know about, spending time with them can help. These moments won't last forever. One day you might wish you could relive them. My heart recognizes that every bedtime story, every shared game, and every curious question answered builds a foundation of trust, love, and self-worth in my child.

The time you invest in your children today is more than quality time; it's a message to them that they're important, valued, and worthy of your attention. Our actions relay a legacy of unconditional love and engaged parenting, which will resonate as they grow, mature, and become parents. In the grand scheme of things, it's not about losing sleep; it's about sustaining irreplaceable connections, understanding their needs, and creating memories that will last a lifetime.

> **REAL LIFE REFLECTIONS**
>
> 1. What strategies can you use to improve your listening skills when communicating with your children?

2. In what ways can you learn from your partner's approach to patience and incorporate it into your own parenting style?

_____
_____
_____

3. How can you work with your partner to create a more patient and understanding environment for your children?

_____
_____
_____

4. What can you learn from your children by practicing patience and actively listening to their thoughts, feelings, and concerns?

_____
_____
_____

5. How can you teach your children the importance of patience in their relationships with others, including their siblings?

_____
_____
_____

8. Encouraging Greatness vs. Demanding Greatness

Encouraging greatness in kids versus demanding it is a delicate balance. It involves nurturing their innate curiosity, promoting self-discovery, and providing a supportive environment for growth. This approach allows children to develop their unique strengths and interests without pressure to meet unrealistic expectations. Whether intentionally or unintentionally, sometimes, we can set those unrealistic expectations and go about our lives not realizing the damage we're doing with the pressure we're placing on our kids.

Encouraging greatness begins with cultivating a growth mindset, emphasizing the value of effort, and embracing challenges as opportunities for learning. When we create a safe space for children to take risks, ask questions, and explore their interests, we're actually empowering them to develop confidence in their abilities and a genuine desire to excel. My parents and RaaShaun's provided that for us.

"We encourage greatness in our kids by focusing on the process rather than the outcome."

We encourage greatness in our kids by focusing on the process rather than the outcome. By praising effort, resilience, and perseverance, you can help kids understand that progress and growth are more important than achieving immediate success. This approach enables children to develop a strong sense of self-worth that isn't solely tied to their accomplishments. With sports, education, extracurricular activities, and anything your kid is doing, give them room to figure out what they love and the path they want to explore. Encourage them and give them the tools to be successful. If you don't have the resources, some programs and organizations, such as the Boys & Girls Club of America, and local churches and clubs can help you by providing opportunities.

You can create a supportive network of mentors, coaches, tutors, and role models who can inspire and guide your kids. If you're a single parent with a demanding job, health issues, or other limiting circumstances, don't think that you have to do all of this alone. You have options that can help your kids develop in healthy ways. Don't let them fall by the wayside because you can't do it. Take the time to do a little research and handpick the network or resources you think will inspire greatness in your kids. By exposing our kids to diverse experiences and perspectives, we're helping them broaden their worldviews and foster a greater appreciation for the value of learning and personal growth.

> **"By promoting a growth mindset, focusing on effort and perseverance, and providing a supportive environment for exploration and self-discovery, parents can help their children reach their full potential and cultivate a lifelong love of learning."**

In contrast, demanding greatness from children can lead to excessive stress, anxiety, and a fear of failure. Constantly pushing your kids to achieve at all costs may develop a fixed mindset, causing them to believe their abilities are innate and unchangeable. This mindset can create reluctance to take risks or pursue new challenges, hindering their growth and potential. If they have to worry about the possibility of failing and disappointing you, they may not even try.

Encouraging greatness rather than demanding it is essential for nurturing well-rounded, resilient, and confident children. By promoting a growth mindset, focusing on effort and perseverance, and providing a supportive environment for exploration and self-discovery, parents can help their children reach their full potential and cultivate a lifelong love of learning.

(RAASHAUN)
Balancing Parental Expectations with Healthy Development

We're not saying anything's wrong with wanting your kids to be great and excel to their fullest capabilities. Who doesn't want their son playing in the NFL for my Giants, their daughter running a company or the country, or their kid becoming an innovator? That's great, but using their childhood to fulfill *your* dreams isn't. We have to manage the degree of pressure we place, intentionally or unintentionally, on kids to succeed. There's a fine line between motivating our kids and applying pressure. And that pressure can cause considerable damage. I want what my kids want. Gia wants what our kids want. And that's enough. When you raise kids to be confident, passionate, and driven, they'll want to achieve greatness for themselves. They'll do what's necessary on their own. If you see they're taking too much on or putting unhealthy stress on themselves, you might have to let them know what you see. Pull them back and help them reset, slow down, or refrain from being too hard on themselves. You don't want to be the ones applying that pressure. The pressure of demanding greatness can strain your relationship and set them on a course that can be damaging.

Gia and I see parents at sports competitions and school events treating their kids like they're valued only for their achievements—only if they win, or come in first place. Some of those kids don't even look like they're enjoying it. They look overly stressed or irritated that they're even there. Some take it out on their parents by showing blatant disrespect. This pressure can cause your kids to resent you, and they may not want to be around you because of the pressure you create. That stress can undermine the trust and emotional connection needed for their healthy development. The goal is healthy and happy kids, not kids who meet your expectations.

TOP: Gia and RaaShaun at fifteen and sixteen in Queens, New York (1994)
BOTTOM: Gia and RaaShaun in the high school cafeteria, St. Francis Prep, Queens, New York

TOP: RaaShaun and Gia's first kiss as husband and wife, Oheka Castle, Huntington, New York (2001)
BOTTOM (left to right): Gia and RaaShaun at the hospital with their second-born, Logan, after his birth (2003); RaaShaun at the birth of Brooklyn (2016)

TOP: RaaShaun with Madison at her christening (2002)
BOTTOM (left to right): Madison and Logan (2004); Jaxson and Logan (2017)

TOP (left to right): Brooklyn and London competing in their dance competitions (2024); Peyton as a newborn (2021); London and Jaxson, Isla Mujeres, Mexico (2023)

BOTTOM (left to right): Pouty Peyton at two years old (2024); London and Peyton (2023); Madison and London at Disney World (2018)

TOP: Madison and Gia (2022)
BOTTOM: Logan, Gia, and RaaShaun at the Super Bowl, Hard Rock Stadium, Miami (2020)

TOP (left to right): Madison's high school graduation (2020); Logan's senior prom (2023)
BOTTOM: Madison, London, Logan, and Jaxson (2018)

A Casey Crew Christmas (2020)

TOP: RaaShaun's birthday trip to Riviera Maya, Mexico (2019)
BOTTOM: A Casey Crew Halloween (2022)

Family vacation in Puerto Morelos, Mexico (2023)

London, Jaxson, and Brooklyn in Puerto Morelos, Mexico (2023)

TOP: Gia and Payton in Isla Mujeres, Mexico (2023)
BOTTOM: RaaShaun and London in Ocho Rios, Jamaica (2019)

Gia, Logan, RaaShaun, and Madison in Bora Bora (2017)

Cover for *ALPHA Magazines*' Father's Day issue, 2024

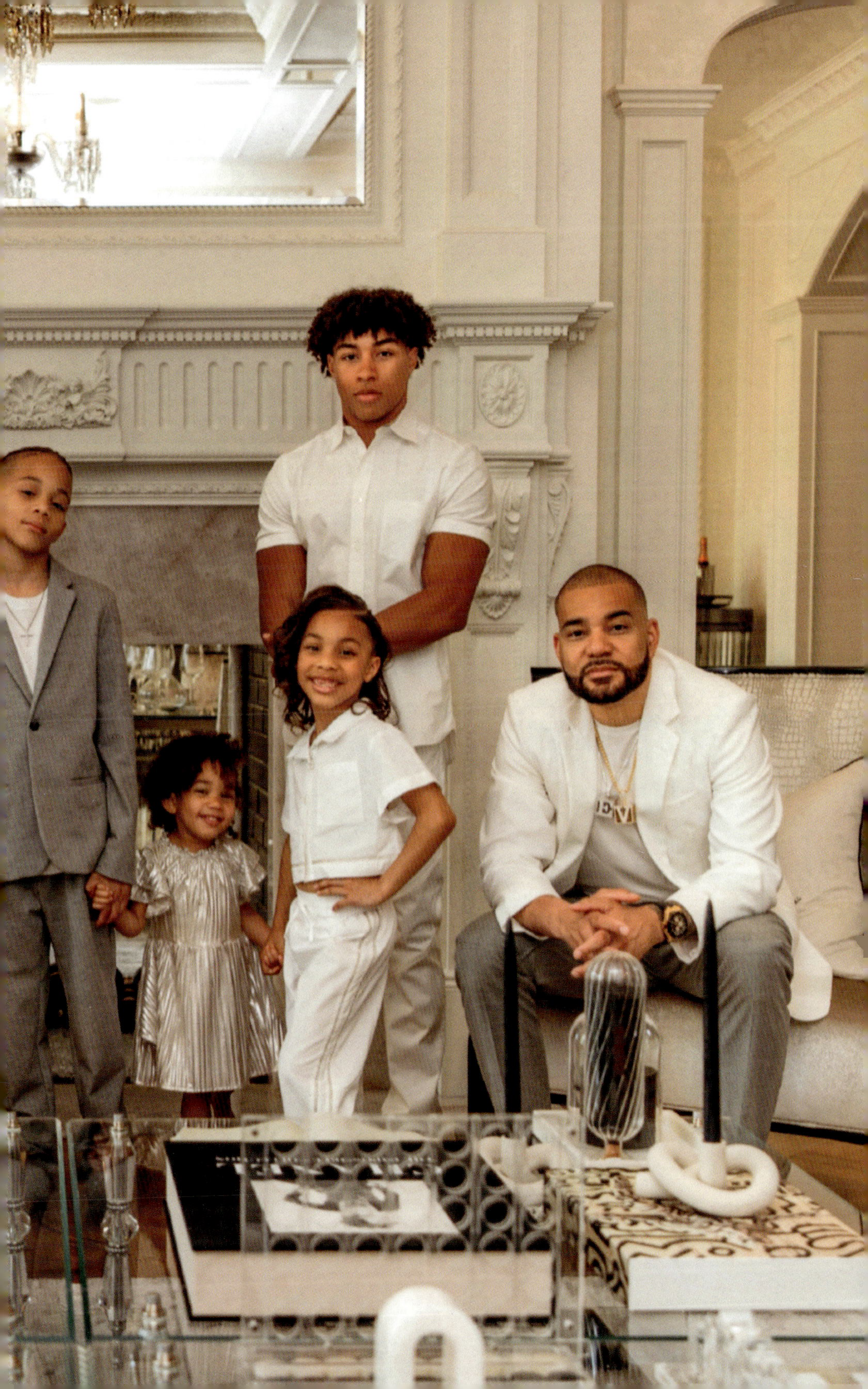

Sunset in Isla Mujeres, Mexico (2023)

REAL LIFE REFLECTIONS

1. How can you involve mentors, coaches, tutors, and role models in your child's life to provide guidance, inspiration, and diverse experiences and perspectives?

   _____
   _____
   _____

2. How can you balance your own aspirations for your child's success with the need to prioritize their emotional well-being and happiness?

   _____
   _____
   _____

3. What are ways to recognize and address signs of unhealthy stress or pressure in your child, and how can you support them in finding a healthier balance in their pursuits?

   _____
   _____
   _____

4. How can you celebrate your child's achievements without attaching their self-worth solely to their accomplishments?

   _____
   _____
   _____

5. How can you maintain a trusting relationship with your child, ensuring they understand your love and support are not contingent on their success or achievements?

_____

_____

_____

Real-Life Stress Kills

Some stress and pressure is good, but in this section, I'm addressing the unhealthy kind. The kind that causes anxiety, depression, and suicide. The kind that makes kids lose their minds and retaliate worse than you would imagine. Demanding greatness and setting unrealistic goals for your kids can negatively affect their emotional and psychological well-being. We see it occurring every day. Every single day! The constant pressure to achieve perfection can lead some kids to unhappiness, stress, anxiety, and depression when they feel overwhelmed by your high expectations or those of others. You need to know what your kids can handle. It's not about making them soft or softer. It's about helping them protect their confidence, strength, and, more importantly, their mental health.

Sometimes, those unrealistic burdens and unnecessary stress drive kids to search for unhealthy coping mechanisms. Substance abuse. Promiscuity. Self-harm to numb their emotional pain. Contemplating suicide. These behaviors can further intensify their mental health struggles and put them at risk for more severe problems later on or cause them to die by suicide. We have to discuss and create ways to better protect our kids. We have to love them the right way. We can't let them do whatever the hell they want thinking that's love. Focus on the foundation of your home. Remember your mission statement. Show unconditional love. Exercise patience. Build their self-esteem. Teach healthy habits. Encourage greatness—don't demand it. We've got to do a better job of protecting our kids' mental health and well-being.

Dual-parent, single-parent, foster parent, it doesn't matter. If your child is pushed to be a high achiever, they won't complain to you, which means if this pressure becomes unmanageable, you might not know it until there's a serious problem or it's too late. Unfortunately, society's proving that we need to do a better job. Look at the suicide rates today among teens; they're higher than ever. Teen suicide is a growing public health problem. In 2021 the Centers for Disease Control and Prevention (CDC) reported that suicide was the second leading cause of death among individuals between the ages of ten and thirty-four in the United States.

When your kids feel they always have to be or appear perfect, they might develop an unhealthy fear of failure that can cause them to avoid taking risks, engaging in new experiences, or stepping out of their comfort zone because they don't want to disappoint you or themselves. Unfortunately, some kids just can't handle failure in today's society. They just can't. Over time, this anxiety about failure can manifest as chronic stress, negatively impacting their physical and mental health. So we need to pay attention to our children even when they seem to be handling things okay. Have those conversations about what's happening and do a check-in or wellness check. Asking them about their stress level and how much of a load they carry at school or college shows you care. It can keep the lines of communication open when they need your advice or help.

> **"We've got to do a better job of protecting our kids' mental health and well-being."**

Kids who are constantly pushed to achieve may begin to associate their self-worth solely with their accomplishments. This narrow focus on success can lead to feelings of inadequacy and self-doubt when they inevitably face setbacks or challenges. They need to accept when the outcome isn't in their favor. These negative emotions can contribute to depression and hopelessness if they start to feel that they're never good enough or that their worth is contingent on their ability to meet unattainable standards.

You don't want to put so much pressure on your kids that it hurts your relationship. They're more important than success—winning—achieving our goals, or keeping up with their peers. Kids can feel that your love and approval are contingent on their success. That can lead to resentment, alienation, and a lack of trust, preventing the emotional bond necessary for healthy development and support during difficult times.

We're saying that demanding greatness and setting unrealistic goals for your kids can severely affect their emotional and psychological well-being. To stimulate a healthy, balanced, and resilient mindset, focus on nurturing their intrinsic motivation, promoting a growth mindset, and celebrating effort and progress rather than solely on achievements, which reduces stress and encourages building character. Place emphasis on acknowledging the journey rather than the outcome. This approach can help kids develop a stronger sense of self-worth, resilience, and the ability to navigate challenges and setbacks confidently and gracefully.

(GIA)
Encouraging Greatness Without Overwhelming Pressure

You can fall into a situation where you can take your partner's role for granted. Even as adults achieving success, goals, or being great in your endeavors can take a toll on you. RaaShaun is constantly on the go, working, traveling, talking, parenting, providing—repeat. Sleep isn't in his routine because he doesn't get enough to begin with, and it takes a toll on his body and health. I've explained to our kids that Daddy focuses on working hard now so that he won't have to work later, and it's important that he knows his limitations. I worry about him and don't hesitate to voice my concerns and try to get him to slow down. But he's always in forward motion, working on what's next. And RaaShaun doesn't sit still long enough to enjoy the fruits of his labor. When you step into someone's shoes, it becomes a reality on some level, and most can't handle what he does at the pace he does it. The reality is that everything we do is authentic to who we are. But in the same way, pressure can negatively affect adults, it can have that same effect on your children, and because they aren't adept at handling stress, it can be worse.

When we look at our beautiful little babies, we can't imagine not providing unconditional love and emotional support, ensuring their safety and security, guiding and teaching them, encouraging social and emotional development, and fostering independence and responsibility in them the way RaaShaun and I have. That is because we want the absolute best for them. However, as parents, it's our role to balance aspirations to ensure our children are not pressured to be perfect and constantly driven until they hit a wall or go off a cliff.

From a very young age, we noticed that London tends to become anxious quite easily. She consistently aims for top performance in school, sports, and social situations, placing significant pressure on herself. Sometimes, the onset of pressure derives from the meaning and interpretation placed on what is seen. For example, RaaShaun is a high achiever, and London has only ever seen her daddy working hard, setting and achieving goals. She may be trying to mirror his behavior. Recognizing this early on, we promptly taught her that striving for perfection is not the ultimate goal. Instead, the objective is to pursue one's personal best.

"We don't see what children internalize or the other pressures and stress their peers, teachers, or society places on them."

London doesn't need to score 100% on every test or seek approval from others, including us, if she has put forth her best effort. If she desires good grades, she should pursue them for herself. Should she receive a low grade, we are there to support and encourage her to work harder to improve. In our home, mistakes are stepping-stones for growth and personal development. Encouraging greatness rather than demanding it and applying overwhelming pressure removes the emotional stress that comes with it. We don't see what children internalize or the other pressures and stress their peers, teachers, or society places on them. When we detect any indication of unnecessary stress or too much self-imposed pressure, their behaviors change; it's our responsibility for the sake of their well-being to remove it. Encourage what you want, but demanding greatness of a child can be damaging. *We can do better.*

REAL LIFE REFLECTIONS

1. How can you foster an environment that values personal growth over perfection?

   _____
   _____
   _____

2. How can you help your child cope with low grades, not winning a competition, or setbacks while maintaining their self-esteem?

   _____
   _____
   _____

3. What are some methods for creating a healthy balance between encouraging excellence and avoiding excessive pressure?

   _____
   _____
   _____

4. How can you be more aware of the pressures and stressors your children may face from their peers, teachers, or society?

   _____
   _____
   _____

5. How can you, as a parent, model a healthy approach to handling stress, setbacks, and the pursuit of personal bests?

   _____
   _____
   _____

9. The Alchemy of Actively Listening

We've all been there. When your child is going on and on about a topic you're completely disinterested in. You have a to-do list that will keep you up until midnight, and you just want out of this never-ending conversation. However, as parents, we must keep our eyes on the prize, which is our children's sense of security and belonging. We have to be enthusiastic about our conversations with them and remain engaged. When children feel that you're not actively listening to them, they may experience disappointment, frustration, disconnection, low self-esteem, or resentment, or simply be misunderstood. Conversely, actively listening fosters a supportive and nurturing environment where children feel heard, valued, and understood. That's part of the magic in our house—everyone is heard, respected, and understood. Regardless of your level of interest, you're the parent and the example—always make your children feel as though they are the only thing that matters.

Choosing to actively listen without interrupting your children is vital to their respect and trust in you, and this is overlooked and underrated. Actively listening means fully concentrating, understanding, responding, and remembering what is being said during a conversation rather than merely hearing the words passively. It involves engaging with the speaker verbally and nonverbally to demonstrate genuine interest, empathy, and understanding. Your children want this from you.

Verbal and nonverbal cues that signal deep engagement are maintaining consistent eye contact, such as nodding, facial expressions, mirroring their body language, paraphrasing or summarizing their main points, asking open-ended questions, and brief verbal affirmations. This will let your children know they have your complete and undivided attention, which helps build self-esteem by making them feel heard, interesting, and important. This is essential in their pursuit of self-worth because nothing stresses anyone, child or adult, more than feeling like they're not being heard or, worse, not worthy of being heard. Children who are heard develop into adults who feel like their words have substance. By actively listening, you create an environment where your children are confident and comfortable coming to you with anything.

(GIA)
The Effects of Active Listening on Child Development

Hear me out—if you are not deliberate about parenting, it can get away from you. Something that seems to be as insignificant as listening without interrupting is vital to raising healthy children who are resilient to stress because it fosters a supportive and nurturing environment where children feel heard, understood, and valued. In addition, you create a safe space for open communication and emotional expression when actively listening to your children without interruption. This has several benefits in raising low-stress children.

You can validate your children's emotions and experiences by listening without interrupting, helping them feel understood and supported. This emotional validation can reduce stress levels by allowing them to process and express their feelings. Cutting them off can make them feel you "think" you have it figured out or are disinterested and are rushing them through the conversation.

Active listening helps build trust between parents and children. When children can openly share their thoughts and feelings without being judged or dismissed, they're more likely to confide in you, allowing for a closer and more trusting relationship.

Listening without interrupting allows children to express their concerns, challenges, and problems. Parents can then guide and support their children in finding solutions, helping them develop problem-solving skills that will serve them well throughout life.

If you want to foster emotional intelligence, active listening encourages them to express their emotions and reflect on their feelings. This skill helps children manage their emotions, build resilience, and cope with stress effectively.

One of the biggest mental health concerns is anxiety. When children feel heard and supported, they are less likely to experience anxiety about discussing their concerns or worries. This reduces stress and helps them feel more confident in navigating life's challenges.

> **"Children who are heard develop into adults who feel like their words have substance. By actively listening, you create an environment where your children are confident and comfortable coming to you with anything."**

When RaaShaun and I listen without interrupting our children or one another, we have set the stage to deliberately encourage our children to feel comfortable discussing their thoughts, feelings, and experiences—and they do. This open communication helps children develop healthy coping mechanisms and reduces the likelihood of them turning to unhealthy means of dealing with stress.

A beautiful and natural way of strengthening your bond with your children is by promoting empathy, understanding, and an emotional connection. A strong parent–child relationship helps raise children who feel loved, secure, and supported.

We've recognized that listening without interrupting fosters trust, encourages open communication, and builds essential life skills, ultimately contributing to children's well-being and emotional health. Despite the availability of time, some parents are still choosing not to prioritize spending quality time with their children. This is a concerning trend that must be addressed, as our children need us to be present and engaged in their lives.

> **REAL LIFE REFLECTIONS**
>
> How can I do better?
>
> 1. Assess interruption or dismissal of your child's concerns.
> 2. Improve active listening skills for your child's needs.
> 3. Encourage open sharing of your child's concerns and challenges.
> 4. Validate your child's emotions and guide them toward problem-solving.
> 5. Foster emotional intelligence and stress management in your child.
> 6. Recognize and address your child's anxiety or signs of stress.
> 7. Strengthen your bond through empathetic listening and understanding.
> 8. Ensure comfort in discussing thoughts, feelings, and experiences.
> 9. Support your child's emotional health through open communication.

(RAASHAUN)
Your Undivided Attention Can Transform a Parent-Child Relationship

When your kids come to you and have something they want to talk about, or if they just want to hang out with you, make the time. We always say we don't have the time. We're busy. We have work to do. Okay, but think about how you can manage time to text or talk to a friend over the phone. I'm all for self-care, but if you have the time to get your hair or nails done, do yoga, or work out, you have time for your kids. Self-care is incredibly important. So yes, make yourself a priority. If you're not good for yourself, you're not going to be at your best to actively listen to your kids and give them the attention they deserve. Without a thought, I'll sacrifice those things to spend time with my wife and kids. I'll cut my hair myself and wear a hat if that'll give me more time with them. They're fun!

It's easy to dismiss our kids when they need to talk to us as though we know what they're going to say, or it's meaningless, and it can definitely wait. While we might have an idea about what they want to tell us, we don't know where they are emotionally. Even asking a few questions, like what they wanted to talk about, allows us to gauge where they are mentally and emotionally and, at least, ask if it's important. Whatever you're doing, it only takes a minute to assess the severity or impending need. Just looking at our kids, Gia and I would know if it was serious or not—because we know them. Let them know you're interested in hearing what they have to say or want to talk about. Then, ask them if they can wait until you finish what you're doing, so you can give them your undivided attention.

I know a lot of dads who claim, "I'm a Giants fan. I watch the game every Sunday." Trust me, I'm a Giants fan too. But my kids are more important than anything. Even if I'm watching the game or attending it, my children are my priority, and they know it. Some parents might not have the best relationship with each other. However, when you're reading a book on parenting to learn how to be a better parent and raise healthy kids, it's crucial to let your kids see both parents working together to improve your parenting skills. Even if there's an uncomfortable situation, try to work together for the benefit of your children.

The point is when you can encourage greatness in your children, do it together. Keep the rest of the drama away from the kids and work it out between the two of you because it affects them. All of it. They may side with one parent over the other, but more often than not, it's hurting or damaging them. If your honest goal is to encourage greatness in your children, it starts with you—be a great parent! If you have that drama in your relationship, you have to put that bullshit aside and ask yourself, "How can we co-parent our kids to make them the best out there because we're already working against a society aimed at destroying them?"

When traveling for work, I use the computer or my phone to play games with my kids. I play pool with London and tic-tac-toe, and we go back and forth, laughing just the same as when I'm at home. Even if I'm not with them because I'm working or traveling, I feel like I am with them because I make the time personal. I actively listen and respond as if I'm right in front of them. We schedule our life with everything centered around our faith and kids.

"Successful parenting emphasizes the importance of being deliberate in making time for your children, understanding their emotional needs, and maintaining your family as a priority."

Successful parenting emphasizes the importance of being deliberate in making time for your children, understanding their emotional needs, and maintaining your family as a priority. Despite the busy, multifaceted lives many of us have, finding a way to be present for our children is paramount. It involves a delicate balance between necessary self-care and the undivided attention that children require. It's not about being physically present but understanding their emotions and responding appropriately, even when separated by distance. Healthy collaboration between parents is necessary for sustaining a positive environment in challenging relationship dynamics. Showing a united front in parenting presents a successful model of cooperation and shared values that can help guide your children's growth. It's about shaping your family life around your core principles and values that guide you and set a clear path for your children to follow. The message is clear: Nurturing and encouraging greatness in our children requires consistent, compassionate effort, well-aligned priorities, and a willingness to maintain our children's needs as priorities, even when it means we have to make personal sacrifices or navigate complex interpersonal dynamics.

REAL LIFE REFLECTIONS

1. How do you prioritize spending time and talking with your children in your daily schedule?

2. How do you ensure your children feel heard and valued when they approach you to talk or spend time together?

3. How do you model effective communication skills and active listening to your children?

4. In what ways can you work on building a stronger emotional connection with your children so they feel comfortable coming to you with their thoughts, feelings, and concerns?

5. What strategies can you use to ensure a healthy co-parenting relationship, even when there is conflict or disagreement between parents?

   _____

   _____

   _____

10. Building a Safe Environment

Back in the day, building a safe environment for children was a relatively straightforward task. As I said, for the most part, we did what our parents told us, and we were safe—end of story. Our parents taught us not to talk to strangers. Dad said to make some noise before entering the house. There weren't a lot of other rules because I knew what my parents expected, and I used common sense. Our environment was safe. Gia's environment was safe. However, today's society is more complex and diverse, and building a safe environment for your kids requires a nuanced approach. Whether you are part of a single-parent, dual-parent, or more diverse kind of family, there are steps you can take to ensure your children are safe and secure.

First and foremost, creating an open and honest dialogue with your children is essential. Talk to them about the dangers they could face, whether bullying one another, bullying from online predators, or the risks associated with drug and alcohol use. Talk to them about their mental health and how they're feeling. Then pay attention to them and monitor their behaviors. Make sure your home is their safe place by encouraging them to come to you with *any* concerns or fears, and make sure they know you're there to support and protect them.

Though our parents didn't have to worry about us buying drugs online or connecting with predators or bullies online, we have those issues today and need to address them. If your kids are young and impressionable, lack confidence, or are followers, don't allow them free range and access online. Monitor their screen time, make sure you have their passwords, and take the time to look at their browsing history to see what they're viewing and what chat groups or other groups they're in. Put parental controls or privacy settings on the computer, phone, and television. Filter and block harmful and unsafe content. If they're a little older, having frequent, honest, and direct dialogue about the dangers on a higher level can help keep them safe. Engage in conversations and ask them what they see as dangerous or misleading content. Find out what's going on with their friends and whether they're having issues online. Seeing your kids every day isn't a measurable indication that you know they're safe and their well-being is protected or what's going on in their lives. Adversity can infiltrate your home environment even while you're in it!

Another crucial element of building a safe environment for your kids is setting boundaries and guidelines. This can mean establishing rules around internet and social media use, imposing curfews, and monitoring their activities at home. It's important to strike a balance between giving your kids the freedom to explore and make their own decisions while also ensuring they aren't putting themselves in harm's way.

In a single-parent household or one with parents who are both working and aren't able to be home as much, creating a supportive and trusted network of friends and family can also provide a safe environment for kids. Surrounding your children with positive influences and supportive people who can help to build their resilience and self-esteem can provide a buffer against potential risks and negative experiences.

In a diverse family, it is essential to celebrate and embrace each person's unique background and culture. Encourage your kids to learn about and appreciate the differences between themselves and others through food, music, traditions, or what they believe because it can help build a sense of empathy and understanding and promote a safer, more inclusive family unit. Don't allow division. Promote unity and discourage discord or separation within a family, particularly one that is diverse in terms of culture, background, beliefs, and so on. This implies avoiding any behaviors, actions, or attitudes that may create a sense of segregation or isolation among family members based on their individual differences. This can involve preventing discriminatory practices, discouraging favoritism, and actively addressing any conflicts or misunderstandings that arise due to these differences. By not allowing division, you're creating an environment of acceptance, understanding, and respect for all family members, regardless of their unique traits or backgrounds. It's about promoting a family culture where differences are not just tolerated but are celebrated and seen as a source of strength and enrichment for the family as a whole.

It's essential to model safe and responsible behavior yourself. Whether that means practicing healthy and respectful communication, being mindful of your alcohol consumption, not using drugs, or not allowing people in your environment that do, whatever your lifestyle is, take a look around, assess the environment, and determine what's safe and what isn't. Your kids will learn by example. So make sure you lead by example and demonstrate the behavior you want your kids to emulate.

Building a safe environment for your kids in today's society requires a multifaceted approach. By creating an open and honest dialogue, setting boundaries and guidelines, creating a supportive network, embracing diversity, and modeling responsible behavior, you can give your children the tools and support they need to navigate an increasingly complex world.

(RAASHAUN)
Why Honesty and Mutual Respect Are Key to a Safe and Happy Home Environment

Creating a safe environment doesn't mean there won't be disappointment and pain; that's a part of life's experiences—the same with disciplining your kids. What's important is that you handle those things with love. Your home and everything and everyone in it must contribute to maintaining a safe environment. What helps make it safe is when honesty and accountability are encouraged, which breeds mutual respect.

Overreacting or disciplining from a place of anger can instill fear in children. And if they live in a fearful environment, it's not necessarily safe for them. As parents, we should concentrate less on fear and more on creating mutual respect. Children who fear their parents often don't tell the truth, which causes their relationship to deteriorate because of diminishing trust. When you create an environment where you have open communication and reward honesty with positive reactions, you're raising truth-tellers who will grow up to be teens and young adults with integrity, honesty, and authenticity because they didn't grow up under the hand of fear. You don't want there to be punishment at every corner. Give them room to express themselves freely and listen without judgment. You can give them advice without making your kids feel that no matter what they do, they're always wrong. Give them examples to show they're not.

Children who are not afraid of the truth but own it instead practice accountability and responsibility. Because your children can benefit from this deliberate and active interaction, they will be eager to confide in you with the truth. Providing a safe and soft place to land makes children feel comfortable and feel they don't have to handle problems alone. You can address everything within the family unit with unconditional love. A safe environment is paramount.

REAL LIFE REFLECTIONS

1. What steps can you take to encourage honesty and accountability in your children?

   _____

   _____

   _____

2. How can overreacting or disciplining from a place of anger affect your child's sense of safety in the home?

   _____

   _____

   _____

3. What are some effective strategies for creating a safe place for your children to confide in you?

   _____

   _____

   _____

BUILDING A SAFE ENVIRONMENT

4. In what ways can an environment of fear impact your child's long-term emotional and mental health?

_____

_____

_____

5. How can you foster a sense of mutual respect between you and your children while still maintaining authority and boundaries?

_____

_____

_____

Staying Vigilant and Navigating Today's Society to Keep Your Kids Safe

Conversations with your kids are critical. You can learn so many things from them if you take the time to actively listen. They'll drop clues on what you need to be concerned with, and you can address those things. Don't ignore them. If your kids join any groups or organizations and someone asks to meet with them, find out what that's about. Explain risky behavior, online flirting, and sending sexy selfies and where they can end up. If someone starts sending your kids pornographic images, that's a red flag—they could be grooming your kid. Don't assume your kids have the common sense not to do these things. This environment, the society we're living in with young girls disappearing, stress and hateful acts toward our kids causing them to die by suicide—it's putting tremendous pressure on them to conform or feel isolated. It's your responsibility to know what your kids are doing even when they're on their computer in the privacy of their room. They can do drugs right up under your roof.

As busy as I am, when I'm home, I go through my kids' things. I said it. In today's society, I want to know if they need me and what someone else could be putting them through. I make sure I know what they're doing and where they are. When we say we're honest and trust one another, this is the checkup to make sure I'm still doing my job. Now, I do have limits as to how far I'll go. There's a difference between respecting privacy and ensuring their safety. For instance, I may search their backpacks but not read conversations among their friends. But this isn't the same society we grew up in. The risks today are much higher. *Trust but verify.*

There are predators online. Sex trafficking wouldn't be as prevalent as it is if predators couldn't access your kids. Know who they're talking to and on what sites. If you suspect your kid is talking to someone, and they have too much information about your kid, they are too nice, or the language is inappropriate, contact the FBI and let them intervene. You don't know how old that individual is, or who they really are. That's not a safe space for your kids. People having negative conversations with kids or teens can cause them to feel socially isolated. That alone can cause them to be reluctant to socialize, attend school, or participate in extracurricular activities. When it's too much and too painful, some die by suicide.

REAL LIFE REFLECTIONS

1. How can you balance respecting your children's privacy with ensuring their safety and well-being?

   _____

   _____

   _____

2. What are some effective strategies for talking to your children about risky behavior and the dangers of online predators?

   _____

   _____

   _____

3. How can you stay informed about the groups and organizations your children are involved in?

_____

_____

_____

4. How can you recognize and address social isolation in your children, and what impact can it have on their mental health?

_____

_____

_____

5. What resources are available if you suspect your child may be in danger of being trafficked or groomed online?

_____

_____

_____

Neglect and Lack of Parental Support Can Lead to Dangerous Situations

Real Life Struggles: When you don't prioritize your kids, they will get that love and guidance or whatever they need from those you don't want them to get it from. That's usually how young girls end up with an abusive boyfriend. They think he's only abusing them because "he loves me," when in actuality, he's dangerous to them. They don't know what love looks like when they don't get the love or self-esteem they are supposed to have from you.

From DJing in strip clubs, I've seen a lot of negative situations with girls. While they were waiting for the club to get packed, they would tell me their stories. Many of them came from messed-up backgrounds. Some had parental responsibilities for their younger siblings without any guidance. They didn't have a parent to teach them to have self-respect and self-love or encourage them to do or be anything. They were raising themselves the best they could. "I had to braid my little sister's hair and take care of my two little brothers," one girl told me. "I did the cooking and cleaning and took care of my three sisters because no one else would do it. What was I supposed to do?" another explained. "Mom got sick, and I had to make a dollar." "No food, no clothes, we were about to lose our apartment. I had to do something." These were the things they shared with me. When I'd ask how they started working at the strip club, many had the same response, "I didn't have a dad," and their words resonated with me—how could they not? Boys without male role models face their own unique challenges. While fathers can model healthy emotional regulation and self-esteem and help form an identity to navigate the diverse world, a negative father figure can do more harm.

I learned that many of the young women had a kid or two and were doing their best to support them. But the majority of them were doing it on their own. They've told me, "The best thing I could do is sell my body, so I became a dancer." Others have said, "I'm trying to better myself, and this is the only way I know how to make money to do it."

Those experiences taught me what my daughters—all my children—needed at home. As their father, I needed to build a safe, encouraging environment. I am responsible for knowing who their friends are and who they are talking to on the phone, where they are going, and where they are at all times. Your kids will give you the respect you deserve and earn when you first build a relationship with them. Even when they live under your roof, they're not going to confide in you or tell you what's going on in their lives if they don't trust you. They won't come to you if you don't actively listen and show unconditional love and support. All of this is about creating a safe environment. They may try to create their own without proper guidance and support if they don't have one with you at home. They won't want to leave home and look for anything else if your home is a safe, happy, encouraging, and fun environment.

REAL LIFE REFLECTIONS

1. How can you recognize and address the signs of isolation, loneliness, neglect, or lack of guidance in your children's lives?

2. What changes can you make to better provide your children with a higher sense of self-respect and self-love?

3. How can you provide your children with a safe and supportive environment while also fostering independence and self-reliance?

4. How can you address the challenges of being a working parent while prioritizing your children?

> 5. How can you model positive behaviors and values for your children to follow?
>
> _____
>
> _____
>
> _____

(GIA)
Preparing Children to Handle Life's Challenges Begins in a Safe Home Environment

Who doesn't want a safe environment for their children? When your children walk through the door, you want them to breathe a sigh of relief that they're home and it's the best place ever! You want them to feel safe, protected, and loved by you. When I thought about having children, I knew building a safe home environment would always be a top priority. As mothers, it's our responsibility to protect our children. They need us to see them and see right through whatever they're trying to conceal. It doesn't matter if we have a career outside of the home or in the home. They need us to ask them, "What's wrong? Come here. Sit down and talk to me." When you communicate with genuine sincerity and interest, they will because they know how they're feeling or what they're going through matters to you. You've shown them that they are the most important person in your life. Each of our six children feels that way. Of course, I'm taking the liberty of speaking for the littlest, Peyty-Choo. With so many dangers and negative influences present in today's society, creating a safe and nurturing home is one of the best things we can do for their well-being and development.

As RaaShaun has touched on, communication is critical to building a safe home environment. Open and honest communication fosters trust and respect between parents and children. When I say I love my children, I actively listen to what they say because even if it seems insignificant, it's not to them. When we were kids, our words were important. We wanted to be heard and understood—and so do they. It's why I encourage them to express their thoughts and feelings and address any concerns or issues in a calm and supportive manner. This creates a safe place for our children to come to me with anything, knowing Mommy will listen and help them find a solution, laugh, cry, or listen when words are unnecessary.

Another critical aspect of creating a safe home environment is setting clear boundaries and expectations. This provides structure and consistency for our children, which helps them feel secure. It also helps to create a sense of responsibility and accountability, which are excellent traits for them to develop as they grow.

We also stay informed about the latest trends and risks in today's society, particularly those related to technology and social media. Children can have a public social media profile that parents are privy to and a private profile that truly reveals what is going on in their life—including cyberbullying, so know where to look. While our children know which social media platforms are trending, the media knows *what* they are propagating on social media and what is transpiring because of it. This allows us to educate our children on how to stay safe online and in the real world and to have open conversations about potential risks and dangers.

"We also stay informed about the latest trends and risks in today's society, particularly those related to technology and social media."

Building a safe home environment requires unconditional love, patience, and understanding. There is no way to circumvent it. We must remember that what our children deal with outside of the home—hate, anger, racism, jealousy, dysfunction, whatever they face—we will feel it at home if we haven't prepared them to rise above what society is showing and teaching them. We must instill confidence at every turn. We must also ensure that they are stalwart in their convictions. By creating a positive, nurturing, and safe environment, we aim to help our children grow into confident, resilient, and happy individuals equipped to handle whatever challenges life may bring. When you raise your children in a safe environment, they will want to sustain that as they grow up.

REAL LIFE REFLECTIONS

Ten ways to prepare your kids to handle challenges:

1. Create and sustain a safe and nurturing environment.
2. Actively listen.
3. Set boundaries and establish expectations.
4. Address today's risks.
5. Model healthy communication.
6. Promote self-esteem.
7. Teach your kids about consent.
8. Provide emotional support.
9. Encourage open-mindedness.
10. Maintain balance.

PART 3

Individuality

11. Prioritizing and Savoring Quality Time with Your Family

It can be challenging to prioritize and savor quality time with our families. However, doing so is essential for building strong and healthy relationships and promoting positive development and well-being in our children as individuals.

Quality time is so important because it allows us to connect with our loved ones on a deeper level. When we spend time together, we can engage in meaningful conversations, share experiences, and create lasting memories. These experiences strengthen our bonds with one another, foster a sense of belonging and connection, and provide a source of support and comfort in times of need.

We don't just encourage spending time with your kids because the value is in the "quality" of that time. Are you with them but on your phone, having lunch, or preoccupied with work, or are you looking at them and only hearing a few words they say, which isn't enough to understand or engage in the conversation? The quality of time we spend with our kids promotes positive development and well-being and strengthens the parent–child dynamics. That quality time allows us to give them guidance and support, reinforce positive behaviors, and help them to develop important skills such as communication, problem-solving, and emotional regulation. These experiences can help build their self-esteem, resilience, and overall well-being.

So, how can we prioritize and savor quality time with our families in today's environment? One approach is to be intentional about setting aside time for family activities and making them a regular part of our routines. For example, you can have family dinners, cook together, have game nights, or go on weekend outings like hikes. We can also disconnect from technology and other distractions during these times, allowing us to engage and connect fully.

We're not expecting anyone to change their entire life, but making slight additions to how you parent can garner considerable results. If you don't have much time to spend with your children, focus on making the most of your time together. But commit to being completely present during conversations, actively listening to your loved ones, and expressing your love and appreciation for them regularly.

Overall, prioritizing and savoring quality time with our families is essential for building strong and healthy relationships and promoting positive development and well-being in our children. By being intentional and present during these times, we can create lasting memories and strengthen our bonds with one another, even in today's challenging environment.

(GIA)
Making Your Children Feel Special in a Few Minutes

In addition to regular family meetings and spending time together as a unit, we've learned that it's equally important for each parent to create opportunities for one-on-one time with their children. For families with three or more children, it's not uncommon for individual needs to be overlooked or for one child to feel overshadowed by the others. It could be because of their academic or athletic accomplishments, the demand they have on your schedule, they're most like you, or they have health issues or particular needs that require your time. There are numerous reasons that cause children to feel they don't matter, are not special, or are not loved the way you love another child. But when you create moments, experiences, or occasions where you engage with each child individually, you can make all of them feel seen and loved in a unique way.

All six of my children are my priority. I can be in the presence of every one of them and look at each one as though they are my only child. I have the mental capacity to home in on that one child at a time knowing how to make each of them feel equally important, no more or no less than the others, just by the way I engage. I may ask Brooklyn to draw me a picture. And I can tell she feels special and takes pride in me wanting something beautiful from her. She thinks, *Mommy loves my drawings.* And I do love them.

Each day, I take the time to do that with one of our children. My goal is to make that a habit. One would think it's unnecessary because it's really an extra dose of what they already get, but when I see their responses, I can see that I'm savoring our time together the same way they are—and it's delicious! When we had just Madison and Logan, I didn't need that reset button to make sure I was making them feel special, but now that our life is hectic with six kids, I hold myself accountable for making our children a priority. They didn't ask for life to be hectic. Children still have needs. They want Mommy and Daddy. And they shouldn't pay the price because of our schedules.

When I'm talking about making your children feel special and carving out time for them, the beauty of doing this is that it doesn't take hours to make your children feel seen, loved, heard, and special. You can do that in a few minutes with a sentence comprised of uplifting words, a few beautiful kisses, a single question about something important to them, or a warm hug. And none of that costs anything.

Our girls are in dance, their schedules change, and Logan has games out of town. He's playing football and into his education. Madison is in college, and we're constantly connecting and spending time together. RaaShaun's time is limited, and everyone wants Daddy. I do a great job managing everything. Of course, everyone gets their love and kisses. But the magic comes in when you stop moving and treat each of your children like they're the only one in the world. The response is priceless, memorable, and hard to convey, so it's worth doing.

Jaxson's special power is that he's filled with love. London is as well. Brooklyn shines. We've given them all extraordinary characteristics, which makes them happy to know we acknowledge it. My mother did that with me, and I love feeling special. What child doesn't? If you have a child with particular needs or who requires special care, you can also give them a special type of love. They'll feel it. It doesn't matter what it is, as long as it's unique to your children. The way my parents hyped me up, I thought I was the most beautiful girl in the world. I believed them even if it was the furthest thing from the truth. When your children feel great about themselves, they give off incredibly confident and positive energy.

REAL LIFE REFLECTIONS

1. How do you currently prioritize quality time with each of your children?

2. What unique characteristics of your children can you acknowledge and praise?

3. How do you balance hectic schedules and travel with spending time with your children?

4. Do you feel like your children get enough one-on-one attention from you? If not, how can you make changes to prioritize them?

5. How can you continue to make your children feel important and valued as they grow older and face new challenges?

_____

_____

_____

The Importance of Nurturing Individuality in Children

Encouraging children to pursue their interests is one of the most important ways to foster their senses of individuality and self-worth. It allows them to develop their own unique talents, skills, and passions, which can be a source of pride and fulfillment throughout their lives. As parents, it's our job to support and encourage our children in their pursuits, to help them navigate the ups and downs of life, and to be there to celebrate their achievements.

In today's busy world, balancing our children's activities with the rest of our responsibilities can be challenging. However, by attending their games, performances, and events, we show our children that we value their interests and are invested in their success. Doing this can help to build their self-esteem and create a stronger bond between parent and child.

Encouraging individuality also teaches our children the power of choice and the importance of taking responsibility for our actions. By allowing them to explore their interests, we will enable them to develop their unique identity and learn from their successes and failures. This can help them become more resilient and self-reliant.

At the same time, it's healthier to balance encouraging our children's interests without overwhelming them with too many activities. It's important to give them the space and time to recharge and pursue other interests, and that can help them to maintain a healthy sense of balance in their lives and to avoid burnout or stress.

REAL LIFE REFLECTIONS

1. How do you support and encourage your children's interests, and what steps can you take to show your enthusiasm and recognition of their passions?

2. How can you foster a sense of individuality and self-reflection in your children, and why is this important for their overall growth and development?

3. What role do your children's interests and passions play in shaping their future goals and aspirations, and how can you help guide your children toward achieving them?

4. How do you model healthy habits and behaviors for your children, and how does this impact their well-being?

5. How can you encourage your children to take responsibility for their choices and actions while providing guidance and support as they navigate life's challenges and opportunities?

_____

_____

_____

The Ultimate Act of Self-Love

It's beautiful to talk about our children and focus primarily on what their needs are and how we can contribute to their well-being. With that responsibility, we have a hundred other things to do in a day that are significant in the scope of things. Whether balancing work and family, paying bills, taking your children to school or their activities, running errands, dealing with emergencies, family issues, and financial stress, providing academic support, caring for aging parents, managing unexpected events, whatever it is, doesn't matter. We still manage to find time to do everything else. Our children are a priority, and if they have disabilities, special needs, health issues, or mental health concerns or are fighting addiction, they need more of our time, empathy, love, and care. But being a loving, caring parent doesn't mean you're supposed to neglect yourself, your well-being, or your happiness. Be an amazing parent. Love your kids unconditionally, but you can't let it be at the expense of your well-being.

When you look at your life and the responsibilities that come with it, don't let them weigh you down so much that you can't manage to take time for yourself. Your physical, mental, and emotional well-being and happiness matter. You've heard this, but are you doing it? We know what matters when it comes to our kids, but believe me, you matter! You can't take care of anyone to the best of your ability if you're mentally or physically exhausted, depressed, unhealthy, or struggling.

When you're taking inventory of what others need, you have individual needs too, so every day, make it a priority to take care of yourself. If you are married or in a relationship, take care of each other. When you make a list of the things you have to do, put yourself and your spouse or partner at the top of that list. If you aren't taking care of yourself as a single parent, or you're neglecting your spouse or partner, that's unhealthy, and it can only cause other issues. There's a difference between asking, "How was work?" versus "How are you feeling?" "What do you need?" and "Are you happy?" Effective and intentional communication, emotional support, and quality time to continually feed the relationship are a few examples of how to care for each other.

It's even more important for you to be in good health mentally, emotionally, and physically. Keep in mind we are relentless in saying to be an example—so be healthy and happy, know when your body needs rest—take care of your *mind, body, and soul.*

The terms "self" and "I" refer to different aspects of your identity. "Self" generally refers to your sense of identity, which includes your beliefs, values, and personality traits. It's the part of you that remains stable throughout your life and is often shaped by early life experiences and socialization.

"I" refers to your sense of agency and your individual subjective experience. It's the part of you that experiences the world and makes decisions based on your own desires and goals. "I" is often associated with your conscious mind and is closely tied to your sense of self-awareness. In other words, "self" is the sum total of your beliefs, values, and personality traits, while "I" is the subjective experience of being a unique individual with agency and autonomy. Understanding the distinction between these two concepts can be helpful in developing a more nuanced understanding of human identity and behavior. You are prioritizing loving yourself first. How can you love others or your children if you don't love yourself?

"Self-care" emphasizes taking care of yourself physically, mentally, and emotionally, to improve your overall well-being and quality of life. "I-care" emphasizes a more individualized approach to self-love and self-care. "I-care" underscores taking responsibility for your needs and desires, prioritizing self-love, and making choices that align with your values and goals.

"I-care" is fundamental. It emphasizes the importance of caring about oneself. It's a reminder that I am an individual. I come first. I care to be happy. I care to enjoy life. And I am going to care about whatever I feel I need because while I care about and love you, I love me too!

Don't you dare feel guilty about making the same investments in yourself that you give everyone else. Caring about your needs as an individual can help you become the best possible version of yourself, and that self-love and joy will naturally transfer to your family. The transformation in your parenting style will be healthier and better for your children and your relationship. You will have removed a tremendous amount of stress and pressure.

"Don't you dare feel guilty about making the same investments in yourself that you give everyone else."

As a couple, taking time for one another is vital in maintaining a healthy and strong relationship. Being a parent doesn't mean the fun and excitement between you and your spouse or partner have to slow down or end. Be fun adults and make time to love each other the way you did before you had children. Be adventurous, and laugh rather than discuss negative situations. Set time aside for date nights and weekend getaways, or hold hands and talk about fun things while taking a walk—imagine being genuinely connected and happy and operating as one to raise your children as one. RaaShaun and I do these things. Time spent together helps to strengthen the bond between parents and couples, which can make you better equipped to handle the challenges that come with parenting. If you're single, give yourself what you need and schedule time for yourself. Recharge and rejuvenate, which can improve your physical and mental health and reduce stress, even if you take just a few minutes a day to meditate. Read a book, listen to music, get a massage, journal, spend time in nature, take a hot bath, see a therapist, go to a gallery and immerse yourself in art, but continue to do something.

I-care acknowledges and prioritizes self-love. And when you model healthy habits for your children, you teach them the importance of loving oneself—and everything begins with how you feel about yourself.

(RAASHAUN)
Supporting Your Child's Interests and Passions

It doesn't take much. It really doesn't. Just tune in and pay attention to what makes your kids happy. Then do what you can to support their interest and passions. If you don't think you have the time, you do. In today's society, and with the current demands, we all have busy lives juggling careers, household duties, health concerns, and other responsibilities. As a result, it's easy to fall into the trap of thinking that there isn't enough time to spend with your kids. But the reality is that there are many small pockets of time throughout the day that you can utilize to connect with your kids. And technology takes whatever excuse you have out of play.

While driving your kids to school, turn the music down, put your phone on silent, and take the opportunity to engage in conversation and ask questions about their day ahead that show them you're in tune with their lives. Name their favorite teacher and ask what's happening in that class. Ask about their friends, the projects they're working on, and what they have planned for the weekend. Ask what they'd like to do with you on your next day off. During mealtime, turn off the television and other devices and have a family discussion. Even bedtime can be a special time to read a story or share something about your day. Quality time doesn't have to be a grand gesture or take up an entire day. Simple activities like playing a game, walking, helping them with a problem, or building something together can be meaningful. If you can take them to work with you so they can see what you do, even that can have tremendous value. If you knew how much your kids want you to be a part of their lives, you'd realize you have more time to give them than you think.

Some of you may not want to make cookies or bake with your kids, but they enjoy those little things. Games, laughing with Mom or Dad, playing a video game, or going out to lunch. I wouldn't say I like arts and crafts. Okay, I hate them. But it's not about the activity. It's the bonding time that has value. We play Taboo with our kids, and it gets really serious. London plays with the adults, and she's learning to think critically without saying things. And Gia and I know these characteristics are necessary now and as young adults. These are just some of the many things we do to make our home a place they want to be. To make it safe. Educational. Healthy. And, of course, fun.

One weekend, my Giants were playing, but Logan wanted to go to see the Holy Cross Crusaders play soccer. So the following day, while my Giants were playing, we went to Boston to see Holy Cross play, and then we went back to New York so I could do *The Breakfast Club*.

I have to do whatever I have to do to encourage his interests and help make sure that it happens. Spending that time is worth everything.

"Building meaningful connections with our children doesn't necessitate grand gestures or elaborate plans; it's about being present and actively participating in the activities they love."

I remember, when I was younger, Dad and me building a remote control car. Bit by bit, we put it together every Sunday. Dad taught me how to wash cars and do many things, but I realized it was about something other than the activity. It was about being next to him at that moment. It was about enjoying being around each other. We need to do that with our kids and enjoy those moments. I am trying to learn soccer. I have been studying FIFA and the game to enjoy with Logan when he watches it.

Building meaningful connections with our children doesn't necessitate grand gestures or elaborate plans; it's about being present and actively participating in the activities they love. Whether it's a conversation during lunch, playing a game, or working on a project together, these moments build emotional connections that have significance beyond the activity itself. Just as you may recall a specific activity you did with your parent(s) just to have quality time together, we can create those treasured memories with our children. In a world of distractions, simple acts showing we're present, understanding, and encouraging will resonate and make a difference in your child's life.

Although we might be tired, have other things to do, or don't want to, the truth is that we need to do whatever it takes to have those moments. I want my kids to remember building Legos with me.

REAL LIFE REFLECTIONS

1. How do you balance your own interests with spending time with your children?

2. What are some unique ways to bond with your children that don't involve typical activities?

3. What are some strategies for making the most of the time you have with your children?

PART 3: INDIVIDUALITY

4. How can you ensure that each child feels equally important and loved if you have health issues, a disability, or limited time due to work or other conflicts?

_____

_____

_____

5. How can you make sure that the time you spend with your children is both fun and educational?

_____

_____

_____

12. Cultivating the Seeds of Greatness in a Complex World

Cultivating the seeds of greatness in your kids is a multifaceted process that requires intentionality, patience, and a deep understanding of the complexities of the world around us. I discuss them on our show and in talking with people throughout my day; they're in the news, and I pay attention because I have to navigate them. And in today's world, many adversities and problems can impede your kid's development and prevent them from reaching their full potential. As parents, it's our responsibility to help them traverse these challenges and develop the skills and traits necessary to thrive.

(RAASHAUN)
The Traits of Successful Children

Gia and I work hard to be successful and, more importantly, to raise successful kids. What "successful" means to you may not be the same to someone else, and that's okay. People have diverse perspectives on what success is. That may be excellent health, being happy, overcoming challenges, achieving academic excellence, or achieving goals that align with passion and interest. Kids with disabilities or special needs could be developing self-advocacy skills and gaining independence to the best of their abilities, having strong social and emotional skills toward helping others, preserving cultural traditions, achieving financial stability, innovating, and overcoming substance abuse or other addictions. What success looks like to you is defined by you. It could be getting out of bed when dealing with depression. And depending on how it's defined, it can be measurable, but it's not always quantifiable.

Some of the things that you can observe in your children is whether they possess key traits that have helped them achieve their goals. As a parent, it's important to cultivate these traits in your kids to help set them up for success. For example, successful children have confidence, resilience, perseverance, self-discipline, creativity, and curiosity, which leads them to having a growth mindset.

We have addressed confidence in nearly every section of this book because if they don't have it, they won't reach the level of success they could. If you take one thing from this book, it's that helping your children develop confidence will flow into other critical areas of their growth. When a child has confidence, it's not just at home around Mommy and Daddy, when you're big brother or sister is around, or you're with your crew. It's in any room, around any group of people, in any environment, regardless of all else! Confidence isn't fleeting. I've had some tough conversations on *The Breakfast Club*, and I still have them. But I never lose my confidence, even when I interviewed President Obama. Having indomitable confidence is a part of success.

We want our kids to be resilient because that means they can bounce back from setbacks and challenges, and it's an essential trait for success in any field. For example, if they fall off a bike and get back on it instead of saying they don't want to ride it again, that indicates they possess resilience. So, what do you do? Nurture it. And continue nurturing those moments and situations that help your kids become increasingly resilient. To cultivate resilience in your children, encourage them to view challenges as opportunities for growth and learning rather than insurmountable obstacles.

Perseverance is another key trait of successful kids. They're not quitters. Instead, they follow through and stick with something even when it's difficult or tedious. If they're running hurdles in a track meet and fall, they'll get up and finish the race even if they come in last. You can help your children develop perseverance by encouraging them to set goals and work toward them steadily, even when progress is slow.

When your kids have homework, practice after school for sports, sports events, chores, or other obligations, and they don't need you prodding them along to get things done or remind them to do what they need to, that's self-discipline. They exhibit self-discipline when they can wake up and prepare for school without you having to wake them up. Their friends want them to hang out, but they have a previous commitment or test to prepare for; resisting temptations and distractions in pursuit of long-term goals—that's self-discipline. Recognize and encourage it. To cultivate self-discipline in your children, encourage them to set priorities, make plans, and stick to them. You can also model self-discipline in your behavior.

Creativity is not putting yourself in a box that you have to think yourself out of; instead, it's developing innovative solutions to problems. So encourage your children to engage in creative activities like those arts and crafts I hate. Encourage drawing, writing, playing music, or building and innovating. You can also encourage them to think creatively by asking open-ended questions and encouraging them to explore different perspectives.

"All these things lead to your kids having a growth mindset."

When your kids are curious, they desire to learn and understand new things. When they ask questions, explain them. When Logan wants to learn something about DJing, I tell him or show him. It's fostered such an innate curiosity that now he is showing me things, and he's pretty good. He knows how to use new technology and things I may not know about. Encouraging your kids to ask questions and explore their interests allows you to expose them to new ideas and experiences to spark their curiosity. And when we actively listen to our kids and respect their perspectives, we can learn things from them.

All these things lead to your kids having a growth mindset. They believe they can develop their abilities through hard work and dedication. And you want this. Encourage your kids to view their abilities as malleable and to embrace challenges as opportunities for growth and learning. Cultivating these six traits in your kids can help set them up for success in all areas of their lives.

REAL LIFE REFLECTIONS

1. What are some examples of self-discipline in your children that you can acknowledge and encourage?

2. How can you model self-discipline for your children?

3. How can you encourage your children to think creatively?

4. How can you encourage your children to be confident, ask questions, and explore their interests?

5. What are some practical ways you can help cultivate these traits in your children?

Unlocking Your Child's Full Potential

One critical aspect of cultivating greatness in kids is providing them with a safe, nurturing environment that encourages growth and learning. Creating an atmosphere of love, trust, and respect allows kids to feel comfortable expressing themselves and exploring their interests more freely. It also means setting clear boundaries and expectations that provide structure and consistency, which can help kids develop a sense of responsibility and accountability.

Another critical component of cultivating greatness in your kids is supporting their interests and passions. If Gia so much as thinks the kids want to do something, she's on it. She supports whatever they want to do, but she ensures their commitment is there. I support them by making sure they can do the activities they're interested in. Don't overextend yourself because of societal pressures that will cause unnecessary stress—you'd be the one who pays the price. Support your children based on your ability. And if your resources don't allow you to do some of the things you would like, find community opportunities for your kids. You have access to find community resources that are available by going online.

Look for community centers or after-school programs that offer free or low-cost activities aligned with your kid's interests. For example, find art classes and music lessons, or put them in an intramural league. Libraries offer free events that can be educational and fun. Volunteer with your kids at community events that align with their interests. Attend community events or festivals where they can learn about and experience diverse cultures and foods. Call on businesses and ask if they would be willing to sponsor your child. Look into government-funded programs and grants that can help support their interest and drive. Take them to museums. They can join a basketball league at the YMCA or Big Brothers Big Sisters to have a mentor, or attend science or sports camps through their school. Ask the administrators about funding and available opportunities for your children to help them reach their full potential. Engage their minds and provide continuous support in their learning journey to instill valuable educational principles. Get them on an athletic team if they can physically participate. Being part of a team can help foster relationship skills, and in this society, they need them. Kids sit alone and play video games for hours, and when they have to go out and communicate, express themselves, or build relationships, they don't know how. We need to change this.

If your kids don't exhibit any interest, help them identify what aligns with what they are passionate about or talk about. We won't know what they enjoy or what interests our kids if we don't take the time to understand what drives and motivates them. If we want to unlock their full potential, we have to help unlock their passions—find ways to support or encourage their interests. Sometimes, they want us to take an active interest in what they're doing.

"You can instill greatness in your kids by just giving them the opportunity or helping them learn how to get it independently."

When you see an article that may interest them, give it to them and tell them to read it so you can discuss it later; tell them you want their opinion. Doing that can help develop their critical thinking skills and create intelligent dialogue about the world, politics, other countries, innovations, stocks, and investments. Giving them articles to read and topics to research and discussing them will help them form opinions, understand perspectives, and develop their critical thinking. Unlock the door to their minds and teach them how to overcome and circumvent challenges. Help your kids see ways to move forward after setbacks and stay motivated and focused. Enhance their communication skills by reading to them and having them read to you. You can instill greatness in your kids by just giving them the opportunity or helping them learn how to get it independently.

If you have the time to cultivate greatness, give it to them. If you don't, it doesn't take much, but it requires something.

Overall, cultivating greatness in children is a complex process that requires a thoughtful and intentional approach. We can help our kids navigate a complex world full of adversities and problems by prioritizing their needs and having effective, thought-provoking conversations about life. Real life. Providing a safe and nurturing environment, supporting their interests, helping them sharpen their skills, and pushing the boundaries of their learning and development is setting your kids up to thrive in this complex world so they can reach their full potential.

> **REAL LIFE REFLECTIONS**
>
> Eight keys to unlocking potential:
> 1. Foster a nurturing environment.
> 2. Support interests and passions.
> 3. Utilize community resources.
> 4. Identify passions and interests.
> 5. Develop critical thinking skills.
> 6. Set clear boundaries and expectations.
> 7. Foster resilience and a growth mindset.
> 8. Prioritize children's needs and conversations.

(GIA)
Teach Them to Traverse Boundaries with Their Minds

Cultivating the seed of greatness in children and nurturing young minds starts by creating a close-knit family unit where every member is encouraged to contribute to the family's well-being. In our household, we have little entrepreneurs who are always thinking beyond boundaries. As parents, we are responsible for challenging our kids' minds and encouraging them to think outside the box. Exposure to new experiences, cultures, and outlooks helps our children develop critical thinking skills, appreciate diversity, and have varied perspectives about worldviews from their experiences rather than what someone has told them. That's why we love to travel as a family, even if it's just day trips or staycations, as it allows us to explore new cuisines and museums nearby. It's all about experiencing life together, forming strong bonds, and encouraging our children to develop a broader perspective on the world. It's important to note, you can give your children an incredible experience in the city you live in. Teach them about the culture and food, art, history, architecture, and anything that evokes curiosity about the world around them. They will learn to appreciate the differences and similarities between cultures and people, which can help them become more empathetic and open-minded. It may inspire them to learn another language or dream bigger and think outside of what they ever imagined they could. During conversations, travel, sports, academics, whatever it is, teach your children to traverse boundaries with their minds.

REAL LIFE REFLECTIONS

1. What are some ways to encourage your children to think beyond boundaries and develop critical thinking skills?

2. How can exposure to new experiences, cultures, and outlooks help your children develop varied perspectives and appreciate diversity?

3. What role do you play in helping your children develop a broader perspective on the world?

4. How can you instill an appreciation for differences and similarities between cultures and people in your children?

　_____

　_____

　_____

5. How can you nurture your children's curiosity about the world around them and inspire them to pursue their dreams?

　_____

　_____

　_____

13. Recognizing Individual Needs Through Heartful Parenting

Your parental support can profoundly impact your child's well-being and success in today's society. Children with supportive parents tend to have higher self-esteem, greater resilience, and better academic achievement than those without parental support. When parents take an active interest in their children's lives, it can create a sense of security and belonging for the child, which can positively influence their overall mental health.

For example, imagine two children who have a passion for music. One child has parents who encourage their musical pursuits, attend their performances, and invest in music lessons and instruments. The other child has parents who are indifferent to their musical interests and don't prioritize supporting their passion. The first child will likely have a greater sense of self-worth, as their parents have validated their interests and invested in their development. This child is also more likely to continue pursuing music as a hobby or even a career, which can lead to a sense of purpose and fulfillment in life. The other child may feel unsupported and discouraged, negatively impacting their confidence and sense of self. This child may eventually abandon their musical interests, leading to a lost opportunity for personal growth and fulfillment.

When we are supportive of our children's interests, it can lead to better outcomes in other areas of their lives. But, unfortunately, we can see the difference. Some of the children we know who are supported and validated by their parents tend to take healthy risks and pursue new opportunities, such as trying out for a sports team or applying for very competitive academic programs.

Their willingness to take risks and put themselves out there has led to them achieving greater success and personal growth.

In contrast, some of the children we've known don't have parental support and have struggled with insecurity and uncertainty about their abilities and interests. Many are talented and have extraordinary academic, athletic, or artistic skills. If a teacher or mentor doesn't recognize or encourage the development of their talents, skills, or interests, and their parents don't or cannot support them, these children will fall by the wayside. Not recognizing, supporting, and guiding our children can lead to a lack of motivation and poor performance in school or other areas of life. Children who don't feel supported by their parents may also be more likely to engage in risky behaviors, such as substance abuse or delinquent behavior, as they may lack a sense of purpose and direction. Communities, schools, and the streets are full of them.

We're saying that parental support plays a critical role in your children's well-being and success in today's society. When you take an active interest in your children's lives and support their interests and passions, it can lead to greater confidence, resilience, and success.

(GIA)
The Impact of Parental Support on Your Child's Well-Being and Success

The Choo Crew are multifaceted individuals with diverse interests spanning from sports to music, academics, volunteering, and even film. As parents, we understand the value of encouraging and supporting their passions to help them develop a strong sense of individuality. We need to be present, rooting for them on the sidelines or in the auditorium seats and recognizing their accomplishments.

In today's society, where external pressures such as work demands and technology distractions can take away from quality time with our children, heartfelt parenting is a reminder to focus on the essential elements of parenting that contribute to the emotional security and self-esteem of your children. We see it as an approach that emphasizes the power of *unconditional love*, open communication, and consistency in *positive reinforcement* to create a lasting bond with your children. Despite the busyness of life, we must prioritize our children's passions, create schedules that enable them to participate in activities that speak to them, and provide the support they need to thrive.

With six children, we have to create a schedule that allows all of them to engage their interests and participate in activities that speak to them. And we do that knowing we must be present on the bleachers, in the auditorium seats, and on the sidelines whenever possible, as sometimes schedules may overlap. Our children need our support, and though unspoken, they expect it. Whether yours is a single- or dual-parent household, as parents you have many other considerations such as your health, work demands, travel, and different schedules, but you can still be engaged by asking your children to provide you with the details—and when they tell you, be excited for them and ask questions to show you're listening. When you can't make a game or event, show up to their practices to let them know you see them and you care about their progress. Be honest with your children about why you can't make an event. When you have a conflicting schedule, asking how you can make it up to them or what you can do to be supportive can make all the difference. Don't just call it a day and say, "I can't make it." Most may understand, but it doesn't mean it won't adversely affect them. And you don't want to discourage them from playing, as supporting their individual passions and skills is beneficial to them.

Encouraging your child to develop their individual skills and passions is crucial for their overall growth and development. When children engage in activities that they enjoy and are passionate about, it helps them to build their self-esteem, self-confidence, and a sense of accomplishment. It also allows them to explore their interests, talents, and abilities, which can lead to discovering their life's purpose.

Encouraging children to pursue their interests and passions teaches them the value of hard work, dedication, and perseverance. They can learn that success requires effort and that setbacks and failures are a natural part of the learning process. Encouraging your children to pursue individual interests can help them develop a growth mindset that benefits them in all areas of life.

In addition to personal growth and development, encouraging individuality fosters a sense of belonging and connectedness, and this helps with relationship skills. When children feel that their interests and passions are understood and supported, it strengthens their bonds with their family, friends, and community.

Encouraging and supporting our children in developing their skills and passions is beneficial for their personal growth, academic success, and social and emotional well-being. It allows them to discover their unique strengths and talents, build their self-esteem and confidence, and develop the skills and mindset needed to succeed.

Individuality produces children who look at themselves introspectively and understand the power of choice and the responsibilities that come with those choices. And when they have our support, it's even better!

REAL LIFE REFLECTIONS

1. In what ways can you encourage individuality in your children and help them understand the power of choice and responsibility?

   _____
   _____
   _____

2. How do you ensure that you are present and supportive of your children's activities and events, even when you have conflicting schedules?

   _____
   _____
   _____

PART 3: INDIVIDUALITY

3. Can you think of a time when you had to miss one of your child's events? How did you make it up to them?

   _____
   _____
   _____

4. How can you use your own interests and hobbies to connect with your children and encourage their passions?

   _____
   _____
   _____

5. What impact can supporting and encouraging your children's interests have on their self-esteem and overall development?

   _____
   _____
   _____

6. In what ways can you show your children that their individuality and passions are valued and respected in your family?

   _____
   _____
   _____

(RAASHAUN)
Correcting Behaviors Through Firm and Fair Communication

Parenting isn't about yelling or screaming at your kids, or abusing them to get them to do what you want. Good parenting takes patience and time. Yelling is easy, but kids become immune to it, and it becomes ineffective. We manage our kids with a parenting style that takes love, empathy, and deep emotional connections to guide their development. It means we have to tune in to our children's emotional and physical needs and respond with understanding, affection, firmness, and fairness when needed. As Gia would say, "It prioritizes the nurturing of the parent–child relationship to help with healthy emotional and psychological development."

As parents we have to tune in and recognize that a strong parent-child bond is critical for our kids' overall well-being and that it involves consistent and positive interactions with them. It encourages us to be present and actively involved in our kid's life, to listen and communicate effectively, to set boundaries, and to provide consistent guidance and support, especially when we see it's needed.

When a child has needs, it will come across in their behavior or communication. They may be withdrawn, unusually quiet, agitated, picking on a sibling, or mouthing off to you. But it's our responsibility to recognize these changes because it tells us what their individual needs are.

When a child misbehaves, it's often because they want attention. They may be seeking more of their parent's time and attention, and this behavior is usually more visible when you take your kids to school. The kids who don't listen or fall on the floor and roll around are generally looking for a reaction. It's not necessarily because they're that angry but because they want to elicit a response from their parents. Adults do this, too, especially in relationships.

Gia and I try to nip that in the bud early on with each of our kids. The only reaction they will get is one they don't want. You have to teach kids; if they want a positive reaction, you must approach it differently. When you see a kid cursing their mom out, falling on the floor and rolling around, doing things they see at home or other kids doing in school, you cannot allow that negative behavior to persist. We don't. I had to have a conversation with Jaxson because what he doesn't like other kids in school doing to him, he was doing to his sister. And he was doing it because he thought he could.

Jaxson is genuinely a friendly, polite kid. However, the kids were making fun of him and taking advantage of who he was because he was so nice. If he raised his hand in school, another kid would jump in front of him and do it or do other annoying things that bothered him, and I realized that he was doing these things to his sister.

"As parents, we have to be vigilant in addressing behavioral issues and little situations as we see them arising as preventive measures."

As parents, we have to be vigilant in addressing behavioral issues and little situations as we see them arising as preventive measures. We don't want them to become habits or behavioral problems. Instead of letting his behavior evolve, I had to have a stern conversation with Jaxson. There was no yelling or screaming. The key to parenting is *love, understanding,* and *correction.* Jaxson and I had a *firm and fair* discussion where I explained, "The same things kids are doing to you, you're now doing to your sister. Why would you do this to your sister if you don't like how it feels? You should know how your sister is feeling right now. So what you're going to do is you're going to turn around and apologize to your sister. And you're going to make sure that you don't do it again. If you do it again, you will have a problem with me next time." He understood.

We see a lot of this with kids, and parents let these behaviors progress. They clearly don't stop them at home because the kids are doing it out in public. We have to manage what's going on in our households so that good and healthy behavior is natural when our kids leave home. If you're not correcting little negative behaviors early on, they can turn into habits that can become worse and adaptive in other areas of their life. Our kids often emulate behaviors they see or experience at home or from the people they are around the most and may repeat them in school. Parenting is heartfelt. When you're in tune with your kids, these bad behaviors will not go undetected.

Loving our kids is seeing and hearing them and correcting their behaviors.

REAL LIFE REFLECTIONS

1. What are some common behaviors that your children display when they have unmet needs, and how can you address these needs?

2. How can you differentiate between genuine anger and attention-seeking behavior in your children?

3. How can you effectively communicate with your children about negative behaviors without resorting to yelling, screaming, abuse, or harsh discipline?

4. How can you ensure your children don't emulate negative behaviors they see in the home or from those around them?

5. What strategies can you use to manage your children's behavior both in and outside the home?

_____

_____

_____

14. Challenges of Raising Children with ADHD, Autism, or Diverse Diagnoses

As parents, we all have challenges. Often in today's society, and for many reasons, families are dealing with issues some know nothing about, and it serves us all to be kinder and gentler.

Some of you are raising a child with ADHD, autism, depression, anxiety, or other diverse diagnoses, which can be an incredibly challenging and complex journey that requires a great deal of understanding, patience, and perseverance.

Attention-deficit/hyperactivity disorder (ADHD) is one of the most common mental disorders affecting children. Autism is a neurological developmental disability that one in one hundred children has been diagnosed with. Keep in mind, these are just two out of the many mental disorders that can affect children, but these diagnoses can impact a child's behavior, learning, and development in ways that aren't always immediately apparent. While we all love our children, for some parents, navigating the various symptoms and challenges that come with these diagnoses can be an uphill battle.

One of the main difficulties of raising a child with ADHD or autism is the unpredictability of their behavior. Children with these diagnoses may struggle with impulse control and hyperactivity and have difficulties with social interaction, which can make it difficult for them to adhere to routines, follow directions, or stay focused in school. This alone can lead to a great deal of frustration for both the child and the parent, and it requires a constant effort to manage symptoms and behaviors in a supportive and structured way.

Another challenge is the social stigma that can come with these diagnoses. Children with ADHD, autism, depression, anxiety, or other diverse diagnoses may struggle to fit in with their peers or be misunderstood by others, which can impact their self-esteem and mental health. As a result, some parents may need to work harder or require assistance to create an environment that is supportive, understanding, and accepting while also advocating for their child's needs and educating others about these diagnoses, as not everyone understands.

Additionally, there may be other medical or therapeutic interventions that are required to help manage some of their symptoms and improve a child's quality of life. This can include medications, therapy, or other interventions that may require a great deal of coordination, expense, and effort.

Despite these challenges, raising a child with ADHD, autism, or other diverse diagnoses can also be incredibly rewarding. Children with these diagnoses often have unique perspectives and talents, and with the right support and interventions, they can thrive and succeed in their own ways. It requires a deep commitment to understanding and supporting their needs, as well as a willingness to adapt and be patient in the face of challenges. But ultimately, it's a journey that can lead to incredible growth, resilience, and love.

REAL LIFE REFLECTIONS

Five tips for raising children with ADHD, autism, or diverse diagnoses:

1. Be patient and understanding.
2. Create a supportive and structured environment.
3. Advocate and educate.
4. Coordinate necessary interventions.
5. Celebrate their unique perspectives.

(GIA & RAASHAUN)
The Heart of Parenting and Dedication to Raising a Neurodiverse Child

Real Life Challenges: Candace, Will, and their two children are a very loving and close-knit family that we have met on several occasions through friends of ours. Despite their personal challenges, they are incredibly compassionate and are always willing to help someone in need. Their thirteen-year-old daughter, a beautiful girl with big honey-colored eyes, has autism. Their seventeen-year-old son is kindhearted and a talented athlete. Although difficult, he works hard to achieve academic success, given his professional diagnosis of ADHD during childhood by a therapist.

When their children were little, Candace and Will noticed that their daughter struggled with eye contact and didn't respond to her name. Then social interactions and communication weren't developing normally. At the same time, their son with ADHD had trouble focusing, finishing tasks, and staying still. They did their best to support their children and provide them with the care and attention they needed. They even took classes on autism and joined support groups.

But within the confines of their home, Candace and Will faced many challenges. There were times when their daughter would have a meltdown, and her parents would struggle to calm her down. Other times, their son with ADHD would become so hyperactive that it was hard for the parents to keep up with him. They put their son in behavior therapy to help him gain better self-control and turn negative energy into positive thoughts and behaviors. Love and consistent patience seemed to help.

"Despite these challenges," Will explained, "we feel that we're persevering. We've been through some difficult times and adjustments, but that's life, isn't it? Everyone has challenges at some point, and theirs are no less than ours. Candace and I work to support our children together as a team. When one of us is overburdened, the other picks up the slack, so we ensure our kids constantly have what they need. They need us to be attentive—to come up with solutions and to guide and protect them. We get to the heart of parenting and do the best we can. Sure, it takes away from our time together, but regardless of what's going on, we squeeze in time for ourselves and each other. Regardless of the diagnoses our children have, we value our time with them. And having each other to lean on has brought us closer.

"We've had to learn and create a love language for our daughter, which has helped us communicate with her better. We've enrolled her in applied behavioral analysis (ABA) therapy, and it's been incredibly beneficial to her development. We've been patient with our son, and he attends behavioral therapy, which we felt was a good alternative to medication. These interventions help our kids learn skills to cope with their diagnoses, such as social skills and self-regulation techniques.

"It's taken time, but we've done workshops and seminars to better understand their diagnoses and how to continually support them as they grow. We researched articles with our son and processed them together. Gaining understanding can give our children some power over their diagnoses as well as the ability to face them. Working through this with them can alleviate them researching a diagnosis on their own and finding inaccurate information or making them feel they are incapable of normalcy. Every little bit of knowledge helps, and often there are new processes or things that can help us better understand our children's diagnoses and how to support them at home.

"Over time, we've found ways to adapt and work together, even developing routines and rituals that help our children feel comfortable and secure. For example, our daughter has a set bedtime routine that includes reading a story and listening to calming music. The one thing Candace and I have found is that our family never lost sight of our faith, love for each other, and the love and protective nature we have for our children. We've supported each other through tough times and celebrated each other's achievements, no matter how small. We learned to see the beauty and unique qualities in both of our children and celebrate them for who they are."

Candace, Will, and the story of their two children vividly portray resilience, love, and intentional support in parenting. Despite their multifaceted challenges, the family's relentless commitment to understanding, loving, and supporting each other's uniqueness genuinely stands out. They have sought professional therapies, engaged in workshops, and embraced unique communication strategies, reflecting a thoughtful approach to their children's needs. However, their unity, adaptability, faith, and love resonate powerfully. They have worked as a unit, leaning on each other to provide consistent care and create comforting routines while celebrating each child's individuality. Their story isn't about coping with challenges. It's about transforming those challenges into triumphs through empathy, education, and unwavering dedication. They are a beautiful example of the power of compassionate parenting. It reminds us that challenges are part of every family's narrative, but facing them with dedication, understanding, and love truly defines us.

REAL LIFE REFLECTIONS

1. How can you identify if your child is showing signs of ADHD or autism?

   _____

   _____

   _____

2. Are there any specific challenges you've faced in raising a child with diverse diagnoses?

   _____

   _____

   _____

3. How can you create a supportive and inclusive environment for your child at home?

   _____

   _____

   _____

PART 3: INDIVIDUALITY

4. What strategies have you found helpful in managing your child's behaviors or symptoms?
   _____
   _____
   _____

5. What resources or support networks are available to help you as a parent of a child with diverse diagnoses?
   _____
   _____
   _____

6. What role do you think early intervention plays in improving outcomes for children with diverse diagnoses?
   _____
   _____
   _____

7. How can you approach discussions with your child about their diagnosis and any associated challenges they may face?
   _____
   _____
   _____

8. How can you prioritize self-care and manage your own emotional well-being as a parent of a child with diverse diagnoses?
   _____
   _____
   _____

9. What steps can you take to advocate for your child's needs and ensure they receive the best care possible?

10. How can you celebrate your child's unique strengths and abilities rather than solely focusing on their diagnoses and challenges?

PART 4

Discipline and Self-Discipline

15. The Unbreakable Bond of a Parent and Child

The bond between a parent and child is one of the most unique and unbreakable relationships in the world. And we treasure ours. It's an emotional and physical connection that's developed through years of love, trust, and nurturing. To create and maintain this bond, we must provide our children with emotional support, physical safety, and a secure environment. Love isn't enough. Ensuring their well-being, happiness, and personal development—that's love. It's important to understand that creating a strong parent–child bond is not an overnight process. What we have with our children takes consistency and years to reinforce. We're not entitled to having a strong, unbreakable bond even when birthing our children. It derives from a continuous effort that lasts a lifetime. Love and being committed to your children aren't fleeting. They are forever.

In today's society, where you and your children are often pulled in many different directions, building a strong bond can be challenging. However, it is essential to make time for your child and to be present in their lives. This involves active listening, showing interest in their daily activities and interests, and providing emotional support during difficult times. It doesn't mean that we as parents won't have challenges, but it does mean we have to rise to the responsibility of being excellent parents. We should strive to create a safe and secure environment that allows our children to express their emotions without fear of judgment or rejection.

Building a strong bond with our children is the establishment of healthy communication patterns. The way you communicate sets a precedent for whether they will respect you. If you talk in any kind of way to your children and are disrespectful in your communication, expect that it may come back like a boomerang when you least expect it. It's your responsibility to create an open and honest dialogue with your children, allowing them to express their thoughts and feelings without fear of repercussions. This requires active listening, empathy, and validation of your child's feelings.

It's crucial to create a strong sense of trust between parent and child. You can establish trust by setting clear boundaries and following through with consequences when those boundaries are crossed. Refrain from disciplining your child when you're frustrated or having a difficult day; be consistent and remove negative emotions from your communications. Trust is also built by being honest and transparent with your child, sharing your thoughts and feelings with them, and demonstrating that you're dependable and reliable.

Building an unbreakable bond between you and your child requires consistent effort and dedication. Constant. It involves creating a safe and secure environment, fostering healthy communication patterns, and establishing a strong sense of trust. By prioritizing these elements, you can create a lasting bond that will benefit both you and your child for a lifetime.

(GIA)
Understanding the Importance of Trust in Parenting

In today's society, with deteriorating social skills and exposure to greater trauma and risks than in the past, it's natural for parents to worry about their teens sneaking out and engaging in risky behaviors. For some families, these risky behaviors are occurring at younger ages. RaaShaun and I are not concerned about our children sneaking out or engaging in risky and dangerous behaviors because they already know the outcome will far outweigh the fun they think they may have. This has been instilled in them from the beginning of their lives, and they know our morals, values, and disciplines are in place to protect them. They trust us and have seen evidence of that trust benefiting them, just as your children have seen with you. However, building a strong foundation of trust and communication with our children can go a long way in preventing these issues, as trust is discipline.

We've never had to worry about our teens sneaking out because we have established relationships built on trust and mutual respect, which requires our children to be disciplined in their behaviors. More importantly, they have self-love, self-respect, and self-discipline, which must be taught early, especially in a society where these values are diminishing. By giving our children the freedom to make safe and appropriate choices while also providing guidance and support, we trust them to make the right decisions. This trust allows children to have fun, gain new experiences, and live their lives to the fullest.

> **"By communicating with our children and fostering trust, we can guide them toward safe and fulfilling choices."**

This trust is something that can be passed down from generation to generation. For instance, we learned about trust from our parents and understood why certain choices were being made. This approach helped us develop critical thinking skills and provided valuable life lessons. We have the advantage of foresight based on our own life experiences. By communicating with our children and fostering trust, we can guide them toward safe and fulfilling choices. Creating relationships built on trust deactivates the need that many teens and young adults have to disobey and disrespect their parents, leading to a stronger and healthier parent–child relationship. In essence, the parent–child trust relationship is a crucial component of a healthy and nurturing family dynamic, allowing you to provide guidance and support while giving your children the freedom to grow and learn. This is a way of helping them become better decision-makers who are less likely to give in to negative influences.

REAL LIFE REFLECTIONS

1. How can you build trust with your child from a young age?

   _____

   _____

   _____

2. How can explaining your reasoning behind decisions to your child strengthen your relationship?

   _____

   _____

   _____

3. How can you foster an environment where your teen feels comfortable coming to you with any issues or concerns they may have?

   _____

   _____

   _____

4. What are some ways to establish boundaries while still fostering trust with your teen?

   _____

   _____

   _____

5. How can trust be used as a tool to prevent rebellion in teens?

   _____

   _____

   _____

The Art of Effective Discipline

Raising children can become complex regardless of how financially secure the parents are. Some parents are naive to the fact that because their children are in affluent circles, they don't do drugs; others consider their children don't have money for drugs; and some simply believe their children would never do them. But access to disposable income or negative influences can lead to drug abuse, and once addiction takes hold, it can be difficult to regain control of your child's behavior. However, as a parent, if you teach your children to have unwavering self-discipline and to be comfortable in their own leadership and morals, you can rely on your child's decision-making and confidence that they don't have to partake in drug use, even if they are around it. We need to prepare them for it because access to drugs can be unavoidable.

It's important for us to plant the seeds of discipline and strong morals early on so that our children can resist peer pressure and make intelligent choices. This is why we are sharing preventive measures to implement early on or adapt now. Think of it the same way we explained building a foundation for a house. If you miss a step, you may have to backtrack and reinforce that foundation. But with patience, love, and guidance, you can create an unshakable foundation for your child's well-being. Don't forget the value of developing and implementing a mission statement that bonds your family so closely as a unit they don't need anything from anyone else as they trust and rely on family!

Remember, drugs—fentanyl, prescription drugs, anything a child may want—can be found anywhere, but a strong foundation of values and discipline can help your child navigate these challenges successfully.

REAL LIFE REFLECTIONS

Eight ways to practice effective discipline:

1. Teach resistance to peer pressure.
2. Understand personal beliefs.

> 3. Educate children about the dangers of drug use.
> 4. Monitor children's behavior.
> 5. Take action if drug use is suspected.
> 6. Create a safe discussion environment.
> 7. Utilize community resources.
> 8. Instill responsibility and accountability.

When Parenting Isn't Enough: Navigating the Challenges Beyond Your Control

We never told our children not to drink. Instead, we educated them about the consequences and issues related to drinking and asked if they were curious. That set the tone for later because they've had this and other necessary conversations relevant to their development. They understand our perspectives and intentions and the "why" behind our rationale. RaaShaun and I also understand the reality of peer pressure and societal pressure our children face, so we're honest and direct in our communications about how they can navigate situations beyond our control as parents.

When hanging out with friends, Madison and Logan know how to respond to peer pressure or adverse situations because they've been taught and had the value of good decision-making instilled in them early on. It continues to shift as society changes, and there are even more concerns for us to address. So how do you teach these practices? Through direct conversations, examples of what you or others have experienced, and having real talk about consequences and their impact. How a child or teen navigates uncomfortable situations when a parent isn't present matters the most.

When Madison was in high school, we encouraged her to have these experiences, testing her resolve and allowing her to attend parties, even though we were aware kids were drinking. We explained, "You must be able to separate yourself from others. You have to be strong and confident to be around people who choose to drink. And you don't have to be judgmental. Take people as they are. Value them for the things that you appreciate. If you don't, you will ostracize a whole host of people who may be good and kind and bring value or diverse insights. You will never need their decision-making in certain areas, and that is your power. I went through life never really believing I was above anyone, but my decision-making was firmly set in my beliefs."

In this society, the key is to try to raise your children to be strong-minded leaders, capable of making informed decisions rather than succumbing to the influence of their peers. The objective is to help them adopt self-confidence and independence, precluding the need for external validation. I didn't have my first drink until around my sophomore year in college, and after that, I might have had a drink three times in college. I was secure in my thoughts. I knew my life was good, so I had fun alone. I took pride in ordering an ice-cold Coca-Cola when practically everyone else drank alcohol. Sure, kids would joke about it, but it didn't shake my confidence or elicit insecurity.

> **"In this society, the key is to try to raise your children to be strong-minded leaders, capable of making informed decisions rather than succumbing to the influence of their peers."**

On the contrary, I felt emboldened to do what I wanted because I carried myself as a leader, not a follower. That's why I encourage our children not to limit their experiences because of others. That isn't reality because you can't keep them tucked away forever. They need you to help guide them and instill confidence in their decision-making and leadership so they can have fun the way we did, but in this environment, however, it's essential to teach them to continually assess the environment, minimize risks, and remove themselves from danger.

It's not always the parent's fault when kids adopt a certain mindset; however, kids have their own unspoken goals, expectations, and influences. It's not your fault when your children do things beyond your control, teachings, or reach, as with co-parenting, one parent can't control what the other parent says, does, or allows. We do not want you to carry the burden of thinking you've done something wrong when you have done everything possible or within reason to love, protect, and guide your children. As we've addressed, other people, their environment, social media, and television can influence children in negative ways.

Regarding social media and television, although you can set parental controls, have conversations, give examples, and teach them what they should not do, they can still gain access or have negative influences, which doesn't diminish your parenting. Pressure, social media, and things children are told can influence them or carry weight—in their world—outside of their homes. Many situations beyond our love and control affect our children. Being sharply in tune can help alleviate or balance these effects on our children and allow us to catch them before they fall, but unfortunately, the truth is that sometimes, the ability or opportunity to save them isn't in our grasp.

REAL LIFE REFLECTIONS

1. How can we empower our children to make their own decisions and build their confidence?

   _____

   _____

   _____

2. How do you navigate situations where your child's mindset may be influenced by social media or television?

   _____

   _____

   _____

3. When your children make decisions beyond your control, how do you cope with the feeling of parental responsibility?

   _____
   _____
   _____

4. How can you ensure your children can separate themselves from negative influences while valuing others?

   _____
   _____
   _____

5. What can you do to support your children through their challenges and ensure they know you are always there for them?

   _____
   _____
   _____

(RAASHAUN)
How to Handle Challenging Parenting Situations with Patience and Love

I had an associate who told her fourteen-year-old son, Andre, he couldn't go out with his friends because he didn't do what his father had told him to do. Andre was supposed to take the trash out and help his mother around the house while his father was out of town. What he was asked to do was reasonable, especially since his mother was eight months pregnant. I asked her how that worked out, and she said, "He went and hung out with his friends anyway," which created another level of issues when the dad returned home and the garbage was still piled up on the side of their home. The bottom line is that Andre disobeyed his parents because respect wasn't taught as part of his foundation, and he clearly wasn't concerned about the consequences.

Positive reinforcement, such as rewards or encouragement, and negative reinforcement, like removing a restriction, are helpful approaches to shaping behaviors. However, core issues, such as creating respect, enhancing the parent-child bond and dynamics, and teaching appropriate behaviors, need to be addressed. Since there were no consequences for Andre's behavior, there was no respect, just anger. When you have unemotional communication, make sure there's a mutual understanding of the entirety of the situation and come up with a resolution. When there's understanding, and your child contributes to their discipline, they are less likely to exhibit disrespect. They will come to understand the consistent way you operate and why.

Keep in mind that it's good to have rules, but measure the severity of the problem and make sure it aligns with the disciplinary actions. I'll give it to my wife—she taught me the value of this lesson when it comes to raising kids. Yes, I'm always working. And I have a lot of things on my mind and in progress, but it takes more energy to diffuse a situation that becomes fuel for a debate or negative because of the lack of communication. First, listen. Process what was communicated. Ask questions. Then give your response. Remove the potential of your kids being frustrated or angry with you when you won't let them do something because they understand what was expected. When you take the time to break things down for your kids, letting them know the reasons behind your decisions without anger or an attitude, they'll be less likely to look at you as just having a bad day. They won't view you as being dismissive of their perspective or not understanding them, which is one of the worst situations to create. You never want your kids to feel that you don't understand them. Why? They'll start looking for answers and solutions from others, which can harm them.

Gia is great in her communications with all our kids because she thinks about what she's going to say before she says it. My way doesn't always work, especially as they get older and want you to understand their perspective. When I think back to the times my father said no, there were many occasions I wanted to know why, but I wasn't going to challenge him. Remember, it was his way—or the highway—and "no" was "no." But aside from that, I respected my dad.

In today's society, and through the effectiveness of Gia's parenting style, I've come to realize that consistently explaining to your children the reasons and methods behind your protective actions as a parent can significantly benefit their emotional development. This process helps them grasp the consequences of their actions in various aspects of life, such as societal norms, self-respect, discipline, financial responsibility, and personal safety. To truly instill these lessons, maintain a consistent approach in imparting this knowledge because they'll learn to respect your decisions and grow to trust your wisdom. Andre would have put the trash on the curb if his parents had taught him to respect their decisions. No excuses.

Share an example of what you're teaching your kids or something that supports your decision, even if it's something you see on the news or hear about. Talk about situations until they get it. Eventually, if your methods are conveyed out of love rather than out of anger, they will be less likely to challenge or intentionally disrespect you. When you're confident in your decisions, your kids can learn to be too. I could see the change in how Madison and Logan responded to me, even when my decision wasn't necessarily in their favor. When I explained why I made a decision one way or the other, they respected it. And sometimes, they made sense when I listened to their logic, and I conceded. At the end of the day, if you're coming from a place of love rather than anger or dismissiveness, they're less likely to intentionally disrespect you.

REAL LIFE REFLECTIONS

Eight essential skills and strategies for effective parenting:

1. Teach respect and discipline.

2. Take appropriate disciplinary actions.

3. Use effective and honest communication.

4. Diffuse negative situations.

5. Be consistent in teaching life lessons.

6. Explain decisions.

7. Balance actively listening and decision-making.

8. Nurture trust and respect.

PART 5

From Theory to the Practice of Living with Purpose

16. Unleashing the Power of Critical Thinking in Children

Teaching children to think critically is an essential part of their overall development. Critical thinking skills enable our children to solve problems, make informed decisions, and analyze complex situations. When our children learn critical thinking skills, they develop a deeper understanding of the world, which helps them to navigate it with confidence.

There are numerous ways to encourage your children to think critically. One effective way is to ask thoughtful questions that go beyond surface-level conversations. For example, instead of asking generic questions, ask open-ended questions to encourage conversations. Asking "How was your day?" can give you a response of "Good," and that's the end of the conversation. Saying "Tell me about your day" leads to a conversation. Posing these types of questions can prompt your child to delve deeper into their experiences, reflect on their learning, and articulate their thoughts and feelings. Additionally, this type of communication can help offset the influence of social media and playing video games, which can often hinder meaningful conversations. Ultimately, getting your children to engage in thoughtful discussions can enhance their critical thinking skills and strengthen their communication abilities and overall personal growth.

Another way to promote critical thinking is by encouraging children to ask questions. When your children are curious about something, feed into it and be excited because that's an opportunity for them to learn and develop new skills. You can inspire children to be curious and ask about topics that organically interest them, such as cooking, science, nature, politics, art, or current events. This helps to develop analytical skills and encourages exploring diverse perspectives.

We love having fun, and playing games that require critical thinking skills is an effective way to accomplish two goals at once. There are several new strategy-based games that can help your children develop logical thinking, problem-solving, and decision-making skills. We play games almost every day. London's, Brooklyn's, and Jaxson's skills are impressive because we started early and played competitively. Playing against parents and siblings makes them bring their A-game. Our children don't subscribe to losing. Playing UNO with Jaxson is another story! He is a critical thinker and plays to win. This is why we say "fun" is a big part of our lives. There are benefits to having fun. We grow closer while laughing, spending time together, and solving problems.

"We love having fun, and playing games that require critical thinking skills is an effective way to accomplish two goals at once."

These games also help our children to understand the concept of cause and effect and how their actions can impact their outcomes. It's important to teach children to examine and evaluate information critically because that's what real life is about. In today's world, where there's an abundance of information available, it's essential to teach children how to analyze information and evaluate its accuracy and reliability. Encouraging your children to read books and articles from different sources and comparing their viewpoints helps them to understand multiple perspectives and develop their own opinions.

The benefits of teaching children to think critically are numerous. It helps them to develop a deeper understanding of the world around them, encourages them to become independent thinkers, and enables them to make informed decisions. It also fosters creativity, innovation, and problem-solving skills, essential for success in all aspects of life. In addition, when children learn to think critically, they become better equipped to face real-life challenges and overcome obstacles, which leads to greater confidence and resilience.

We've learned that teaching our children to think critically has become a vital component of their overall development.

(RAASHAUN)
Encouraging Our Children to Think Critically in Preparation for Their Future

Critical thinking can be fun! When implementing it with fun, love, and creativity, critical thinking goes a long way. When my kids build something creative, play with a toy, or play a video game, I always tell them, "Show me how you do that." "Show me how your toy works." "Tell me about that book." Why? It causes them to think. I won't give them a win when we play games, but I will teach them how to win.

In the new UNO game, you can swap your hand with anybody. The Choo Crew were together playing, and Jaxson had so many cards he looked like he was collecting them! But as soon as one of us yelled, "Uno," Jaxson said, "Well, you're going to have a tough time," and he'd give one of us his hand. The entire game, Jaxson exercised critical thinking to determine how to beat all of us and won. When we were playing Monopoly, Logan hid money and thought of ways to win. He got some of us to trade this and that, and he could outthink everybody. Why? From when Logan was little, we taught him not to put himself inside a box, and he won't have to think his way outside the box. We also led him to stay three steps ahead of everybody.

We love our kids, but we don't baby them; we did that when they were babies, but even then, we spoke to them like they were adults. You can't turn babied kids into critical thinkers. Our approach is to be open and honest about everything. It causes them to listen, evaluate, and think critically to follow our logic. Whatever happens in our life, we tell them. We're constantly challenging them to think on our level because when they're walking around the world, we want them to pay attention and think critically about everything! When we go to a restaurant, just like my father taught me, I want them to know where the exits are in case there is an emergency. I want them to think about their exit strategy if needed. This isn't a stretch of thought in today's society—watch the news and look at what's happening in schools and across the country. In emergency situations, critical thinking can save your life.

Besides that, we do real-life situations and role-play to see how they would think and respond in various situations. For example, I'm open about my income at home, and I tell them how much things cost so they know. That means for me to be able to pay the bills, Daddy has to have this, this, this, this, and this. Unfortunately, too often some parents and children are oblivious to what things cost, which precludes them from preparing for the future. Parents must be more transparent with their kids about finances, and what it takes to have the material things or investments they want, early in their lives so they're already prepared when they get to that point. Encourage them to think about things to help them plan, prepare, and succeed.

Gia and I prefer to be open and honest with all of that. Gia is constantly teaching Madison and Logan real-life lessons, and we started teaching them early. We give them an allowance and let them determine how they want to spend it. When it's gone, it's gone. My daughter London saves. Brooklyn gives everything to Daddy. Madison has a boyfriend that she has been with for a while. Good kid. I like him. Around Christmas, she said, "I want to buy my boyfriend something."

I said, "Buying him something, that's your choice. If you need money for your mother or me, I'll give you more. But not him. That's what you use your money for."

REAL LIFE REFLECTIONS

1. Encourage questioning to foster critical thinking.
2. Use board games and strategy games for cognitive development.
3. Develop critical thinking through diverse reading materials.
4. Incorporate critical thinking in daily routines.

> 5. Address challenges in teaching critical thinking and solutions.
>
> 6. Understand benefits of critical thinking for personal and academic life.
>
> 7. Use critical thinking to promote independence and confidence.
>
> 8. Build resilience through critical thinking skills.

We'll Figure It Out at Home

When you think about the dangers in the streets today, that's not the place to resolve issues. It's not the place to walk around as a badass because there's always someone who doesn't care about risking it all—even if they don't know they are. Emotions run high and crazy. I taught my kids to be smart and get out of a bad situation first. It's what Dad taught me. He said, "You can't win out in the streets. You cannot beat them in the streets. But if you make it home, we can figure out how to fix the problems." And Dad was right. Too many of us are locked up or dead because of this statement alone. This goes for police officers too.

When our kids were little, I didn't want them to be bullied. I didn't want anyone stripping them of their confidence, instilling fear, or making them believe they weren't good enough. So my rules are that if someone lays their hands on you and shoves you, shove them back. Stop that behavior because if you don't, no one will. When you teach it early, it prevents kids from being bullied. I don't want them to start anything, but they have my permission to defend themselves. We don't condone bullying or being mean to other kids. In fact, Gia has a list of words she doesn't allow our kids to use. She doesn't let them curse, and they are not allowed to call anyone anything that is hateful. We make sure we use an opportunity to teach them that we don't judge people for disabilities or things they cannot change. Our kids don't see the humor in someone's pain or plight—our kids aren't like that. And they aren't afraid to stand up for themselves. When we take that away from kids and tell them to walk away and turn the other cheek growing up, they sometimes develop self-esteem issues. Sometimes, it's good for a bully to realize someone will stand up to them. Hopefully, it will stop that behavior, whether learned at home or elsewhere.

Logan had an incident where he was at school playing, and another kid started yelling and screaming at him, so he gave it back, and they went back and forth until the kid shoved Logan pretty hard. Logan kept his footing and pushed the kid back so hard that he knocked the kid down. His parent was on the playground and witnessed the entire exchange without stopping her child from acting out and pushing my son. It wasn't until Logan stood up for himself that she decided to say something, which escalated the issue. The woman spoke disrespectfully to my son, chastising him. Logan and that kid were kids, they could handle their situation, but when the parent intervened—when I got the call and heard what happened, DJ Envy from Queens, New York, showed up. As a parent, she should have informed the principal of what happened without bias, called Gia and me, and let the matter be handled internally without inflammatory negative emotions. We're constantly teaching our kids how to handle situations through our own actions. I knew that dialogue would have been different had Gia or I been there because when we got to the principal's office, the woman's and her husband's demeanor changed when they saw we were not passive, uncaring, uninvolved parents.

We're adults. It's not our role to intimidate or yell at someone else's child. Address it with the parents, do it respectfully, and come to a solution, or apologize if warranted. When our children get older, we must teach them to be diplomatic. When I was younger, I had road rage. I used to keep a cup of pennies to throw at cars if they cut me off on the road. What caused me to calm down was getting my gun license later in life for protection and learning about the rules and responsibilities that come with it. There's no benefit to owning a gun and being hotheaded. You have to understand the rules and regulations of being a gun owner. Many people move off of emotions, and you think about things more critically when you have a lot to lose. Today, up and down the highway, I don't let it affect me if someone cuts me off. I want to be a positive example to my children, so as a rule, I try to be diplomatic first and let it go. This isn't the same world. Our kids aren't us.

A Real Life Analogy: Navigating life is like playing a strategic board game, where critical thinking is essential to outmaneuver challenges and diffuse volatile situations. Imagine life as a chess game. Each piece on the board has unique movements and characteristics, representing different elements of our lives—emotion, intellect, courage, fear, aggressiveness, and defensiveness, among others. The game doesn't unfold randomly but is based on thought-out strategies, just as we use critical thinking to navigate our lives.

Consider a scenario where a pawn, a less powerful piece representing a relatively innocent or less experienced individual, such as your child, is threatened by a more powerful piece (representing a bully or a conflict situation). The initial reaction might be to confront the opponent, progressing with all the firepower one possesses—to react to road rage, throw a punch, or exchange heated words. However, a seasoned player knows that this reactive response might lead to a short-term win but could set the stage for a loss in the long run.

Instead, a skilled player, equipped with critical thinking, chooses to tactically move the pieces, retreat when necessary, create a safe environment, and strategize a counterattack. It's like how we handle real-life situations: We teach our children to stand their ground but not to instigate, to respond but not react, to defend but not assault. This strategic play enables us to maintain dignity, ensure safety, and reduce potential violence or harm.

Remember, the king in chess, the most valuable piece, often moves cautiously and thoughtfully, avoiding direct confrontation unless absolutely necessary. So likewise, in life, we should aim to be more like the king, using our critical thinking skills to maneuver through challenges and conflicts to make it home where we can evaluate and devise a plan to overcome the problem.

In chess, as in life, the board can change rapidly, and emotions can run high. But as we teach our kids the game's and life's rules, we teach them how to navigate this world rather than to win every battle but to play the game with dignity, empathy, and critical thinking. As a result, our children learn to value their inner kings and queens more than the perceived power of the rooks or knights, creating a life that reflects respect, resilience, and thoughtful decision-making.

(GIA)
A Parent's Approach to Critical Thinking

I've always been one to sit back and listen to everything that's said, then I lean in and present scenarios. I present the oppositional story, what the truth might be, and provide different contexts so our kids understand the opposing views. I will ask them, "If you are in either of those opposing views, how do you look at it now?" The responses cause them to think critically and honestly. I sometimes role-play to see how they would feel at that moment. I do it with everybody. Sometimes people need to vent, and I let them do that. People want and need to be heard. It's helpful to do that because it can give them time to reflect on a situation without the emotions.

After they have said what they need to express, I'll say, "Let's go through this, but I want you to have an open mind. Look at it from his point of view." You can see how things will sit with people when you're logical and present opposing scenarios they may not have thought of. Then when I say, for example, "Now that he says XYZ to you, does he sound crazy?" Their perspective typically changes to one that reflects more understanding. It doesn't always mean they're wrong. That's not the goal—it's for them to understand what causes people to think and feel the way they do. Often, it's not being understood. In my dialogue, we take left turns, right turns, and U-turns until we've looked at the situation as a whole. When people are in their feelings, they don't think of things logically, with fairness or empathy. When you think beyond your own parameters and reality, you'll grow in your ability to understand others as a critical thinker.

When our children or those close to me ask me a question, they know I'll always tell them the truth because I have hurt their feelings in the past. Madison, Logan, and all of our children know that trust is there. Your friends won't tell you the truth when they don't trust you can handle it or that trust just isn't there. Even in these situations, you have to think critically and be around people who think and respond with integrity.

With London, even at ten, she's extraordinarily mature. She's in a gifted and talented program. Most people who meet her and have a moment to engage in conversation say, "Wow, this little girl is so mature." Because of her maturity, London loves what she calls "grown-up business." London has a vast understanding of many things. What I realized I can do for her is to take a situation on television, a show, or the news and say, "Let's talk about it." We have a whole dialogue around a specific topic. My goal is to help sculpt her psyche so she looks at things in a way they're applied in the real world. We talk about something, and she knows there are certain things she won't tolerate.

"The ability to pause, reflect, and see situations from multiple perspectives is invaluable in a world often driven by snap judgments and polarized opinions."

The profound and relative value of engaging with children or anyone in this thoughtful, reflective manner is cultivating empathy, critical thinking, and emotional intelligence. By presenting various viewpoints and encouraging our children to step into the shoes of others, we're not just teaching them how to think; we're guiding them in how to feel, understand, and navigate the complex social dynamics of human interaction.

The ability to pause, reflect, and see situations from multiple perspectives is invaluable in a world often driven by snap judgments and polarized opinions. It transcends the limitations of personal biases and facilitates a deeper understanding of people and situations. Pausing nurtures an environment where trust, honesty, and integrity develop, forming bonds that can withstand adversity.

The dialogues and the role-play aren't little intellectual exercises; they're pathways to personal growth and ethical maturity. They shape how children perceive the world and how they act in it. The lessons from these conversations prepare them for real-world challenges and equip them with the intellectual and emotional tools to be compassionate, fair, and insightful human beings.

This approach to communication and understanding extends beyond parenting; it's a philosophy that can enrich friendships, marriages, professional relationships, and our broader societal discourse. It's about recognizing the humanity in others, acknowledging our shared complexity, and striving for a world where empathy and critical thinking are not rare commodities but the common currency of our interactions. In nurturing these qualities in our children, we invest in a more intelligent, compassionate, fair, and humane future.

> **REAL LIFE REFLECTIONS**
>
> 1. Actively listen and absorb all perspectives.
> 2. Present contrasting scenarios for understanding different views.
> 3. Use role-play for emotional awareness and empathy.
> 4. Allow space for others to vent and express themselves.
> 5. Foster an open-minded approach to discussions.
> 6. Understand the roots of people's thoughts and emotions.
> 7. Explore all possible directions in conversations.
> 8. Promote logic, fairness, and empathy amid high emotions.
> 9. Encourage thinking beyond immediate reality for growth.
> 10. Be honest and truthful to build trust and enhance critical thinking.

17. Navigating the Boundaries of Domestic and Public Spaces

When it comes to teaching your kids how to navigate the boundaries at your home and other people's homes, you can start by creating an environment where emotions are validated and feelings are respected. When we teach our children that it's okay to experience a range of emotions, from joy and excitement to sadness and anger, we can show them, through our behavior, or help them understand how to express these emotions in a healthy and constructive way. This might be by talking about our feelings, using calming techniques when we're upset, or finding joy in simple things when we're happy.

In the public realm, we have to help our children understand that different settings may require different behaviors. For instance, the way we express our emotions at a festive birthday party may be different from how we behave in a quiet library. We do this not by suppressing our children's emotions but by equipping them with the tools to adapt to various social contexts. We encourage our children to observe and learn from the behaviors of others, and we remind them that it's essential to respect others' feelings and personal space.

We also communicate openly with our children about the differences between private and public behaviors, explaining that some actions and expressions of emotions are more suited to the home than they are to public spaces. Navigating the differences between private and public behaviors is like knowing the appropriate attire for different occasions. At home, you might feel comfortable lounging in your pajamas, similar to expressing your emotions freely within your safe space. But when you go to a formal event or a professional setting, you're going to wear suitable attire, which means modifying your behaviors and controlling your emotional expressions to fit the norms of public spaces. Just as you wouldn't wear your pajamas to a business meeting, there are certain behaviors and emotional expressions that are best kept within the privacy of your home.

It's also great to discuss the importance of empathy in all spaces—understanding and respecting the emotions and differences of others. We remind our children that just as they have their own unique feelings and reactions, so too does everyone around them. This recognition of shared emotional experiences can foster understanding, tolerance, and kindness, essential skills for navigating the complex world of human emotions.

Teaching our children to navigate various spaces involves a blend of open emotional education, modeling appropriate behavior, clear communication, and fostering empathy. By providing them with these tools, we equip our children to handle their emotions in a healthy manner and to respect the feelings and differences of others, no matter where they are.

(GIA)
101: Establishing Boundaries and Maintaining Respect

As a kid, I was always a little fresh with my mom, like I was the little boss in front of my friends. In hindsight, it was unfortunate that I'd talk back.

Mom would say, "Gia, I want you home at seven."

"Well, I'll be home at nine."

"No, you'll be home at seven. I need you to help me with some things around the house."

"That can wait. I'll be home at nine."

Somehow, I had a subliminal way of trying to show my friends I was the boss. If my mom had stopped it and gone upside my head, I might not have done it again. Of course, she wouldn't have done this, but if she had given me a course correction in front of my friends at the onset of this behavior, she would have taught me what I needed to know, and I would not have continued behaving disrespectfully. But since she wouldn't, and I knew she wouldn't, I could, and I did. If you had similar disobedience or disrespect, why did you continue? Most likely because you could.

These lessons were born from the foundation of my youth, and they stayed with me. I've taught and explained that if our children act out of line or disrespect me, I will stop them. With our boundaries and the respect for one another in and outside of the home our children have been taught, there's no room for error. We've seen many parents who try to de-escalate a situation shrink and disappear—and ultimately do nothing. They don't discipline their children—they don't want to make a scene or appear abusive. People might record it on their phones, and it could become another issue from there. But you have to remember, you are the parent. Record me because I will course-correct negative behavior. That's a big part of the problem. Kids don't think Mommy or Daddy will embarrass themselves. Regardless of where I've ever been and no matter who I am around, I am always the parent. You can discipline in public without abusing or hitting your children when you are consistent in your demand for respect and discipline in the home. Do not place perception over parenting.

REAL LIFE REFLECTIONS

1. Promptly correct disrespectful or disobedient behavior.

2. Prioritize parenting over public perception.

3. Demand respect and discipline universally.

4. Use nonphysical methods of asserting authority, such as taking away privileges.

5. Address negative behaviors immediately.

6. Apply discipline consistently, including in public.

> 7. Communicate reasons behind disciplinary actions.
>
> 8. Maintain your parental role firmly in all situations.

(RAASHAUN)
Equipping Your Children for a Safer Journey

I tell my kids to preplan before they go. Know where you're going. If you feel awkward or uncomfortable, leave immediately. I tell them to call if anything has happened, whether right or wrong—call us. Even if they did drink or made a bad decision. No judgment. As I've mentioned, I show them to look at the front door of a restaurant and the back door to know how to get out.

Equipping our kids means having boundaries to protect them. They don't have to like the boundaries, but they have to respect them. It's easier for kids to accept boundaries when you teach them to also see and understand the *why* behind our boundaries, rules, and protectiveness. We don't want them to learn the hard or dangerous way. I couldn't live with myself if I had chosen anything over the safety and well-being of my children and my wife. We need to teach our children the realities of life outside of the home, and we have to make sure that home, their safe space, is just that!

We're busy, constantly stirring multiple pots on the stove—one pot is our work, another is our family, and others are personal hobbies, health, and friendships. Each pot needs attention and care, but not all can be attended to simultaneously. In the manner a chef uses their skill and judgment to decide which pot needs stirring or which dish needs seasoning, we're constantly making decisions about where to invest our time and energy. The goal is to create a harmonious meal where all the elements come together and, in this case, a balanced and fulfilling life where work and family coexist happily.

REAL LIFE REFLECTIONS

1. Promote forward-planning and environmental awareness.

2. Cultivate trust in your child's instincts and prioritization of comfort.

3. Develop judgement-free communication lines.

4. Educate on practical safety protocols.

5. Value your child's safety above personal luxuries.

6. Instill understanding of safety boundaries.

7. Prioritize child safety and well-being.

8. Reinforce home as a safe space while preparing your children for external realities.

18. Living Deliberately by Design

Living with purpose: Ah! We love the sound of that, as we've learned to do it. It means you are deliberately choosing the direction of your life, taking ownership of your actions and their consequences, and creating a meaningful existence. Why wouldn't you want to do that?

As parents, it's essential to understand the dynamics of cause and effect and the power of designing your destinies. Living deliberately enables us to cultivate a meaningful and satisfying life for ourselves and our children. One benefit of being deliberate in your behaviors and actions is the ability to take control of your life. For example, embracing a healthy lifestyle involves more than isolated actions. It's a cohesive approach that integrates thoughtful decision-making, regular exercise, adherence to beneficial practices, and a conscious understanding of the motivations behind these choices. Combining physical well-being and self-awareness can help you live a more fulfilling and balanced life.

The cause of everything you do has an effect. When we live with deliberate intent, our choices are more likely aligned with our values and goals, and we are less likely to be swayed by external factors. For example, our mission statement is a protective layer for the Choo Crew. It causes us to focus on what truly matters to us, and the effect is that it helps create a meaningful life. By modeling intentional living, we can also help our children develop purpose and direction because we are the example.

Living deliberately not only allows us to align our values and desires with our vision but also enables us to experience a sense of wholeness and satisfaction. By intentionally choosing our actions, thoughts, and beliefs, we can create a life that feels complete. Rather than feeling discontented or unfulfilled, living deliberately allows us to tap into our inner potential. RaaShaun and I have done that. And we continue to do that.

Taking control of your life is exciting because you set the vision and the goals that are meaningful to you and work toward achieving them. You may achieve only some goals you set, but be persistent; set another and another until you recognize that you have created the life you want. Of course, this is real life, so it doesn't mean it will be without challenges, pain, loss, or hardships, but continuing to move forward means you are resilient and can persevere. Having purpose and direction can be empowering and fulfilling. As parents, you can teach your children to do the same by initially setting goals for them. Then encourage them to continue setting goals independently and working toward achieving them.

"Living deliberately not only allows us to align our values and desires with our vision but also enables us to experience a sense of wholeness and satisfaction. By intentionally choosing our actions, thoughts, and beliefs, we can create a life that feels complete."

Purpose also allows us to be more mindful of our actions and their consequences. Thinking before we act and making choices that will produce healthier results must be the goal. Mindfulness can lead to healthier relationships, better decision-making, and greater self-awareness. We can teach our children the importance of mindfulness by practicing it ourselves. When they see us exercise this behavior, it can help them understand the impact their actions have on themselves and others.

The prevalence of violence, anger, hate, and isms such as racism, sexism, ageism, and ableism in our society is a stark reminder that we may not be instilling in our children the values of self-awareness and compassion toward others. To foster a healthy and constructive society, it is imperative that we actively pursue avenues to encourage and cultivate mindfulness, positive mental health, and a sense of wholeness rather than perpetuating a culture of pain and brokenness. We must also acknowledge when there is a missing piece in our own lives and our children's lives and work to address it. It could be empathy, compassion, faith, love, self-love, self-respect, joy, drive, or resilience, but whatever it is, find it and fix it or get help so you can work toward being whole; that's when you'll find happiness.

(GIA)
Organic Respect and Reciprocity in Relationships

In relationships, especially between married couples, there's often a focus on equality and sharing responsibilities. One of the aspects that we have to factor in is the importance of mutual respect and reciprocity rather than a strict division of tasks and money. The idea is that if two people genuinely care for each other, they will naturally want to help each other and work together to maintain a healthy relationship. Everything you do for one another isn't measurable, and we can't take one another for granted.

It's crucial to the success of the relationship to recognize that everyone has their strengths and weaknesses. Instead of forcing a balance, focus on your strengths and contribute what you can to the relationship. For example, if one partner is better at cooking, they may take on the majority of the meal preparation, while the other partner takes on other tasks they excel in.

By avoiding strict expectations and tit-for-tat debates about who is doing more, you focus on care and mutual support. You can create a stronger bond and avoid the stress that often comes with measuring and balancing each other's contributions if you're moving with purpose and impact. It's important to recognize that specific tasks or responsibilities may be more valuable to one person than another and that both partners should feel appreciated for their efforts, regardless of who is doing what.

We've always organically done things out of respect for one another. Outlining one another's roles was never discussed. If I love and care for you and know you don't derive pleasure from doing certain responsibilities, I'll handle it. If I don't like to do it, I'll find a way to get it done. Let's keep things progressing.

PART 5: FROM THEORY TO THE PRACTICE OF LIVING WITH PURPOSE

Regardless, things work well, and nothing is left undone. Out of mutual reciprocity, we do the same for one another with everything.

We don't have to ask, "Can you take the trash out?" It's out. Can you buy groceries? They're in the fridge. We're adults and know what needs to be done. When we see the need, we handle it. When couples or partners feel they must have equal roles, some of these relationships have serious problems. What has worked well for us is that it doesn't matter if it is seventy-thirty or sixty-forty as long as what needs to be done gets done, and it's done out of care. Sure, there are things I expect my husband to do as a man, and then there are things he may expect from me, but we don't demand them or voice them. Our respect for one another doesn't require that dialogue. We have those expectations of one another because I am inherently better at things, and he is innately better at others. When someone is working and they expect you to bring equal contributions to the table, that feels like a partnership in a more accurate sense of the word. If you want a healthy relationship, you can't measure what one another does. You can't place a dollar value on raising children. You can't put a price on someone working so hard that they barely sleep and put their well-being at risk.

Living with intention and purpose means striving toward shared goals as a

"Living with intention and purpose means striving toward shared goals as a family while consistently demonstrating and reaffirming organic respect and reciprocity."

family while consistently demonstrating and reaffirming organic respect and reciprocity. Cultivating an environment of caring and mutual support promotes well-being and is a positive model for our children. Parents must actively tune in to each other's physical and emotional needs and take proactive steps to meet them. By being attentive and responsive, you're promoting a healthy and supportive relationship between you and setting a positive example for your children. Your nurturing environment shows that it's important to prioritize each other's well-being, recognize when one partner may need extra support or a break from work or the kids, and act with kindness and empathy. It's a partnership where mutual care enhances the entire family's well-being. Your partner wants to be seen and respected. If you are a single parent—pay attention to what you need, and give it to yourself!

> **REAL LIFE REFLECTIONS**
>
> 1. How do you and your partner recognize and balance each other's strengths and weaknesses in your relationship?
>
> 2. Have you ever felt unappreciated or undervalued for your contributions in the relationship? How did you address this?
>
> 3. How do you recognize and appreciate the unmeasurable contributions that your partner makes to the relationship, such as raising children and keeping them safe and healthy?
>
> 4. How do you and your partner model healthy relationship dynamics for your children?

> 5. How do you communicate with your partner about your expectations and contributions to the relationship without creating tension or resentment?
>
> _____
>
> _____
>
> _____

Believe Even When Things Are at Their Worst

We pass people every day without knowing their struggles, their history, pain, or losses, or the path they're on at that moment. But we truly understand that we must be a kinder, gentler society and execute that thought process. In return, we teach our children how to do the same. When we say, "Look at the world today," we really want you to do so. There are undeniably beautiful, kind, caring, and generous people out there, but those who do not have good intentions are evolving, and society is getting worse. When we can consistently insert positive reinforcements into our children, they will take them out into the world, and when we invest in doing good, it's reciprocated in ways we wouldn't expect. We're saying just be good human beings and contribute to building a better society. We have watched the loss of life through COVID, gun violence, natural disasters, and hate crimes. We see the warnings and rise of sex trafficking, mental health concerns, suicide, and the lack of empathy, knowing we can do more to protect and teach our children how to navigate this world before they leave our homes to create their own. We need them to be stronger and wiser.

We know another parent, Shawn, a motivational speaker, always uplifting others, sharing words that will empower someone who feels broken so they begin to heal and turn their life around. Her faith and love for her children are unbelievable, and she's helped countless others. Shawn has been deliberate in the way she speaks, inspires, and lives.

After raising two intelligent, kindhearted, and purpose-driven children who intrinsically care about others, raising tens of thousands to help police and firefighters after 9/11, donating clothing to homeless individuals, and receiving many awards and honors for their leadership and compassion, Shawn was proud of the way she had raised her children and had high expectations for them. However, they didn't know that their close-knit family unit had an unbreakable bond that was about to face their biggest challenge. Everything they had been taught about faith, love, and resilience was tested. Without warning, their mom was diagnosed with three brain aneurysms and given a poor prognosis. Yet, deliberate in how she lived and loved her children, she relied on her faith to carry her through the craniotomy, as did her husband and their four children.

Shawn explained, "When I had the surgery, I knew that if I survived, the expectations were that I would lose my speech and short-term memory. But the doctors said it would take a lot of effort if I got it back."

During the surgery, the surgeon put a stent in one aneurysm and wrapped another in a membrane that was in a cavernous area, and the third, he couldn't fix. But overall, the surgery was successful. Then the work of recovery began.

Shawn had only been married two years when she had the surgery, and her husband, son, and daughter were incredibly supportive. Her blended family, two preteen sons, also dove in to help wherever they could. They had her guidance, discipline, and love in a way that brought the family much closer together, causing them to adjust seamlessly—as a unit. The love Shawn had poured into them was instantly and freely returned. In her words:

"The discipline in how our household was sustained was precisely what I expected. My family trusted God and moved without fear. They knew everything that needed to be done, they catered to my needs, and it was humbling to see how flawlessly and lovingly they hit every one of them. My daughter even put up my inspirational daily post and returned emails to my clients, so I didn't miss a beat. No one outside of my immediate family knew I had the aneurysms or surgery. Everyone pitched in to take on my parental responsibilities and others I had. They did all the chores, cooked, kept the house clean, cared for one another, and took excellent care of me. They helped me walk, get dressed, eat—and did anything they thought I needed without me having to ask. When it came to helping me get my speech and memory back, my family pitched in to help me learn to read and write again. No one said, 'This isn't my responsibility,' or 'I don't have the time.' Everything that needed to be done was done seamlessly, and it allowed me to focus on healing. When you're deliberate in how you live, you will see the fruits of your labor everywhere you turn—and so will others. However, practice humility and gratitude in the midst of it all."

Humility is like the soil in our garden of life. Rich, healthy soil provides the base from which our plants or our actions and achievements can grow. The soil doesn't take credit for the plant's growth, but without it, the plant couldn't thrive. Similarly, humility grounds us and allows our accomplishments to stand out without our egos overshadowing them. It keeps us connected to our roots and reminds us of our human limitations, just as soil anchors the plants and provides them with vital nutrients.

Gratitude can be compared to the cool, refreshing rain. Just as plants need water to grow, our spirits need gratitude to flourish. Rain helps the garden bloom, allowing it to bear fruit or flowers. Similarly, gratitude nourishes our spirits, helping us recognize and appreciate the good in our lives. It refreshes and revitalizes us, encouraging positivity and contentment, just as rain brings life to a garden.

But remember, both soil and rain are needed for a garden to truly thrive, just as both humility and gratitude are required for a well-balanced, fulfilling life. With these, we're equipped to grow, bloom, and bear the fruits of kindness, contentment, and happiness in our lives.

> **REAL LIFE REFLECTIONS**
>
> 1. Cultivate empathy in your children by acknowledging everyone has personal struggles.
>
> 2. Promote goodness and kindness in your children, especially during hard times.

3. Model how positive deeds can lead to unexpected rewards.

4. Equip your children with resilience to face diverse worldly influences.

5. Showcase individuals who exemplify empathy and resilience.

6. Use challenges to build resilience, faith, and love in your family.

7. Create a home of shared responsibility and mutual support.

8. Emphasize how intentional parenting fosters strong family bonds and reciprocal care.

9. Show gratitude and practice humility.

(RAASHAUN)
The Intersection of Work and Family

I work a lot, and I'm constantly on the move. But I am deliberate in my decisions to do so. I love spending time with my wife and kids. I love the fun we have together and seeing them grow and develop in different areas. Although I'd like to make it to every practice or event, and I try to be there as much as possible, it doesn't always work the way I would like. I'm at the intersection of work and family, but I'm there building a bridge to happiness because I work and live for my family—I really do. Some of you may be doing the same, and my why is that I'm setting the future up for them.

My parents did that for me by making sure I got my degree. The one thing they knew was that I needed an education. That was them living for me. It was because of my education that I figured out a couple of other things. I wanted my kids and my wife to be happy. That's why I work. But you might think if I work hard, but my kids don't see me as often as they would like, how does that work? If they didn't see me but I wasn't impacting their lives and providing for them, that's a moot issue. My work is for them. My free time is for them. Some parents spend time with their kids, and that's great. If you can give them all your time, that's great too. But I want my kids and my wife to enjoy life, so I work harder than most. Since we're transparent with our children, they understand why Daddy's always working and respect what I do. I removed the option to have any financial stress. Do what you love and be happy with yourself. Knowing my family is well taken care of and have everything they want and need to be happy and they're successful in life—that makes me happy.

Balancing work and family life is like being a traffic officer at a busy intersection. Work and family are two major roads, each bustling with obligations, opportunities, and challenges that demand your attention. It's your job to manage the flow of traffic, ensuring that both roads get the appropriate time and space without causing congestion or neglecting either route. Sometimes, this might mean allowing work to take the right-of-way to secure the future. Other times, it means stopping work traffic to let family life move smoothly. Throughout it all, you're continually building a bridge overhead, symbolizing the happiness and security you strive to provide, connecting these two crucial parts of your life harmoniously.

> **REAL LIFE REFLECTIONS**
>
> 1. Strike a balance between work commitments, your personal health, and parenting responsibilities.
> 2. Take proactive measures to secure your children's future.
> 3. Ensure you are present at key moments in your children's lives.
> 4. Make sacrifices for the happiness and well-being of your family.
> 5. Assess your children's understanding and appreciation of your hard work.
> 6. Manage family life stresses, like finances.

7. Foster a family environment where your work and its value is understood and appreciated.

8. Identify personal happiness and its correlation with your family's happiness.

PART 6

A Parenting Guide to Course Correction

19. The Beginning of Disarming Potential Bad Behaviors

One of our primary goals as parents is to guide children toward positive behavior and disarm any potential for bad behavior in and outside of the home. We want to shape them into kind, respectful, and responsible individuals, and this journey isn't always a straightforward one. However, with the right approach and understanding—it's achievable.

It's essential to appreciate that all children are unique, with their individual temperaments, interests, and ways of understanding the world. So the strategies to encourage good behavior will be as unique as each of our children. Being flexible and adjusting our expectations based on our child's personality and developmental stage is crucial.

> "It's essential to appreciate that all children are unique, with their individual temperaments, interests, and ways of understanding the world."

One effective way to disarm potential bad behavior is through fostering a warm, loving relationship. Children who feel loved, secure, and understood are more likely to behave well. Building this relationship involves spending quality time with your child, listening to them, understanding their feelings, and showing them that they are your priority.

Be consistent in setting clear, consistent boundaries. Your children need to know what you expect of them. Clear rules, delivered in a straightforward and gentle manner, can prevent misunderstandings that lead to bad behavior. It's also good to ensure that the boundaries are fair and to explain the reasoning behind them so your children understand the importance of following them.

When we model good behavior, it's a way of teaching them what that looks like, and it creates good habits and more respectful communication and actions. We can't stress how much our children learn from watching us rather than what we say. When we display patience, kindness, and respect, our children are likely to do the same.

Another way to disarm potential bad behavior is to encourage your children's sense of responsibility and independence. Little things like cleaning up their toys, taking care of pets, or helping around the house can boost their self-esteem and contribute to their sense of belonging.

When your children misbehave, it's crucial to address the behavior right away, but don't attack your child's character. It's important to communicate it's the negative behavior—not your child—that isn't acceptable. Constructive criticism should be given in a way that maintains your child's self-esteem.

"In real life, everyone has off days, including children. Sometimes, a child's adverse behavior may just be their way of expressing stress, frustration, or confusion or that they are not feeling well."

In real life, everyone has off days, including children. Sometimes, a child's adverse behavior may just be their way of expressing stress, frustration, or confusion or that they are not feeling well. In these situations, empathy and understanding go a long way in disarming potential bad behavior.

Encouraging positive behavior in children is an ongoing process that requires patience, understanding, and a whole lot of love. The reward is when you see your child grow into a caring, responsible individual.

(RaaShaun)
A Journey Toward Self-Control, Respect, and Progress

When your kids are toddlers, you course-correct them right away. "Don't touch this. It's hot." "Don't climb the stairs." If they fall down, you tell them to get up so they're tougher. If they fall down and throw a tantrum, you're going to be there to stop it. Then as they get older, things pretty much go on cruise control, right? Wrong. We still have to course-correct our kids. It's something they need until they don't, and it's an element of respect and healthy progress that teaches self-control, respect, and personal growth. As a parent, it's good to leave a little element of fear. I do, so they know when Dad gets serious, don't play with Daddy. They respect boundaries. They respect my work. They respect me.

Gia, Madison, and I went to a gala. I had to be there by seven P.M. We went to pick up Madison. And when I told Madison, "If you're not down by six P.M., Daddy is leaving," she knew I was a man of my word. Daddy will cuddle you, laugh, and play kickball, but they know when Daddy says something—it's serious. When you create an environment where respect is not an option, they love you but understand that you have boundaries, and you're beginning to disarm bad behaviors.

Many times, when you have a problem with your kids, it's due to a lack of respect. My mom is seventy-eight, and she can talk to me any way she wants, and I will display that respect. I will never challenge my parents. I feel a lot of times, kids don't treat their parents the right way—respectfully. Yelling and screaming isn't the way to gain respect, but as a parent, you have to take a stand. When you are setting a precedent, disciplining your kids, or implementing a rule and they are grounded in what they want, don't back down. It can turn around. At some point, they will learn to respect you.

Kids look at the relationship between parents or partners, and if the parents don't respect one another, your children may learn not to respect you. Especially if they see your spouse, partner, ex, or friends running all over you. Learning to set that example is important. If you can't correct your children, they may end up in trouble. There is always someone out there to teach them a lesson they're not ready to learn. If I tell my kids, don't go somewhere, they won't go there. When you gain that respect in your household between adults and kids, they will learn from you. If your landlord talks to you crazy and you don't speak up and demand respect, they know you're a sucker. I'm not saying go out yelling and screaming. I'm saying demand respect, and that will teach your children to do the same.

Every kid wants someone to support them, and unless you want your kids to struggle, you have to make that time. You can disarm bad behavior by listening and being passive. Set the example. Be the example. For every bad behavior, there is a reason—and we have to get to the bottom of those reasons. We can do that by actively listening and working through these issues respectfully. When you see bad behavior, stop it in its tracks, and ask why they are doing it. "What's going on with you? What is this really about?" Begin that conversation and show them that you are in tune with them and care.

REAL LIFE REFLECTIONS

1. Course-correcting children is an ongoing task, from toddler to self-regulation.

2. For children to respect parents, mutual respect within the family is important.

3. Establishing clear boundaries instills respect and security.

4. Accountability, even in minor scenarios, teaches your children about consequences.

5. Respectful environments lead to better behavior by setting clear norms.

6. Children often mirror parents' behaviors, underlining the need for positive role models.

7. Open communication and active listening are key in addressing root causes of bad behavior.

8. Consistent support and guidance help your children navigate their emotions and behaviors.

(GIA)
Transformative Parenting

I've observed, read about, learned from, and spoken to parents about how their children go off course. The commonality is that they didn't create a solid foundation to raise them. Our children know we do everything we can to keep from disappointing them, and they don't want to disappoint us. Even if they didn't understand something and became upset, they would talk to me about an issue instead of doing something disrespectful or wrong. They respect our family, our values, our mission statement, each other, and themselves.

Over the years, and six children later, we've learned to disarm or prevent negative behaviors by spending time with our children, and they love spending time with us. They don't want to be away from us, and they don't want to leave my bedroom. They love being around the people they trust and love. Even with Madison's and Logan's busy schedules, we're constantly on the phone or spending time together. Our children will confide in us when they need to. When you have kids that generally like and trust you, they don't go wayward. When they don't have those things, you have to build them. Trust, respect, unconditional love, time—all of these things are staples in this book because they are interconnected, and they work from the toddler years on. They are necessary for every aspect of parenting. We can guide our children away from negative behaviors thanks to our deep bond and understanding. Their receptiveness came from our considering their psychological, emotional, and spiritual needs. They do what we ask because they trust us and value our relationships as we do our relationships with them. When you cultivate this transformative parenting, it will effectuate change in your children.

We have fun with our toddler, Peyton, often taking an interactive approach to preventing potentially negative behavior, such as tantrums, wanting things she shouldn't have, or natural toddler behavior where they will explore and test their boundaries and you. Instead of becoming frustrated or angry, you can make it fun for your toddler while teaching them about boundaries and the concept of delicate objects or things that can harm them. Try distracting them and remove whatever is harmful or substitute it with something positive. Or creatively tell them an age-appropriate story to explain a lesson. I have encouraged communicating with our children through positive reinforcement and maintaining a light, engaging tone. When they make the right choices, I let them know. I demand respect, but it's done in a consistent and approachable manner. This constant reinforcement of lessons, coupled with an approachable demeanor, lays a better foundation for receptiveness to communication and contributes to having a respectful relationship between you and your children.

Mitigating adverse behavior in your children is a nuanced process, with discipline playing a vital role. Whenever we enforce discipline, we inadvertently provide our children with our attention and, in doing so, facilitate opportunities for meaningful dialogues that may reveal the underlying causes of the undesired behavior. Children desire acknowledgment and affirmation; they want to know they're visible and valued. Do it when you are not angry or frustrated. Take a moment to collect your thoughts to communicate effectively so your messaging is received.

Fostering an environment that provides consistent recognition, respect, and quality time prevents feelings of isolation, loneliness, or rejection—emotions that can potentially propel a child toward risky behavior. Children who experience frequent bullying or rejection from peers or family, or who consistently feel like they don't belong, may have an elevated susceptibility to substance abuse or suicidal ideation.

"Our role as parents transcends beyond merely responding to behaviors. It includes proactive involvement and a commitment to understanding our children's emotional landscape, ensuring they feel seen, heard, and loved."

Our role as parents transcends beyond merely responding to behaviors. It includes proactive involvement and a commitment to understanding our children's emotional landscape, ensuring they feel seen, heard, and loved. We must get better at recognizing and addressing potentially harmful behaviors before they evolve into severe risks. The job in this environment is safeguarding our children's overall well-being.

There are kids from both public and private schools who may lack discipline at home due to various circumstances. But they show respect to their coaches, who can motivate and shape them into hardworking, disciplined, and respectful kids. Why? They give them their time. Coaches, great teachers, and mentors demand respect.

Jayden is a young teenager from a rough neighborhood in an inner-city area. His home environment lacks the necessary discipline due to various socioeconomic challenges, including parents who are often absent due to work obligations, leaving him with little guidance or supervision. This led to Jayden feeling overlooked and lacking a clear understanding of discipline or respect. With access to drugs, gangs, and other vices he'd fallen susceptible to, Jayden was going down a dark and dangerous path.

However, things changed for Jayden when his dad (one of our friends) encouraged his son to join their school's basketball team. Although his parents' work schedules didn't allow much time for Jayden, his coach, Coach K, became a significant figure in his life. Unlike Jayden's home life, Coach K spent ample time with him, listened to his problems and concerns, and genuinely showed that he cared. Coach K demanded respect not just in words but also in his actions and how he treated all his team members. He checked on Jayden's progress with grades and community service, helping build confidence and instilling hope, which kept Jayden out of trouble.

By providing Jayden and the other team members with a sense of structure and discipline, Coach K helped them channel their energy and potential positively. In return, he offered them respect and expected the same, creating an environment where the kids felt valued and heard. Sports and extracurricular activities are excellent ways to keep kids focused on goals rather than wandering through life lost.

Coach K's dedication and commitment motivated Jayden, inspiring him to become more disciplined, hardworking, and respectful. He began to see the value in maintaining a strong work ethic and respecting others, and the benefits of discipline—earning a full scholarship to play basketball at a D1 school. Through the consistent time and effort of his mentor, Coach K, Jayden, like many kids from similar backgrounds, transformed into a more responsible, disciplined individual, both on and off the court. As parents, we must prioritize making time to guide our children toward improved decision-making and behavior.

I have a friend whose young daughter looks at her with disgust. Through her behavior, she's saying, "You're too weak to discipline me," and "You don't care." Her daughter is ten and runs her mother like nothing anyone has probably seen. She acts and behaves far too mature for her age and always seems angry, leaving no semblance of a child other than her small frame. She was on Madison's softball team. When she finished striking out, her mother went toward her to console her. Instead, she yelled at her mom, "Get off me!" and pushed her away as though she were repulsive. Then she threw her bat toward her mother. The bat would have hit her in the face if she had not jumped back. Regardless, it would be a series of games before the girl played again.

On a separate occasion, I watched another girl who didn't score well burst into the room after an event, and she went swinging at her mom, telling her, "It's your fault! I hate you!" When her mom tried to hug her in a calming way, she swatted her away using both hands. My girls looked at me in disbelief as though I should intervene. The key to exercising parental control is to stop it when it begins. Pull children aside and address it like a parent, not their peer.

It's our responsibility to assert appropriate parental control and not tolerate disrespectful behavior. As illustrated, allowing a child to act out without consequence can lead to further escalation. We have to set clear boundaries at home so kids know what's expected in public, clearly articulate expectations, and consistently enforce consequences for inappropriate actions. By doing so, you can establish respect and control, guiding your children toward understanding and expressing their emotions more appropriately.

Preventing potentially bad behavior requires patience, understanding, and a consistent approach. Encourage positive behavior by rewarding it and modeling good behavior. Again, children often emulate what they see. Like Coach

K did with Jayden, try incorporating regular routines and schedules into their daily lives to help provide more security and predictability.

When your child exhibits unwanted behavior, respond with appropriate and immediate consequences so they can make the connection between their actions and the repercussions. However, try to empathize with them and understand their feelings and the reasons behind their actions.

> "We're parents—we're not psychologists or therapists. If their behavior continues to be problematic despite your best efforts, don't hesitate to seek professional help."

Teach your kids problem-solving skills that can empower them to better handle challenges, reducing frustration and potentially decreasing negative behavior. We're parents—we're not psychologists or therapists. If their behavior continues to be problematic despite your best efforts, don't hesitate to seek professional help. A pediatrician, psychologist, or school counselor could provide valuable insight into underlying issues and suggest effective strategies. Just remember: When enforcing rules about behavior, do it with love and respect.

REAL LIFE REFLECTIONS

1. Set clear expectations and boundaries.
2. Provide positive reinforcement.
3. Model good behavior.
4. Create a structured environment.
5. Use consequences wisely.
6. Empathize and listen.
7. Teach problem-solving skills.
8. Seek mentors or professional help if necessary.

20. Resisting Negative Situations and Worldly Temptations

In the face of ever-increasing societal challenges, teaching our children how to resist negative or dangerous situations and worldly temptations is crucial. However, this education is not a single event but a continuous process of nurturing and guidance.

To start, encourage open and honest communication and create a safe space where your children feel comfortable sharing their feelings and experiences. This will allow them to freely discuss complex and difficult topics, especially when it's painful. These might include peer pressure, substance abuse, negative influences online, or other risky behaviors. It's critical to listen without judgment and respond with empathy and understanding. Then devise and implement a plan to keep them safe.

Instilling a strong moral and ethical foundation is also key. Teach your kids the importance of honesty, integrity, respect for others, and taking responsibility for their actions. This provides a moral compass to guide their decision-making in difficult situations.

> "Instilling a strong moral and ethical foundation is also key. Teach your kids the importance of honesty, integrity, respect for others, and taking responsibility for their actions. This provides a moral compass to guide their decision-making in difficult situations."

It's equally important that your children develop problem-solving skills and emotional intelligence. Teach them to recognize and handle their emotions, empathize with others, and negotiate conflict. Equip them with the tools to analyze situations critically and make decisions that align with their values, even under pressure.

As a parent, it's vital to model the behaviors and attitudes you want to see in your children. They learn more from what they see us do than from what they hear us say. So, embody the qualities you hope to cultivate in them. Prepare them for the inevitability of mistakes. Let them know it's okay to get things wrong sometimes. The important part is to learn from these experiences, make amends if necessary, and grow from them. In essence, we should equip our children with the knowledge, skills (including self-defense), and values to navigate the challenging landscape of their lives. The ultimate goal is to foster resilient individuals who can face negative or dangerous situations and worldly temptations with wisdom and integrity.

(GIA)
Confronting Danger and Instilling Safety

From an early age, we all learn that unfortunate incidents occur, but we often perceive them as something that happens to "others." In children, this sense of invincibility is natural and even expected. However, as parents in today's rapidly evolving and often challenging world, it's our responsibility to temper this innocence with the necessary vigilance and understanding.

Our role extends beyond comforting and providing; it is also about arming our children with the knowledge and tools they need to navigate the complexities of modern society. This includes imparting awareness about potential dangers, teaching them how to identify and respond to uncomfortable or threatening situations, and cultivating a sense of personal responsibility for their safety.

It's a delicate balance—fostering their curiosity and zest for life yet grounding them in reality. But, through open, ongoing dialogue and leading by example, we can make the hard truths of life a little less daunting for our children. By harnessing the strength of this informed resilience, we prepare them to anticipate "bad things" and to handle and rise above them should they ever cross their paths.

My mother was out one day, and she saw a little poodle that was lost or stray. Mom picked the dog up and brought him home. We kept him and named him Pierre. It was my responsibility to walk Pierre. I was nine at the time and played softball on the Pearls. Around eight A.M. on Saturday, I got out of bed, put on my softball T-shirt, white shorts, and sneakers, and walked Pierre like I did every day. For about three days prior, until that day, I had seen a man, the same man, a strange man, walking up the opposite side of the street in the opposite direction. I didn't pay it any mind because he didn't scare me. I just noticed him.

On this particular day, I was walking up the street as he walked simultaneously down the other side. I headed to cross at a diagonal to save steps because it only made sense. No one would think anything about it. But when crossing perpendicularly, the man began walking directly toward me. I could tell his attention was focused on me, and he was coming at me. As soon as he did that, I turned and walked back toward my house. As I picked up my pace, he quickly approached me, grabbed me, put his hands around my neck, and started choking me. He didn't say anything. He didn't try to pick me up right away. Instead, he was trying to knock me out by strangling me. While staring at the sociopathic evil in his eyes, I screamed as loud as possible, "Help! Help!"

My dog bit his ankle, causing him to lift me to one side. He kicked Pierre so hard that Pierre went airborne into the street! I kept screaming for help while I grabbed him and kneed him in the groin hard enough for the man to let go of me for a second—long enough to run to my house. He initially grabbed me in front of my friend Shauna's house, and I lived two doors down. I ran from Shauna's house, past my friend Tiffany's, and made it to our porch. Our porch had three or four steps, a landing, another six steps, then our front door. I only made it to the landing before he reached up and grabbed me by my neck again, yanking me off my porch while tightening his grip!

A young guy, Zac, had bought a house across the street two years prior. Zac lived just five or six houses down and was loading furniture into his van when he heard me yelling. I didn't know Zac was out there. But when the guy yanked me off the street again, out of the corner of my eye, I saw Zac running up the road with his rottweiler. Finally, the guy let go of me. I had on a little yellow-gold nameplate necklace that he snatched off my neck before running to the end of the block, where I watched him turn left, and he was gone. I didn't see the man, Zac, or his dog anymore.

I should have been traumatized, but at that moment, I processed the situation more as fight or flight instead of settling into the trauma of the near abduction. So all I said when I walked into the house and ran into my parents' room was, "Mom, Dad, someone just tried to take me."

My father jumped out of bed with high emotions before I could tell him what happened, yelling, "Where did he go?! Let's go! Let's go!"

As Dad ran out of the house, Mom threw clothes at him because he was in his underwear. Then, while Mom called the police, Dad, my older brother Roman, who had on his pajamas, and I all hopped in the car, with Dad still yelling, "Which way did he go?"

I lived on Fifty-Fifth between Church and Linden. Since I saw him make a left down Linden, we made a left down Linden, and our eyes were peeled! We went five blocks down to Utica Avenue, knowing he couldn't have gotten past Utica. Dad turned left on Utica and drove down to Church Avenue. By the time we came down Church Avenue, the police were there, the guy was handcuffed, Zac was there, and Zac's rottweiler was sitting on top of the guy. As I hopped out of the car, the police pulled the man to his feet. I approached him, punched him, and spit in his face. The police had to pull my dad back. Dad was still in his underwear.

The police hauled the man away, and I found out later that his name was Greene, and he was indicted. When I testified against him, we learned that when they caught him, he had a belt with a pouch on it that was filled with jewelry. Greene had thrown it beneath the cop car, but they saw it when they put the car in reverse. He was the guy burglarizing the houses in our neighborhood, and he'd been casing our house.

I told Dad, "That's not what he was wearing!" We lived on a Brooklyn block in New York City, where on one side, there were houses, and behind them were the backyards. As I said earlier, I lived on Fifty-Fifth. On Fifty-Fourth Street, the backyards were back-to-back, with a fence between them. When I couldn't see Greene anymore, he jumped the fence into the backyards and emerged on Church Avenue. He stashed a change of clothes in one of the backyards. Zac couldn't get over the fence with his dog, so he went around and waited for Greene when he came out on Church Avenue. They found the bag of clothes Greene was wearing when he attacked me. It was proven in court that Greene had strategically planned the attack and thought he'd get away with it. We testified, and he went to jail.

This incident has impacted the way I parent. I'm incredibly protective. None of our kids are allowed to walk home from the bus stop. If my younger children play at the park, and it's an enormous space, that could mean trouble. If your child is playing and runs out of range, you can't see them that far away. If an attempted abduction can happen just a few doors down from my parents' house, your kid would be gone by the time a parent would get to the other end of a vast park and baseball field.

I am more aware and do not let my kids out of sight. I don't let my kids go outside to play even though our house sits far back and is gated. I don't let them play outside without me being there. I am fiercely protective. My point is that, in today's world, things are worse. Children are being taken, murdered, trafficked, and unintentionally in the line of fire. Whatever you need to do to keep your children safe, set those rules and boundaries early, and do your best to be vigilant; they expect us to take care of them and keep them safe. At least know where they are at all times and what they're wearing, and have them check in when they are away from you. Track them on their phone for safety.

Being a good parent is not just about saying you love your kids—it's doing everything you can to prove it to them.

Teach your children not to overshare, as disseminating too much information can harm them later. You have to listen to your children in a way that builds trust. Guide them and teach them until it becomes innate—in them. *This is real life.*

REAL LIFE REFLECTIONS

1. Vigilance is key for child safety; preparing your children for potential dangers is necessary.

2. Teach your children to stay alert to their surroundings and unusual behaviors for safety.

3. Quick thinking and self-defense skills, like screaming for help, are critical in dangerous situations.

4. Promptly report incidents to the police with as many details as possible for a quick resolution.

5. Tragedies can guide us toward a more vigilant and protective approach to parenting.

6. Even if stricter than usual, firm safety boundaries are crucial for your children's welfare.

7. Good parenting is demonstrating love through actions like listening, building trust, and teaching safety measures.

8. Teach children about the risks of oversharing personal information in a non-fearful but careful manner.

Conclusion: Real Love and Parenting

In today's dynamic and intricate society, parenting demands an enhanced level of vigilance and engagement. The societal challenges we face, from increased access to technology and social media to heightened safety concerns and even the global pandemic, have dramatically shifted the parenting landscape. As such, guiding our children safely through childhood and adolescence to become responsible, resilient adults requires an ongoing commitment to learning and adaptability.

While the world our children are growing up in might seem more threatening, it is crucial to remember that it is also full of opportunities. We're not implying that our task as parents is to shield them from all harm, but we can continually equip them with the necessary tools, knowledge, and resilience to navigate life's complexities effectively. This preparation involves comprehensive and age-appropriate education about the potential dangers they might encounter, including online threats, bullying, or substance abuse. Simultaneously, we must foster open lines of communication, ensuring our children feel comfortable discussing their fears, problems, or concerns with us.

Empowering our children is another significant component. By fostering their critical thinking skills, we enable them to make informed decisions and resist negative influences. In addition, positive reinforcement and nurturing their self-esteem can strengthen their capacity to withstand societal pressures. Instilling values such as empathy, respect, and integrity will guide them toward positive interactions with others. By being role models for these values, we provide a blueprint for how they can contribute to a kinder, more compassionate society.

Despite the inevitable hardships and challenges, there's a profound beauty in raising our children in today's interconnected world. With the proper support and guidance, our children can become empowered individuals capable of positively impacting society and their families. It's an immense responsibility but also an incredible privilege—and there is perhaps no more rewarding endeavor than nurturing the growth of our children.

Living in alignment with our mission is a way to promote a sense of authenticity and integrity, which is an invaluable lesson for our children. Again—by now, you know, we are the example. We teach them, through our actions, about the importance of staying true to themselves, which is critical in this society, and of making decisions that align with their own life's mission.

When we embrace our life's mission, we also show our children the power of resilience. We're demonstrating that challenges and setbacks are stepping-stones on our path rather than unmovable roadblocks. We're equipping them with the mindset to view difficulties as learning experiences, building their capacity to further bounce back from adversity.

By pursuing our unique life mission, we experience a profound sense of fulfillment and satisfaction that goes beyond mere material success. This teaches our children that genuine happiness comes from within, from living a life that's aligned with their purpose and passion. It imbues their efforts with meaning, fostering a sense of accomplishment that's rooted in self-actualization rather than external validation.

What we're saying is our unique life mission is our personal "why," the driving force behind our actions. By identifying and activating it, we don't just enrich our own lives; we also inspire our children, guiding them toward fulfilling, purpose-driven lives.

Remember, certain core principles can guide you as you work to build your successful family. Crafting a mission statement lays the groundwork, helping you define your family's values and aspirations. Embrace the beauty of adaptability as society evolves. It will empower your family to navigate the ever-changing landscape with resilience. The ultimate goal is cultivating love, happiness, and success within your family. Parenting isn't a task to be completed; it's a transformative journey fueled by faith, love, and the wisdom of lessons learned. Embrace this journey with open arms, as it offers boundless opportunities for growth and fulfillment. Understand the true essence of *Real Life, Real Family*, and allow its wisdom to flow through your life where needed but also shape it to resonate authentically with your unique and beautiful family.

"The ultimate goal is cultivating love, happiness, and success within your family."

As a parent, you'll find that unity and connection within your family are paramount. Encourage practices that foster togetherness, love, and understanding. These are the aspects of creating strong family bonds. Cherish those fun moments of laughter and joy. Yet, acknowledge that no journey is without its challenges, so be open to learning new ways of parenting. Sometimes, parenting may call for support and guidance beyond your current ability—and that's okay. This isn't a sign of weakness but an opportunity to grow. Seek wisdom from those who have traveled similar paths with grace, or seek the counsel of a professional who can help illuminate your way forward.

In the depths of your heart, remember that you are capable, resilient, and ever-evolving. You have the strength to nurture and raise your children with love and purpose. Trust your instincts and the foundation of knowledge and love you've built and embrace the joy and fulfillment of watching your children flourish, knowing that every step of the journey is an opportunity to learn and grow—together.

So, respect your mission, stand on your foundation, and adapt gracefully. You've got this, and you'll continue to thrive as you pour love, dedication, and wisdom into the hearts of your precious family. The path may have twists and turns, but with unwavering love and commitment, you will create your own magic and a remarkable and joy-filled legacy for future generations.

Family Resources

Suicide and Crisis Lifeline: 988

National Mental Health Hotline: 866-903-3787

Crisis Text Line: Text HOME to 741741

Community mental health centers: Google "community mental health center" and your location.

United Way mental health resources: 211

National Domestic Violence Hotline: 800-799-7233

National Domestic Violence Hotline SMS: Text START to 88788

Psychology Today database of therapists and psychologists: psychologytoday.com

Boys & Girls Club of America: bgca.org (Also google "peer support program" and your location.)

Office of Juvenile Justice and Delinquency Prevention mentoring programs: ojjdp.ojp.gov/programs/mentoring

National Federation of Families: ffcmh.org

Our Gratitude

We would like to express our sincere gratitude to Alyssa Curry, a licensed therapist (C.2002418), for her invaluable guidance and expertise throughout the development of this book. Her professional insights and support enriched the content and ensured its accuracy and relevance. We are deeply appreciative of her contribution to this project.

Acknowledgments

We would like to thank God, the architect of our love story. Without Him, nothing in our lives would be possible, and we choose to live each day in deep gratitude for what He has given us.

To our parents: Antonio and Norma Grante and Edward and Janet Casey. Thank you for modeling hard work, consistency, and love. You are models we strive to live up to, and we pray that we make you proud. Thank you for every piece of wisdom, discipline, sacrifice, happiness, and real life lessons that you have given us. You are our greatest teachers.

To our family: Roman Grante, Aaron Grante, Kaitlyn Grante, George Fox, Vivian Fox, Jemal Fox, Lleone Murdock, Carolyn Foye, Brian Foye, Vernon Foye, Eddie Montpleasie, Carmen Montpleasie, and Geran Montpleasie. You have been here since day one and have had front-row seats watching our love and family grow and evolve. Thank you for how you've loved and supported us individually and collectively.

To our closest friends: Carl Blair (June), Ingrid Crossman, Shaun Evans (Lil Shaun), Danny Francis, Kharisma Gonzalez, Brian Grimsley, Dahlia Haynes, Wilfrance Lominy, Rasheed and Sasha McWilliams, Natina Nimene, Reggie Ramsey, Ernesto Shaw (DJ Clue), Danielle Thomas, Renan Thy-bulle (DJ Mono), and Mercedez Walker (Benz). Thank you for knowing the real us, loving us, and always having our backs. Life is amazing with you all riding with us and for us!

To Marala Scott, Tess Callero, Soyolmaa Lkhagvadorj, and everyone at Abrams: Thank you so much for believing in us and helping to bring our lives and lessons to the masses in this way. We are grateful for the blessing.

About the Authors

Celebrity power couple RaaShaun "DJ Envy" Casey and Gia Casey are the very embodiment of partnership, resilience, and ambition. They are the bestselling authors of *Real Life, Real Love* whose love story began in the hallways of Queens High School for the Sciences and has since blossomed into an enduring alliance, both personally and professionally. The dynamic duo has successfully ventured into the world of entrepreneurship with the *Casey Crew* podcast. This trailblazing platform provides a candid examination of relationships and family life, earning accolades and recognition. *Essence* magazine, in acknowledgment of their genuine and impactful discussions, recognized *The Casey Crew* for its authenticity and depth, and it has been distinguished as one of the premier podcasts on Black love and family.

RaaShaun, in his own right, has carved a significant niche in the broadcasting world. As a standout host of *The Breakfast Club*, he collaborates with industry heavyweights like Charlamagne tha God, setting the tone for contemporary cultural dialogues.

Celebrating an awe-inspiring twenty-nine years of togetherness—with twenty-three as a married couple—the Caseys are further blessed with the love and laughter of their six remarkable children, showcasing that both love and determination are at the core of their journey.